Reminiscences by

Staff Officers of

Admiral Elmo R. Zumwalt, Jr., U.S. Navy

Volume I

*****

Captain Howard J. Kerr, Jr., U.S. Navy (Retired)

*

Captain W. Lewis Glenn, Jr., U.S. Navy

*

Admiral Worth H. Bagley, U.S. Navy (Retired)

Copyright © 1989
U.S. Naval Institute
Annapolis, Maryland

Preface

This is the first in a series of volumes containing the recollections of officers who served closely with Admiral Elmo R. Zumwalt, Jr. Admiral Zumwalt has been interviewed for his own oral history, and these interviews serve as a supplement to his recollections. They provide outside perspectives and say things about the admiral that he would not say himself.

Because of the nature of their relationship with Admiral Zumwalt, these three officers discuss him primarily in terms of two tours of duty, his time from 1968 to 1970 as Commander U. S. Naval Forces Vietnam and his tenure from 1970 to 1974 as Chief of Naval Operations. One is struck in all the interviews by the intense loyalty that developed among those close to the admiral. It is a loyalty that is both personal and professional and one that continues to be strong even after the working relationships have ended.

Through the eyes of his subordinates, Admiral Zumwalt is viewed as someone gifted in conceptual thinking, a hard worker, demanding of subordinates, loyal to a fault. A reader learns of the Zumwalt practice of surrounding himself with a small circle of trusted confidants and working around or getting rid of those who weren't willing or weren't able to be team players. One reads also about the striking difference he brought to the in-country war in South Vietnam in 1968: dramatically stepping up Navy involvement in combat, calling for more talented officers to be sent to Vietnam, and demonstrating great personal involvement by making frequent trips to the areas of fighting.

From Zumwalt's time as CNO, one reads in this volume of his drive to modernize the Navy in order to meet its post-Vietnam commitments; to work with a President who was extremely distracted by the growing Watergate scandal; and to bring to the Navy as a whole personnel initiatives that grew out of his experiences with the young sailors fighting the war in Vietnam.

Admiral Elmo Zumwalt consistently operated in ways contrary to the conventional wisdom of his time. Through the recollections of the three officers in this volume, one can learn the reasoning for his actions and the ways in which he sought to implement his often revolutionary concepts in a variety of areas.

Each of the three interviewees in this volume edited his transcript for the sake of accuracy and clarity. These corrected versions are considered the primary source documents. Joanne Patmore of the Naval Institute oral history staff did the smooth typing of the corrected transcripts; Susan Sweeney of the Naval Institute oral history staff indexed the volume.

Paul Stillwell
Director of Oral History
U. S. Naval Institute
December 1988

Authorization

The U.S. Naval Institute is hereby authorized to make available to individuals and to repositories of its choosing the transcripts of two oral history interviews concerning the service of the undersigned, Captain Howard J. Kerr, Jr., U.S. Navy (Retired), on the staff of Admiral Elmo R. Zumwalt, Jr. The two interviews were recorded by the undersigned on 22 September and 9 November 1982, in collaboration with Paul Stillwell of the U.S. Naval Institute.

The undersigned does hereby release and assign to the U.S. Naval Institute all his right, title, restrictions, and interest in the two interviews. The tape recordings of the interviews shall be the sole property of the Naval Institute. The copyright in both the oral and transcribed versions of the interviews shall also be the sole property of the Naval Institute.

Signed and sealed this 26th day of June, 1984.

_____
Captain Howard J. Kerr, Jr., USN (Ret.)

_____
Betty L. Veit, Notary Public

MY COMMISSION EXPIRES 10/29/85

Authorization

The U.S. Naval Institute is hereby authorized to make available to individuals, libraries and other repositories of its choosing the transcript of two oral history interviews concerning service with Admiral Elmo Zumwalt, U.S. Navy. The interviews were conducted on 16 and 22 May 1984 in collaboration with Paul Stillwell for the U.S. Naval Institute.

The undersigned does hereby release and assign to the U.S. Naval Institute all right, title, restriction, and interest in these two interviews. The copyright in both the oral and transcribed versions shall be the sole property of the U.S. Naval Institute. The tape recordings of the interviews are and will remain the property of the U.S. Naval Institute.

Signed and sealed this __2ND__ day of __DECEMBER__ 1984.

W. Lewis Glenn, Jr.
Captain, U.S. Navy

Authorization

The U. S. Naval Institute is hereby authorized to make available to individuals, libraries and other repositories of its choosing the transcript of an oral history interview concerning service with Admiral Elmo Zumwalt, U. S. Navy. The interview was conducted on 16 May 1983 in collaboration with Paul Stillwell for the U. S. Naval Institute. The only exception to the above is that pages 327a, 327b, 327c, 327d and 327e are not to be released outside the Naval institute until ten years from the date on which this authorization is made.

Except as noted above, the undersigned does hereby release and assign to the U. S. Naval Institute all right, title, restriction, and interest in this interview. The copyright in both the oral and transcribed versions shall be the sole property of the U. S. Naval Institute. The tape recordings of the interviews are and will remain the property of the U. S. Naval Institute.

Signed and sealed this 29th day of November 1988.

Worth H. Bagley
Admiral, U. S. Navy (Retired)

Interview Number 1 with Captain Howard J. Kerr, Jr.,
U.S. Navy (Retired)

Place: Captain Kerr's home in Vienna, Virginia

Date: Wednesday, 22 September 1982

Interviewer: Paul Stillwell

Q: This is one of a series of interviews being conducted with those who served with Admiral Elmo Zumwalt, Jr., to get added perspective on his life and career in the naval service.

Captain, before we get to covering your service with Admiral Zumwalt himself, could you start please by providing a little background on your service career prior to that?

Captain Kerr: I enlisted in the Navy in 1960, following graduation from the University of Iowa, and proceeded to the Officer Candidate School in Newport, Rhode Island, where I was graduated and commissioned in December of 1960. Following that, I served successive tours in the carrier Bonhomme Richard and the destroyer Walke. I then joined the staff of Cruiser-Destroyer-Flotilla Nine and in September of 1966 was assigned to the Fletcher School of Law and Diplomacy in a postgraduate program in political science/international relations.

I spent two years at the Fletcher School, and it was upon the completion of this tour that I first served with Admiral Zumwalt as his flag secretary and aide when he was assigned as Commander U.S. Naval Forces in Vietnam in late 1968.

Q: What led you to seek a degree in political science?

Captain Kerr: Well, I always had a deep interest in national security issues, even while I was in college. These had been reinforced during my preceding six years in the Navy until that time. This program which was available to me seemed to fit very nicely with not only my interests, but also with a career path that I saw at that time. So I made application for this specific program, was accepted, and as I said, matriculated at the Fletcher School in September of 1966.

Q: What was the focus of your efforts there?

Captain Kerr: Well, the focus of my efforts there was, the first year was international economic policy, for which I received a master of arts degree. The second year was national policy planning with a basis in international law, for which I received a master of arts in law and diplomacy. I think it's the only school that gives that kind of degree. Fletcher is jointly administered by Tufts and Harvard. And so many of our courses were at the Kennedy School, particularly the second year when we were focusing more on national policy planning.

Dr. Kissinger was still a member of the staff at Harvard, and he taught a course on national policy planning which many of us took at that time.* In 1967 I was a member of his year-long class and, of course, there was a great deal of interest in the Vietnam War at that time. As a master's thesis, I decided to write about the Vietnam War, or I should say about the period that led up to the escalation of our involvement. So I selected the period of 1950 to 1962. That period encompasses the time frame in which we were represented in country by a military advisory assistance group, or a MAAG, as opposed to the military assistance command or the MACV. That organizational change in 1962 represented a significant organizational change, which was necessary to support a larger military involvement. So it seemed to me that was a good breaking point. I wrote about the period just following the outbreak of the Korean War, which changed America's thinking tremendously in the Pacific and resulted in an increase in concern about Communist thrusts into Southeast Asia. At that time, as you recall, the French were, I

---

*Dr. Henry A. Kissinger, who served as special assistant to President Richard Nixon for national security affairs from 1969 to 1973 and as U.S. Secretary of State from 1973 to 1977.

guess you might say, the Western powers' influence or colonialists' hangover of Southeast Asia. They were still there.

Well, to conclude this, I think that our response in Vietnam was driven to a great extent by our perceptions of what had happened in Korea. We moved to assist the French, and when the French failed, the United States moved in. We established a MAAG, and our military involvement began.

I decided to look at that to see if that period would be instructive in understanding the escalation of our effort in the Sixties. So the title of my thesis was "The U.S. In Vietnam, 1949 to 1962: An Instrument of U.S. Involvement." Basically, I concluded that during that period, the dominant influence, or the dominant instrument in U.S. foreign policy in Southeast Asia was driven by military interests and military concerns far more than economic and political. In other words, the military concerns were dominant and they overrode, to a great extent, what should have been more of a balanced mix in terms of our perception of Vietnam and our perception of what our interests were in Vietnam.

So I saw a pattern to the buildup after '62 with the creation of the MACV that was just a continuation of American policy, as opposed to a major change in American policy in 1962 under Kennedy.* It was really just a

---
*John F. Kennedy, U.S. President from 1961 to 1963.

continuum. It was an escalation of that policy, and the increase of U.S. presence was a dramatic change in terms of numbers and the impact that those numbers were to have. But essentially our presence had been dominant in Vietnam through the decade of the Fifties. I guess historians will argue whether or not Kennedy's increase in the number of advisors in 1962 and the creation of a MACV represented a commitment that he was prepared to see through to eventually what we had was 500,000 or whether he would have cut it off at some point in time. But, in my judgment, the decision to create a MACV in 1962, to increase the number of advisors, was a continuum of policy that commenced with the invasion of Korea by the Chinese in 1950, the defeat of the French, and our concern that Communism was on the march in Asia, and the United States had to create a presence there to stop that. We saw it with a compromise solution in Korea with the establishment of the 38th parallel. We saw it in South Vietnam with the creation of two Vietnams, the one Communist and the other so-called democratic. I wrote that paper for the Kissinger seminar that I was attending in national policy planning.

I was under orders at the time to go to Vietnam to take command of one of the PG boats that was assigned to the Market Time operations, stationed out of Camranh

Bay.* I was leaving Fletcher in the late summer months.

I got a call from a friend of mine in Washington who told me that an Admiral Zumwalt had just been named the new commander in Vietnam. I had remembered Admiral Zumwalt from San Diego. He had been the commander of a cruiser-destroyer-flotilla there when I was on the Flotilla Nine staff. I never worked for him and never met him professionally or socially, but knew of him, knew of his reputation in San Diego.

This friend of mine told me that the admiral was putting together a staff and knew that I was going to Vietnam and wondered if it would be all right for him to mention my name to the admiral as a possible candidate to be on his staff.

I told him that, "Well, I have these orders to take command of this ship, but if you want to give my name to Admiral Zumwalt that is fine."

Well, he apparently did. I don't recall exactly now the exact chain of events, but one evening I was at home in Boston doing some reading and I got a phone call from Admiral Zumwalt. He asked me point-blank if I would like to come to Vietnam with him and be on his personal staff.

---

*Market Time was the name assigned to the mission and forces of the U.S. Navy's Task Force 115 off the coast of South Vietnam. Its intent was to intercept enemy forces seeking to infiltrate weapons and equipment into South Vietnam. A PG was a gas turbine-powered patrol gunboat, then new to the U.S. Navy.

I told him at the time that I had orders to command this PG, and I felt it would be impossible for me to turn a command down to accept a staff job, notwithstanding the fact that it would be on his personal staff.

Q: Well, in view of what you had told your friend earlier, that you had expressed some interest, why then the change?

Captain Kerr: Well, just that I had thought through the equation a little bit more and decided that I really didn't want to turn down a command tour.

Q: What was your rank at that point?

Captain Kerr: I was a lieutenant.

Q: A ship command is a real plum for a lieutenant.

Captain Kerr: Yes, it was. At that time it was considered a real plum for a lieutenant.

So, anyway after I'd hung up the phone, I went back and I was reading The New York Times, and I got to about the middle of the first section of the Times, and my eye caught this article that said that the Navy had just named the youngest three-star admiral in its history and that he was going to Vietnam to take command of U.S. naval forces in country.*

I put the paper down, and I thought through that a little bit and I told my wife that I thought I had just made a big mistake. She wanted to know why, and I told her about the phone call and told her about the article in the paper. I said, "I think I'll make a few phone calls tomorrow, and I may reconsider that decision."

Well, I did make some phone calls. I talked to a couple of flag officers that I had worked for. Each of them, without hesitation, strongly urged me to call Admiral Zumwalt and see if that job was still available and take it, as opposed to the command.

As one admiral put it, there's lots of opportunities to command. These PGs are not that significant, but the opportunity to work for and to watch and to learn from Admiral Zumwalt would be of almost inestimable significance to me in terms of my career. It would be almost literally a training opportunity that one couldn't pass up, plus it would expose me to, not only to him, but to an awful lot of senior people in the Navy, which is important in a young officer's career.

---

*When used in connection with the U.S. Navy's participation in the Vietnam War, the term "in country" refers to duty ashore in Vietnam or in Task Forces 115, 116, and 117--all under Commander U.S. Naval Forces Vietnam. Not under ComNavForV were the elements of the U.S. Seventh Fleet. The brief newspaper item appeared in the The New York Times, 26 July 1968, page 38.

Q: Did you find out why Admiral Zumwalt was interested in you individually?

Captain Kerr: Well, I can only assume the admiral must have called the Bureau and asked for my record, which is the usual pattern.* But I think that his primary interest was that I was at the Fletcher School and that the admiral understood that to get to the Fletcher School, you had to go through a fairly significant filtering process in the Navy to begin with. To graduate from the Fletcher School, you had to have demonstrated a certain amount of intelligence and ability to think and write and speak. And he was looking for somebody like that. And, also, I don't know if he had read, but he had been briefed in essence on the paper that I had done. So there was a connection with what I had been doing in the last year. The Kissinger seminar, while it focused on the world, that particular year a great deal of the emphasis was on our current policy in Vietnam, where we dissected it and exposed it and talked about it.

Q: Things were starting to unravel by 1968 as far as public opinion and whether the war could be won. Was any of this reflected in your study on whether it was a worthwhile effort?

---
*Bureau--the Bureau of Naval Personnel, which then handled assignments of naval officers.

Captain Kerr: No, except in my own conclusions of that, I made it clear that in Vietnam where we had failed was that we had too much of a military bias in our effort and that it was a situation that required, first of all, to really understand the character of the situation there and the real nature of that war and required a very sophisticated application of economic, political, as well as military effort. And that over the years the military had been the dominant influence, and it had continued to be the dominant influence in Vietnam. And as a result of that, I felt that the war and our effort there simply could not win with such a dominant military influence unless, of course, we wanted to unleash the military completely, à la World War II. Then there was no doubt in my mind but what we would end the situation in a hurry. But the military was always going to be restricted in Vietnam, and with that restriction you then really needed a very, very careful balance, as I said, a mixture of the political, the economic, and the military. I'm not so sure in retrospect that it was ever winnable in those circumstances. But those are the kinds of conclusions that college students write about in papers, and I was no exception to that.

Q: Well, what happened then when you reconsidered?

Captain Kerr: I called the admiral back and told him that I had thought about his offer and that my response had been a kind of a knee-jerk one. I told him also that I had read the article in The New York Times, and that had influenced me considerably and if he was still interested in my joining him, I would be delighted to do so.

He said, "Fine. You will have to contact the bureau and tell them that you do not want this command."

So, I did that. That was not an easy thing. The Bureau of Naval Personnel, in its usual highly structured way, had decided that a command at this point in my career was the most important thing, and the fact that they had said so made it almost theological, and therefore undoing it was heretical.

We went through a number of phone calls. I had to sign in blood that I had, in fact, turned down a command tour and violated all the tenets of the religion that dominated the Bureau of Personnel at that time. Eventually, they agreed to change my orders, telling me that I was making the biggest mistake of my career, that one never turns down a command in the Navy, that I was in line for an executive officer's tour after that of a missile ship, and I would probably not get that. That I was probably giving up early selection to lieutenant commander. And, although it wasn't said to me directly, but through another party, the word of the bureau was that there were a lot of people in Washington who were delighted to see Zumwalt leave town, and where best to send him than off to Vietnam? So that I was really tying myself up with somebody that was on the way out, rather than on his way up. So, for all those reasons, I was buying into a stock that I ought to be selling short on rather than waiting for the up-side.

So, with that barrage of opposition to my decision, I called the admiral back and told him that I wasn't finding much support at the bureau for joining his staff, but nonetheless I intended to do so, and when did he want me to start to work.

He said, "Friday, in San Diego."

As I recall, this was a Tuesday, and I was in Boston. Well, I met him in the airport in San Diego on a Friday morning. He and his family arrived there, and he was commencing a series of briefings that were to last, as I recall, about three weeks. The major commands in California, as well as some of the training commands that were training people that were going to Vietnam. We went out to Pearl Harbor and then to the Philippines and eventually on to Saigon.

Q: Did he get briefed by CinCPac and CinCPacFlt in Pearl?*

Captain Kerr: Yes, there were also meetings with the type commanders in San Diego. The most significant one in terms of the job he was going to was then the Amphibious Force Commander--Vice Admiral Smith was his name--because he owned the amphibious assets in country.** He was responsible, as the type commander, for the maintenance and the training and all the support for those boats that were attached to the 117 operation, that is the armored personnel boats, the Game Warden and the 116, the Swift boats, the PBRs.*** Swift boats were the Market Time operations. Other than the minesweepers and the destroyers, Phib had everything in country. He was the type commander for them, so we went there, and we had a series of briefings there.

What I did basically in those briefings was to take notes, record particularly the admiral's questions and the

---

*CinCPac--Commander in Chief Pacific, a joint U.S. command with responsibility for all military activities in the Pacific theater, headed by a four-star Navy admiral; CinCPacFlt--Commander in Chief U.S. Pacific Fleet, another four-star Navy admiral who is responsible for only the naval activities in the Pacific theater.
**Vice Admiral John Victor Smith, USN, whose oral history is in the Naval Institute collection.
***Task Force 116 (Game Warden) comprised fast river patrol boats (PBRs) which operated on major rivers in South Vietnam to enforce curfews and regulations of the government; Task Force 117 (Mobile Riverine Force) was made up of Navy landing craft converted to armored troop carriers and gunfire support vessels. They worked with U.S. Army units to conduct attacks from the rivers onto land.

answers to his questions and then draft up memorandums for the record that afternoon or evening, whenever I had a chance, get them typed up so that we kept a file of the significant aspects of the briefing, the points that were being made, the questions asked. What I'm getting at is that a pattern of supporting the admiral began to evolve. He'd leave them with a series of questions that he wanted answers to that maybe they didn't have. My job was to record those questions and be aware of the fact that he didn't get the answers to them. And then watch for those answers, and if they weren't forthcoming, to go back to that action officer to make sure that they were forthcoming.

I went with him to MinePac (Commander Mine Forces Pacific) in Long Beach and went through the same procedure there. We then went up to San Francisco. There was a lot of training going on up at Mare Island. We went up there, and then we went out to Pearl Harbor.

Q: What was your specific billet on the staff at that point?

Captain Kerr: Well, at that point I was his aide and flag secretary. We'll see as we get into this, I never really functioned as a flag secretary at all.

We went out to Pearl Harbor. I guess the most

significant thing about the flight out was that the admiral's orders read that upon departure of the continental United States, he was authorized to assume the title and wear the insignia of vice admiral, United States Navy. So I had purchased some insignia. I had contacted United Airlines that we were flying to Pearl Harbor and told them about this. I told them as soon as they lifted off and turned off the no smoking sign that we intended to have this frocking ceremony on board this DC-8.* I told them it was probably a first for United Airlines.

So they got behind it and supported a big party on the airplane for us, champagne for everyone, and they had a cake for the admiral. My wife and his wife pinned the three stars on his khaki uniform, and we had a delightful flight over to Pearl Harbor. We got there and went through a series of briefings at CinCPac as well as CinCPacFlt.

Q: What sort of guidance was included there?

Captain Kerr: Well, I don't recall specifically that there was so much guidance presented as there was just an overview of the war as they saw it at that time.

CinCPacFlt's focus was, of course, the Tonkin Gulf,

---

*In the Navy the term "frocking" refers to the practice of donning the uniform insignia and assuming the title of a higher rank before actually being promoted to it. The promotion would come when Admiral Zumwalt took command in Vietnam.

carrier operations. They paid very little attention to what was going on in country; it was really an insignificant part of the war as far as they were concerned. My impression at the time was that while they didn't look upon it with disdain, it was just sort of an adjunct to what the major war was. The Navy's major involvement was carrier operations in support of the war.

CinCPac, on the other hand, as you would suspect, gave more of a "purple-suiter" approach to the thing.* They discussed all the operations that were going on in country and, of course, touched on Seventh Fleet operations. But they were more concerned about what was happening in country than CinCPacFlt. That merely reflects what the missions were.

But, it was really at CinCPac that we got more of an understanding and briefing of what was going on in country--what the Navy was doing in country. In other words, we had 38,000 troops, sailors, at that time in Vietnam--not an insignificant number of forces.

I don't recall right now anything specific about what was said about the Navy, what it was doing. All I have is sort of a generalized recollection of subsequent

---

*As a Navy-only command, CinCPacFlt would take essentially a "blue-suiter" approach. CinCPac, as a joint command involving all U.S. military services, would have a broad outlook. "Purple-suiter" is a slang reference to the idea that if the colors of the uniforms of the various services were blended, as the services are supposed to be blended in a joint-service command, the resulting color would be purple.

discussions that I had with the admiral about what was happening, which I believe reflected his thinking at the time, which was a product of not only what he had learned in Washington, but also what he had picked up privately from the major commanders that he talked to prior to getting to Vietnam. And that was that the Navy was underutilized. We had evolved into a pattern of static operations, the impact of which had denied the major rivers to the Vietnamese and had interdicted most of his operations along the coast of South Vietnam. Nevertheless--given the nature of the infiltration into South Vietnam, particularly in the IV Corps area through Cambodia--we really weren't having much of an impact in terms of supporting the overall war effort there.* Where most U.S. Navy forces were, in the IV Corps, there was a sense that we needed to bring together the three forces that were there in some sort of coordinated effort to involve those forces in the war effort more, a more creative, innovative way to support that effort.

The commander who was there at the time, Admiral Veth, for whatever reasons, had been unable to supply the kind of leadership and innovation in this area that would satisfy a man like Abrams.**

---
*South Vietnam had been divided into four military zones, ranging from north to south; I Corps (commonly pronounced "Eye Corps") was the northernmost, and IV Corps (pronounced "Four Corps") was the farthest south.
**Rear Admiral Kenneth L. Veth, USN, Commander U.S. Naval Forces Vietnam prior to Admiral Zumwalt. General Creighton W. Abrams, Jr., USA, Commander U. S. Forces Vietnam from 1968 to 1972.

Kerr/Zumwalt Staff - 18

Q: Could you pinpoint where this direction was coming from to be more involved?

Captain Kerr: Well, I think, first of all, General Abrams was obviously unhappy with Admiral Veth. He saw 38,000 forces under one of his component commanders, and he couldn't see them being employed in such a way that was supporting the war effort.

Secondly, they were obviously costing the Navy a great deal to maintain those forces there; 38,000 people had to be supplied. All those boats. I don't think the institutional Navy had a strong sense that we should be there. Riverine warfare, in country--somehow that was the Army's responsibility. That was the Marines' responsibility. The Navy should be to seaward. So it was a drag on the Navy. So in the Navy sense they shouldn't be there to begin with, but we are there, and we're not going to remove ourselves, so we ought to be involved somehow.

Q: Admiral Veth had two stars. Now, Admiral Zumwalt came in with three stars. Was there a significance in that change?

Captain Kerr: Yes, I think there was a significance in

that change for a number of reasons. Number one, all the component commanders under General Abrams, were three stars. In fact, the Air Force was four stars. His Army commanders under him were all three stars. And then you had the Navy with a component commander with two stars. So right away, he was not at the same level as his contemporaries, his peers. And then that worked right down through the chain of command in the Navy. Our task force commanders were captains; the equivalent of that in the Army would have been brigadier or major generals. So the Navy was downgraded in the eyes of the whole MACV structure.* In a structure dominated by the Army, rank was very important.

Q: Is it a fair presumption that Admiral Veth would have been upgraded to three stars if he had been satisfying General Abrams?

Captain Kerr: That's my understanding. But at some point, the Navy was going to upgrade that job to three stars; Veth had been promised that if he went to Vietnam, eventually he would come out of there as a three-star admiral, but he didn't.

Admiral Zumwalt did receive the third star. Of

---

*MACV--U.S. Military Assistance Command Vietnam, which was commanded by General Abrams, was a joint-service organization.

course, there was tension that resulted from his arriving in country as a three-star admiral, whereas the outgoing commander was still two stars.

But before we get to Vietnam, let me go back a little bit and just close off the period of time prior to getting in country. We finished off the briefings in Pearl Harbor, and then we flew to Clark Air Force Base.* During this entire period, the admiral's family was with him, because they were transiting to Clark Air Force Base, where they were going to live while he was stationed in Vietnam.

We got to Clark, and we had, as I recall, some discussions there with the Air Force people. The most significant thing we did was go over to Subic Bay, where we had some briefings from the commanders there. But, then the admiral and I went through survival training together in the jungles not too far outside of the naval base in Subic. The program was to set you down in the middle of the jungle. We had a machete, and that was it. We had Maguire, a small Negroid Filipino. And the admiral and I proceeded to survive in the jungle with this young man's skills. Without him I don't know what we would have done. We found that you could make coffee from nuts that fell off trees. That you could reach in amidst a tangled bunch of vines and find one that had fresh water in it. We found

---

*Clark Air Force Base is on the island of Luzon in the Philippines.

how to fish, without poles or string, in streams. And we had some very good meals and exercised a great deal in our days that we were there. Really, it was the training that the pilots went through as opposed to the training that the surface people went through in a base outside of San Diego before they went to Vietnam.

Q: Did you get any POW training--how to behave if captured?

Captain Kerr: Yes, but just some discussion and lectures. We were told what to expect. I don't recall it as being extensive. This whole training was truncated because of the admiral's schedule.

We finished up in Subic, and then we flew to Saigon in an Air Force T-39 from Clark Air Force Base one day, just the admiral and I.* I remember the trip over to Saigon. The admiral was a little pensive and philosophical about beginning this new tour. He was, as you know, at that time the youngest vice admiral in the history of the Navy. He had jumped over an awful lot of people. That had created strains. I didn't appreciate all those at the time. Those strains actually represented themselves sometimes in terms of bitterness on the part of others. He was going to an area in which no flag officer who had gone there ahead of

---
*T-39--a two-engine Air Force jet trainer aircraft with accommodations for passengers.

him had been able to translate that into anything significant, either for himself personally or for the Navy, for that matter. The impression we had was that he had a second-class staff in Vietnam of people who got up in the morning and read their message traffic and proceeded to the Circle Sportif for lunch and tennis and then returned for a couple of hours in the afternoon and then broke early for happy hour.*

Q: Where had you gotten that impression?

Captain Kerr: Just in talking to people on the trip out. These weren't things that were presented in briefing sessions. These were the private conversations with people who had traveled to Vietnam or had been on one of the staffs. And I think that was the general impression around Washington too, that you had a structure, as I said earlier, that had become very static in its operations. The impact on the war was hard to measure. At best, it was highly questionable, and at worst we really don't even belong there.

Q: Was there any sense on the part of the admiral that he had been sort of kicked out of town, as you said?

---

*The Circle Sportif was originally a country club for French officers in Indochina.

Captain Kerr: I never did get that or infer that from my conversations with him. I don't think that was the sense at all. I think he saw this as another opportunity for himself personally, but also to become involved in the Vietnam conflict, to turn the situation around that had gone sour. The admiral had a sense that this war was becoming an enormous drag on the U.S. military. We were expending enormous funds in Vietnam that we should be expending in terms of modernization of our forces, both strategic and conventional. That the war in terms of its dollar cost was way out of proportion to what benefit we would ever gain from it. That confidence in the U.S. and the U.S. military was beginning to erode as a result of this war, confidence not only at home but internationally. The dollar was being weakened internationally, you recall. We were just beginning to see inflation in this country. The dollar was under attack from abroad. A lot of the opposition of our foreign allies at that time to the war was driven by the economics of the whole thing. And the admiral, in my judgment, had the breadth and the sensitivity and the understanding of these multidisciplinary factors. In other words, he didn't view it just as a military operation. He understood that. We discussed it, and he helped me understand it.

I had just spent a couple of years in an environment that was trying to study all these things. So what I brought to it was not much experience, but that which a young student who's been examining all these things in an academic arena brings to it. So many times I was able to ask a question or amplify on a point he made. But, fundamentally, the point I want to make is that I was impressed with the admiral obviously for a number of reasons. But one of the things that impressed me was that he arrived in Vietnam with an understanding and a sensitivity to this war that very seldom one attributed to a military commander. He was discussing these things on the plane, voicing these concerns and trying to sort through all the things that must have been going through his mind.

As I said earlier, he was the youngest vice admiral in history going into a situation that clearly was bad. So he had a lot of things to prove--to prove himself, to prove that he was up to this third star that the Navy had given him, while at the same time turn around the situation in country.

Q: He was taking along only one handpicked staff member in you. Was he willing to take an open mind about the people he had heard these dismal reports about?

Captain Kerr: Well, we'll get to that. I'll talk about the staff a little bit later on.

But I remember we landed at Tan Son Nhut.* Admiral Veth and some of his staff were there to meet us. Just as the door of the plane opened, Admiral Zumwalt turned to me and said, "Well, Howard, this is day one. Let's get on with it." He left the plane, and Admiral Veth was very gracious at planeside, but the fact is that he and the admiral had very little to say to each other during the entire turnover period, as I recall. It was obvious from the time we arrived at our quarters and got to the staff that there was enormous strain in dealing with Admiral Veth. I wouldn't want to draw conclusions without having firsthand information, which I don't, but I think Admiral Veth was not only a bitter, but almost a defeated commander at that time. Defeated in the sense that he was leaving country having been passed over for a third star; his relations with General Abrams were very strained. I know that for a fact. He was very standoffish and cool to Admiral Zumwalt and just sort of went through the motions until the relieving ceremony.

Q: How long did that take for the turnover?

Captain Kerr: About a week, and that week the admiral and I spent out of Saigon. We left almost immediately for a tour of South Vietnam and all the major naval

---
*Tan Son Nhut--an airport/U.S. Air Force Base just east of Saigon.

establishments--not only the operational ones but also the advisory ones. We also went up to the Tonkin Gulf aboard the carrier and met with CTF 77. Cousins was his name.* Then we went to the major task force commands, 115 at Camranh Bay, 116 which was down in the Delta. Binh Thuy is what I want to say, but I'm not sure that's right. And then down to 117, which was the armored.

At that time Captain Bob Salzer was the CTF 117 commander.** He had been in country the longest, I recall. A very impressive warrior-looking officer. He wore a .45 strapped on his chest and grenades around his waist. He looked like the kind of tough commander you ought to have in the Delta. Also what came through immediately was that he was a very smart person.

Out at Camranh Bay was an officer by the name of Roy Hoffman.*** He was also a very tough, hard-bitten commander. He looked like the kind of guy that should be in charge and running things. But, unlike Salzer he just didn't have the sensitivity or the brilliance; I always felt Roy Hoffman was the kind of guy that would have been a military hero in the Second World War, but this was a little too sophisticated situation for him. Sophisticated in the sense he had to know when to restrain himself. He

---
*Rear Admiral Ralph W. Cousins, USN, Commander Task Force 77. TF 77 was the aircraft carrier striking arm of the Seventh Fleet used in the naval air war against Vietnam.
**Captain Robert S. Salzer, USN, Commander Task Force 117.
***Captain Roy F. Hoffman, USN, Commander Task Force 115.

was a fighter, not a talker, not a position paper guy. I have great admiration for him. He had tremendous courage and guts, but he just wasn't sophisticated like Salzer was.

And the fellow who had 116 was a guy by the name of Art Price.* Art Price was a very pleasant guy who was more of a bureaucrat. He was sort of out of place physically; in other words, he just didn't look the role that Hoffman and Salzer did, but an effective commander.

Q: Well, in Admiral Salzer's oral history he speaks of Price and said that he had an intuitive grasp of tactics. Maybe he couldn't explain it, but he just knew what would work best.

Captain Kerr: Yes. As I said, he was very effective, but when you'd met Salzer and you'd met Hoffman and they were kind of tough, hard-looking guys who fit the image of somebody that was fighting a war in a tough, dirty area, then you came upon Art Price, and he looked like the Assistant Chief of Staff for Planning on the CinCPac staff, although he was a very effective, and a very smart, and a very likeable guy. I'm not trying to denigrate him. I just point out that there were personality differences. Salzer was clearly, clearly--in my judgment--the guy who

---

*Captain Arthur W. Price, Jr., USN, Commander Task Force 116.

had the best grasp overall of--he was the best mixture of the fighter as well as the person who understood the war and could articulate it. I think Admiral Zumwalt shared that feeling, although he had great respect for all of them, and they all responded to Admiral Zumwalt in what he wanted to do very effectively. All of those men showed great resolve and understanding and courage in battle. They served the Navy and Admiral Zumwalt and the country with great distinction during the period in which I was there.

Q: Did Admiral Veth send a representative around with you on this briefing tour?

Captain Kerr: No, he did not. He didn't send anyone around with us. They set up the tour for us, the itinerary. That was about it.

It was an interesting trip. It was our first real view of Vietnam physically--a beautiful country. It was our first opportunity to actually talk to people who were in country. It was interesting to see the different perspectives between people on the staffs as we were being briefed and the people who were actually on the ground. That's generally true in any situation. It's not limited to Vietnam.

But the one thing I do recall is that we came away

from those days with a clear understanding that the staff in Saigon was cut off from the forces out in the field. Their relationship was one of telephone calls and messages. Admiral Veth's presence was not really a factor in country in terms of the troops knowing him and seeing him or having any kind of a dialogue with him or with any of the senior people on his staff. It was kind of like people sometimes describe the type commander's staff in the Navy. You get messages from them and you talk to them occasionally on the telephone, but you never see them--unless there is a problem, a serious one, then maybe somebody will come down to the ship.

But this was a war that was not going our way, one that was constantly under examination, constantly being questioned. You would think that with the commitment that the U.S. Navy had in country that the commander would regularly have to be on top of things in a very personal way, as well as getting out and talking to the people in the field so that he could be in a position to respond and adjust his policies or his strategy. But I never sensed when we got over there that there was anything like that at all. It was just a sleepy, large, moribund staff which had fallen into a static pattern of reading message traffic, pulling out of that message traffic what they considered to be important, briefing it to the admiral in the morning--a panoply of statistics on the number of boats that had gone up the river, the number that had been stopped, the number that had been searched, the number that had confiscated contraband or had not. And there was never anyone who questioned, "Well, what the hell does all this mean? What is the relevance of this to the war effort?"

You know, the fact that last week you stopped 15 boats and this week you stopped 20; does that mean that your war effort has increased by a factor of 25%? What is the real relevance of it? I guess it comes down to the fact that there really wasn't a clearly defined mission at that time. There was a mission, but I mean one that was under examination and that was clearly defined in terms of bringing the Navy in-country effort to bear on those situations in the Delta that that force could relate to and could impact on and thereby support the overall efforts of the commander in Vietnam.*

Q: Well, Market Time had a mission at that time.

Captain Kerr: Market Time had done its mission. Market Time had basically accomplished its mission.

But, remember, the issue here was, as I recall, the infiltration of arms into IV Corps through Cambodia. They were crossing the waterways that the Navy could get on. In

---

*Delta--the Mekong River Delta, an interlocking network of waterways which provided the primary vehicle of commerce and transport in South Vietnam.

other words, you could put a presence without actually having to be ashore. We had three commands that were basically operating independently. If you could bring those together in some sort of an integrated way, you could--and in a mission that would be supportive of the effort, i.e., interdiction of these arms that were coming in, make it more difficult for the enemy to introduce those arms, and make him pay a price for that--that's what eventually was done and was not being done when Admiral Zumwalt arrived there. As I said, they had fallen into a static kind of operation. And the relevance of those operations, although they had accomplished the mission which they had originally been assigned, it was a dynamic situation. The war was changing constantly. And one had to be perceptive enough and creative enough to constantly be employing his forces in a relevant way with regards to the changes.

Now, the one thing that we learned in the Vietnam War is that if you cut the enemy off with one pattern of operations, they are going to see that immediately and just adjust their operations to move around it and minimize the impact of what you've done. So what you've got to do is be prepared to understand that first of all, analyze it, and adjust your operations. We hadn't done that. We had denied the major waterways to the Vietnamese. They didn't need the major waterways anymore. They had found other routes to get their ammunition in country. We had Market Time operations which were successful, but they had end-run those. They were bringing them around to Sihanoukville and bringing them down through the Parrot's Beak and across the other border areas of Vietnam and Cambodia.* So we had to recognize that and adjust our operations accordingly.

Anyway, we finished that week of travel with a sense that we had--well, let me put it this way. We realized the Vietnam War was being fought by young people. It was lieutenants and lieutenant JGs and ensigns. That's the first thing that struck you. I think I was struck by how involved, how committed, how perceptive and intelligent, and articulate these people were. And it was clear that they were just yearning and looking for some leadership. They felt detached from the whole Saigon staff, as I said, and they had basically fallen into this static pattern, and they were looking for somebody who could interject some ideas, some creativity, some innovation, and some dynamism and get them involved, so they had a greater sense of participation in the war effort and a greater sense that the involvement, the commitment, the time, the money, the effort that was being put into that war by the 38,000 sailors that were there was having more meaning than what it was.

---

*Sihanoukville--the principal seaport of Cambodia; "Parrot's Beak"--a peculiarly shaped identification by which Cambodia juts into Vietnam on the border between the two countries.

Q: What was your perception of how General Abrams felt the Navy's role should be in Vietnam?

Captain Kerr: Well, I believe General Abrams felt that the Navy should be more involved. Here again, I am repeating myself, but we had fallen into this static pattern of operations that really wasn't having much of an impact on the war effort. Now, one of the ways in which you can measure involvement in a war is by casualties, and the Navy wasn't taking any casualties in country. I don't know that this conclusion was drawn. I certainly never heard anybody say it. It was never said to me, nor was it said in my presence to anyone else. But the fact is there were a hell of a lot of casualties being taken in 1968, as we know, and very few of them were sailors. People could cynically conclude that the Navy just was restraining itself. What I mean by restraining itself is not that there was a deliberate policy on the part of the Navy to minimize their in-country casualties. Keep in mind that when I talk about casualties here, I'm not talking about Seventh Fleet operations and air operations. I'm talking strictly about the in-country operations which were focused in the Delta. We simply were not engaging the enemy. A measure of engagement is the measure of casualties, not only enemy casualties but your own. So my impression was that General Abrams was not happy with the leadership of the Navy in-country in Vietnam.

A couple episodes that probably reflect more the personal relationships than the professional ones: when I arrived in Saigon, I was in Admiral Veth's office, and I got a phone call from General Abrams' office that was supposed to be taken by Admiral Veth's aide, but I was in the office so I took it. The colonel who was on the other line--General Abrams' aide--said to me, "When are you people going to respond to General Abrams' invitation to have a farewell party for Admiral Veth?"

I wasn't familiar with that and I told him. He said, "Look, this is insulting to the general, and I wish you would get back to us."

It was clear at that time that there had been other phone calls. So I went in to see Admiral Veth and told him that I had received this call and thinking that there had somehow been a foul-up in the office and failure to respond and it was just a question of getting a response from him and then I would pass it on. He basically told me that I could call them and tell them that he wasn't going to be present at any farewell party that General Abrams wanted to give to him.

The other episode that comes to mind was when Admiral Zumwalt went over to make his call on General Abrams,

Admiral Veth accompanied him. We got over to the MACV headquarters, and the call was scheduled for like 2:00 o'clock in the afternoon. And General Abrams kept those two admirals waiting for about 50 minutes. Then when he came out into the anteroom to greet them, both Admiral Zumwalt and Admiral Veth stood up. General Abrams went over and shook Admiral Zumwalt's hand and totally ignored Admiral Veth. He didn't even acknowledge that he was in the room, let alone shake his hand. Then they all went into his office. What happened in there I don't know.

From those two episodes it was clear that there was a strain between Veth and Abrams. What had caused that, people who were there would have to opine on that. But I can assure you that there was a strain, and the chemistry between Veth and Abrams was not good and I think that essentially the situation that I've described here was common knowledge among an awful lot of people who were in Saigon and in country at that time.

Q: How soon did you get on with trying to turn this thing around and provide more bold leadership?

Captain Kerr: Well, the admiral did it immediately. In fact, he had been thinking about it a great deal prior to arrival in country. We had discussed informally a background of circumstances and pressures that called for bold action. I'll give you an example of what I'm talking about. I think I've already discussed the fact that the admiral, in my judgment, had a very broad understanding of the world situation, the domestic situation in this country and what the true cost of this war was to not only the American fighting men in country, but also to America's position as a world leader. And particularly what it was costing in terms of our ability to stay abreast with the Soviet military buildup that was really accelerating during that period, as we now know, in both the strategic and conventional sense.

The admiral believed that domestic politics would drive the situation in Vietnam as much as anything. He believed that one of the major efforts of his command should be to turn the U.S. Navy effort in country Vietnam over to the Vietnamese. I remember him stating that if Nixon won the election, we probably would have 18 months. If Humphrey won the election, we might only have six months.* In other words, recognition that, really, the '68 election was almost a vote on the issue of Vietnam and that, either way, the vote was to get things turned over to the Vietnamese and get out. But the real meaning of the vote was what sort of a window, or time frame, we were going to have to execute that.

---
*In the 1968 election for U.S. President, Republican Richard M. Nixon defeated Democrat Hubert H. Humphrey, then the incumbent Vice President.

Q: What time was the relief? This was maybe a month before the elections?

Captain Kerr: This was in October. He took over then in Vietnam.*

Q: Was there anything noteworthy about the change of command itself?

Captain Kerr: Not really. All the heavies were there--Abrams, McCain, Bunker, all the Vietnamese, all the other countries that were there.** We had an interesting sidelight. We were putting together the seating arrangements for the change of command, and the Taiwanese Government was represented in country with a three- or four-star admiral, but Christ, his date of rank was back in the early Forties, so he had a hell of a lot of seniority. And we had him on the front row, the third seat or something and Admiral Veth called and said, "I want that changed." He wanted a friend of his put in that seat. We tried to argue him out of that on the basis that protocol would be violated. He basically told us that protocol be

---

*The formal change of command for U.S Naval Forces Vietnam took place on board the USS <u>Garrett County</u> (LST-786) at Saigon on 30 September 1968.
**Admiral John S. McCain, Jr., USN, Commander in Chief Pacific (CinCPac). Ellsworth Bunker, U.S. ambassador to South Vietnam.

damned--he wanted that person in that seat, and we put her there and protocol was violated. The Taiwanese admiral was very unhappy about it. But, other than that, the change of command went off without incident.

It was a typical change of command. Admiral Zumwalt gave a very short acceptance address and returned to the office immediately. In fact, I didn't even go to the change of command. I stayed at the office. I was preparing some bullets at that time. Bullets were kind of a precursor to Z-grams.

Q: What was the immediate impact Admiral Zumwalt had on the staff?

Captain Kerr: The impact that the admiral had on the Saigon staff was not too unlike the impact that he had on the Navy when he became CNO. He literally shook it right to its marrow and did it in a very short period of time. The Circle Sportif's memberships fell off. The happy hour participation fell off. People were arriving very early in the morning, were working all day, and staying very late at night. The Saigon operation became a seven-day-a-week operation.

But he had an enormous impact on the staff. And I don't mean just in a sense of shaking them up. He had a very positive impact, particularly people like Salzer and others who could respond to the admiral's kind of creative and innovative leadership and who saw that what he was doing was involving the Navy in a very positive way. They responded magnificently, as did a lot of the members of the staff. But there were a lot who simply did not, who just fought it. Those who fought, they lost. They lost in a number of ways. They lost in the sense that they failed to participate in something that was becoming, in my judgment, a very significant effort in country. They lost in the sense they just became miserable in their jobs.

I saw it probably a little bit closer than the admiral did, because I was down in the trenches with them. A lot of them resented me. They resented the pattern in which the admiral worked, the way he did things. He used me as a person to convey what he wanted done. Not the first time; in other words, he would put out what he wanted done, but a lot of times people didn't understand exactly what he wanted. I would watch that and go down and try to diplomatically tell them that they were on the wrong course. A lot of people were responsive to that in the sense that they appreciated that effort, because they wanted to be supportive, and they wanted to do what the admiral wanted. There were others who deliberately misinterpreted what the hell he wanted. The last thing they wanted was some smart young lieutenant who had the admiral's ear to come down, and who had been in country, by the way, for a week, and who had read some history books on Vietnam, and the last thing they needed was him coming down and telling them how the hell to do their job.

Q: Did he tend to work through you rather than the chief of staff?

Captain Kerr: Well, he worked through a lot of people. The admiral didn't have any set pattern. The admiral tended to go with the people that got the job done, as opposed to living within the structure. And, the first chief of staff we had there just didn't get it done. So the admiral basically bypassed him.

Emmett Tidd came in and took over as chief of staff, and he got the job done.* Then the admiral began working through the chief of staff. So the admiral's bias was to always go with the people that would get the job done, whom he could relate to and related to him, understood what he wanted to do, supported what he wanted to do. Supported in the sense of not just genuflecting to everything he said, but argued with him, gave him their thoughts, their objections, et cetera. He always accepted that. But who essentially moved out and got the job done. And those people who fought the program eventually were cut out.

---
*Captain Emmett H. Tidd, USN.

Q: Captain Orme was his predecessor, wasn't he, as chief of staff?*

Captain Kerr: No. It was a fellow by the name of Joe Rizza who was his--well, Captain Orme was there when we arrived and he stayed on for about two weeks into the Zumwalt tour. But the guy who relieved him was a fellow by the name of Joe Rizza, Captain Joe Rizza, who had been a destroyer squadron commander.** Very delightful guy personally, but he just didn't respond in the time frame that the admiral wanted.

Admiral Zumwalt would suggest something. People who ended up being on the team were the guys that either had the answer then or were back within an hour. But the traditional staff way of running--namely, take it, go back, analyze it, do a memo, send a memo out for comment--was a more bureaucratic approach to things. It just didn't work. And the guy who would get the answer back, the kind of answer the admiral wanted, give him the kind of support that he wanted--that's the guy that the admiral favored.

There were an awful lot of things that had to be done on the staff, just the pro forma work, and it takes a good bureaucratic approach to get those things done. But the admiral wasn't there just to oversee and manage a

---
*Captain Samuel T. Orme, USN.
**Captain Joseph R. Rizza, USN.

bureaucracy. He wanted to turn things around. He wanted to get involved. He wanted some creative, innovative thinking. So he had to reach out--in some cases, go around some of the staff structure and find those people who could respond and assist him in getting done what he wanted to do. And essentially, as I recall, there were three major things that he was out to do. One was to get the Navy involved. In other words, to take the three task forces that were there. Get those three task forces together in a common effort. As I said, they each had their own mission, but to bring them together in some sort of an interactive process that would support the efforts in the Delta. And what grew out of that idea was SEA LORDS. The other thing was to begin to start the planning for the turnover to the Vietnamese. We wanted that to go ahead on an accelerated fashion. The third thing was to get some operations going in what was called the Rung Sat Zone, the Forest of Assassins. It was the one area in Vietnam where the Vietnamese Navy had some jurisdiction and had a mission. So those were three things that he wanted to move on quickly. And he reached out and grabbed Bob Salzer and said, "Bob, I want to do this." And Bob Salzer ran off and started to proceed immediately to plan and put together a SEA LORDS operation. In other words, took the lead on that.

I remember one day he called in his senior advisor, a captain by the name of Paul Arbo, who was senior advisor to the Vietnamese Navy.* He called in the assistant chief of staff for plans. I forget the captain's name at that time. Then he called in another new officer who had arrived in country by the name of "Chick" Rauch.** He told each of them that he wanted to put together a plan that would turn over all the assets that the Navy had to the Vietnamese Navy, plus the mission, in as I recall, it was 6 months, 12 months, 18 months. In other words, those are the three options for your plan.

Q: How big a staff was it overall--Naval Forces Vietnam?

Captain Kerr: We must have had 50 people in the headquarters in Saigon.

But let me just finish up on that point. The Naval Advisory Group basically came back and fought that plan. In other words, said, "There is no way you can do that." The assistant chief of staff for plans, as I recall, didn't say it couldn't be done, but he just couldn't find a way to make it happen. Then Rauch came back and said, "Here's how we can get started on it." So he became the action guy on this. That is significant on how the admiral operated. In other words, you call in two or three people, you give them

---
*Captain Paul E. Arbo, USN.
**Captain Charles F. Rauch, Jr., USN.

each the job, discuss it with them, then see who's going to come back and give you the kind of thing that you want.

You know, just parenthetically here, I think that the response that Captain Arbo came back with, the senior naval advisor at the time, was indicative of the pattern, the psyche, the mentality that all the advisory effort had fallen into at that time in Vietnam-- namely, that it will take us years to get these guys to become involved in this war. Years to turn over this effort to them. In other words, there really wasn't a very good sense of the enormous pressure that there was in this country, and the policy that was evolving at that time, or that was soon to evolve, which was one of replacement. In other words, replacement of troops with Vietnamese and replacement of U.S. mission with Vietnamese mission. And I think that the admiral sensed that. He understood that. He saw it coming. Remember, this is in October before the election. Nobody else did--on the Navy side anyway.

I'll tell you another incident later on which I think will support that, that it really wasn't understood by any of the services in country at that time.

So, just to wrap up these thoughts, the admiral arrived in Vietnam at a time when, I think, morale of the U.S. in-country forces were low. Not universally. There were some units where it was high. There were some units where it was very low. But, I think, essentially the morale was not that high. We were not really involved and the morale was not that high. We were not really involved and engaged in enemy action at the time. The utilization of our forces, I think, was questionable overall. I think there was bad chemistry between the Navy commander and Abrams. I think the Navy's attitude towards the in-country effort was one of, "How in the hell did we ever get ourselves into this in the beginning?" And, "How did we ever let it grow to the point where it is?"

Into this came Admiral Zumwalt, who did a magnificent job of turning that around, of involving the forces, giving them a new mission, engaging the enemy, supporting the overall effort of General Abrams, who conceived and implemented a plan to turn the Navy's war over to the Vietnamese and got out ahead of the other services in that regard, and someone who became an enormous morale boost to all the forces that were in country at that time. And someone who became a dominant force in country. This, by the way, was not the situation early on, because the first couple of months we were there, Navy commanders would come into Vietnam, and they didn't necessarily even come over to see us. After about two months, not only were they coming by to see us, but we even had to get a trailer so that we could house the senior Navy people who were spending the night with us, with Admiral Zumwalt. They wanted to know

Kerr/Zumwalt Staff - 46

what he was doing from him, because he had become a force to be reckoned with in that war effort, in the politics of what was going on.

So, you say, "How long did it take him to get started?" Well, I'd say that he got started right after he returned from his change of command.

Q: It sounds as if he got started even before that.

Captain Kerr: Well, he did, but he had a full head of steam going very shortly. He essentially knew what he wanted to do. The pattern was to reach out and grab the people that could do it, bypass those who, for whatever reason, objected to it or didn't want to do it. And I guess the way to judge it is to look at it now in the perspective of history, and I think that people will judge that what he did was the right thing, and it was the correct thing. And I know that General Abrams particularly was extremely responsive, and impressed, and also appreciative, appreciative in the sense of one military commander appreciating the support he was receiving from a component commander, which he hadn't been receiving in the past.

Q: You mentioned that the Navy was ahead of the other services in plans for turning over assets to the

Vietnamese. Could you go into more detail on that, please?

Captain Kerr: Well, throughout the month of October we had the staff working to put together the outline of a plan on how this would be accomplished, and what it was going to take to accomplish it, particularly from the Vietnamese point of view. Did they have the sailors? Did they have the training? Did they have the organization? Were they prepared to accept these assets, as well as the mission that went with these assets?

The admiral was double-hatted in Vietnam. Not only was he the commander of the forces, in that sense an operational commander or component commander, but he also was the chief of the naval advisory group. As I have indicated, there was a senior naval advisor who ran it day to day, but the admiral was the chief of the advisory group. So he had the responsibility for the overall advisory effort of the naval forces in country.

General Abrams met with these advisors from time to time. It turned out that the first scheduled meeting after Admiral Zumwalt assumed command was very early November, just before the election. I forget the exact date now, but it was just before the November election. As you may recall, General Abrams was called back to Washington by President Johnson for discussions and a review of the war. A bombing halt was declared prior to the election, while

General Abrams was in Washington.* So, against that backdrop, General Abrams returned to Saigon, and he had arrived the morning of this advisory presentation. All three of the services were presenting that morning. The admiral and I went over to MACV headquarters, went in the briefing room. General George Brown, Commander of the Seventh Air Force, was there. I forget the chief advisor on the Army side, lieutenant general. And General Abrams and a host of other staff people.

General Abrams came into the room. He was obviously tired from the long trip. He always had kind of a grouchy look about him. His face was drawn. He had bags under his eyes and jet lag. A big cigar in his hand, and he sat down at the table. It was the first time I had ever really seen him in any environment other than his outer office. As a young officer, I remember I was just enormously impressed with this guy. He came in there and was real tough, a hard-looking guy. He sat down and commanded everyone's attention. He turned and said, "All right, let's get on with the briefing."

The Air Force was up first, and this colonel stood up. He looked like something right out of a picture poster or an advertisement for the Air Force. He looked like Steve

---

*In the spring of 1968, when he announced he would not run for reelection, President Lyndon B. Johnson put most of North Vietnam off-limits to U.S. bombing and shelling. On 1 November 1968, that prohibition was extended to all of North Vietnam, including the southern panhandle.

Canyon. He was perfectly coiffured. His uniform was wrinkle-less. Somehow the colonels in the Air Force never get wrinkles in their uniforms. He got up, and the first slide came on, and it was red, white, and blue with lots of numbers. Up at the top is the logo of the command with thunderbolts coming out on either side of the logo. The first thing that struck me was, "Jesus, they are really going to laugh at us, because we didn't even have a visual arts section over at the NavForV headquarters.* We couldn't have prepared a slide if we'd wanted to. What we had was a flip chart, and either the admiral or myself or both had written what he was going to use as a guide in longhand on these flip charts. As the person who was going to do the flipping and the pointing, I was struck by the fact that they were going to think that we had just fallen off the turnip truck, compared to this good-looking Air Force colonel and the neat slides with all the numbers and the colors and the thunderbolts. And he proceeded to give this flawless briefing that he had memorized. Looking back now, it had probably been drafted by four or five people and he had three or four days to memorize it. And he was going through it flawlessly. I remember now the projections were out through 1976. And, at that moment, in '76, as I recall, most of the Air Force assets would be transferred to the Vietnamese.

---
*NavForV--U.S. Naval Forces Vietnam, Admiral Zumwalt's command.

General Abrams was watching him. I happened to look over. All of a sudden, he put his hand up on his head, and he stared at the table. This colonel was continuing in his monologue. General Abrams put the cigar in his mouth, and he raised his right hand and he made a fist and he hit the table. And when he did, the ashtray in front of him flipped over and came crashing down on this table. The colonel stopped briefing, and everyone at the table turned to General Abrams. He said, "Bullshit, bullshit, bullshit! All I ever get out of the Air Force is a bunch of bullshit." I was in a state of semishock at that time, and this poor colonel was urinating down the right side of his leg. But, anyway, General Abrams got everybody's attention.

I'm paraphrasing, but basically what he said was, "Don't you people understand what's happening? Don't you have any sense for the pressure-cooker environment," and those are the words he used, "that the President is in back in the United States?" He said, "He has no consensus for support for this war. What support he has is dwindling. It's clear that the policy is to get us out of this war and turn it over to the Vietnamese. That policy change will be implemented by the incoming administration, but, let me tell you, that's Johnson's policy right today. I've got a letter in my pocket from the President of the United States that directs me to turn this war over to the Vietnamese, and I can tell you that if anybody interferes with that, that I am to go right around them." And he said, "I can tell you right now, that we're going to give Defense, we're going to give CinCPac, we're going to give anybody that's in between us and the President an opportunity to get on board, but if they don't get on board, I'm going right around them. You are sitting here today and telling me that it's going to be 1976 before you can get these planes turned over to the Vietnamese?" He said, "No way, can't happen. The country won't give us that time. The incoming administration won't give us that time. Besides, I now have direct orders from the President to get this thing over with as soon as possible." Over with in the sense of getting things turned over.

What General Abrams was trying to convey was what was being felt in the country, was being felt by the President, and which, obviously, the people in country were out of touch with, except for Admiral Zumwalt who had, as I said earlier, sensed that and had moved out in advance of this meeting, but who had done so in a cautious way. By that I mean our briefing chart had a lot of caveats in it. We knew that there were a lot of assets that were required to make this happen, and a lot of things had to come together, and some priorities had to be reordered to make it happen. So, what the admiral had put together in this briefing was a cautious briefing. Nonetheless, he had anticipated this as a policy that the United States would adopt. So the general got up and left. General Abrams' chief of staff came up to Admiral Zumwalt, and I was standing there with him. And he said, "Bud, you can see the general's tired and the direction that this briefing went in. It's clearly unsettling him. If you would like to rework your presentation, we could schedule it for another time."

Well, Admiral Zumwalt was sitting there like the guy at a poker table who had just drawn to the inside straight. He said, "No, General, I'd like to go ahead and make my presentation."

The general said, "All right, Bud, if that's what you want to do, I'll go and tell "Abe." Let's give him about 45 minutes to clear his head and come down from the emotional level that he's at right now."

The admiral turned to me. He said, "Howard, get the briefing charts."

I got them, and we went back into a room. We started flipping through these charts that we had, and every one of the caveats we had, we were scrubbing out. All the "maybe's" we were changing to "will," and all the "perhaps's" got taken out. Anything that represented some hesitancy at all or a sense that we might not be able to pull this off was basically redirected to, "If you give us this support, here's what we can do."

Kerr/Zumwalt Staff - 53

So General Abrams came back in, and the admiral started his briefing, and the general was paying attention. And so was everybody else. Some of the people could see some of the flaws in it, and some of the assumptions that in terms of the assets that would be needed to make this happen. We were assuming that we could get those, the Vietnamese Navy would get those. So they began to challenge that. This one Army general thought what would be needed to make this happen was a much larger draw on recruits by the Vietnamese Navy than had been their quota in the past, and those could only come from the Army. So he saw immediately a drawdown in his assets going to the Vietnamese Navy. So he raised that issue, and General Abrams told him to shut up. He said, "The Air Force have already dug themselves into a cesspool here today." And he said, "Young Bud Zumwalt may be doing the same thing, but so far he's making some sense, so let's hear him out."

Well, he heard the admiral out. As usual, the admiral did a brilliant job of briefing. Parenthetically, of all the people I've ever seen get up and give a presentation, he has to be the best. And the reason for that, of course, is that he not only knows the material, but he helps draft his own material. So the guy that sits down and actually drafts his material understands it. The admiral was his own action officer in many cases on these things. So he knew it, and that comes across in a briefing. He not only has good presence and good style and all that, but substantively he knew his material, and that came across. That impressed people.

So the general at the end said, "All right, here is what I'd like to know. I need to know what you as Commander Naval Forces Vietnam can do on your own with the authority that you have and the assets that you have. And I need to know what support you need within the Navy chain of command to make this happen. I need to know what I can do as Commander Military Assistance Command Vietnam with the assets and authority that I have. And I need to know what I would have to go up and get assets and authority from my chain of command." He said, "When can you have that information?"

The admiral said, "Monday." As I recall, this was a Friday, and at that moment the only thing that was on paper was what was on those flip charts.

So the general said, "Fine. I'd like to see it on Monday." And Abrams stood up and everybody got up in the room and started to walk out. He took about two steps and turned around and he said, "Bud, come on with me. I want you to come down to my office."

I walked over to where General Abrams was, and the admiral walked over to him. The general put his arm around the admiral's shoulder, and he walked down to his office. I followed them down there. What was going through my mind at the time was the admiral didn't just guess right; he analyzed correctly. He had seen what needed to be done. He had gotten out ahead. He had chosen the time and had been very lucky. The timing was almost perfect. He had begun to put together the structure of his command and a relationship with General Abrams that just did nothing but improve over the next few months. But he was clearly out front on this issue of Vietnamization. When he arrived in country, he moved quickly to present that idea to General Abrams. As it turned out, the timing of it couldn't have been more perfect.

Q: So did he get it in by Monday?

Captain Kerr: Yes, oh yea--we got something over there by Monday. What was going through my mind was, "How in the hell are we ever going to get this piece of paper done up by Monday?" So we got in the car, and I said, "That was a great performance, Boss, and I know the general is delighted, but how in the hell are we ever going to get anything over there by Monday?"

He said, "Well, we'll put it in sections. Really, the only thing we have to do is get a piece of paper over there, and the first part of it has to be done fairly well. But that big bureaucracy over there will play around with it for a few weeks. So we will redo each section a little more thoroughly and a little more carefully. Then, as we get through each iteration, we'll run someone over there with that section and tell them this is the next draft. By the time it really gets to General Abrams, we'll have plenty of time to have gotten a good plan together.

Well, we worked very hard all weekend and got the shell over there. But basically Vietnamization was off the ground from a conceptual point of view and then proceeded to get into the actual details, which, of course, were far more difficult. We had a lot more problems than were anticipated, but nonetheless it happened. And it gave General Abrams, as a commander who had just been given orders by the commander in chief, an opportunity to feel that he was being responsive to the commander in chief and responsive to national policy. And also, I'm sure, it must have given him a sense that "God, I've finally got someone in the Navy over here that understands my problems and is working to assist me in my problems and is getting involved and is supporting me."

I think from that moment on, you could just sense the changing relationships between the Navy and the Navy command and MACV. When I first got there, I really felt like a second-class citizen. We were treated with disdain. But after about a month or so people returned your phone calls. They were polite. They had nice things to say about you on the phone. They would comment on the whole new image that NavForV was beginning to develop--particularly the Navy guys that were on General Abrams' staff out at Tan Son Nhut. They sensed this right away. They would call you on the phone and tell you, "I don't know what's happened, but at the mess and around the offices, people are beginning to talk up the NavForV staff as opposed to laughing at it."

That meant a great deal to everybody on the staff, and for those people who had seen the admiral's effort as one which they wanted to really get behind and support, this was the kind of thing that gave them encouragement to become even more deeply involved and supportive. For those who hadn't seen it that way, many of them, it didn't make any difference. They were leaving anyway; their tour was over. For some of those who had trouble getting on board, they began to see the positive aspects of the admiral's leadership or of his policies. Really there were many of them like the guy who just missed the train. He got on a later train, but he had missed that first train. But basically the staff was very supportive. Of course, along these lines, the admiral had been working very hard from the beginning to try to upgrade the staff as well as to reward those people who had come to Vietnam and spent a tour there.

Q: How did he upgrade the staff?

Captain Kerr: Well, I think that there was a general perception that an in-country tour didn't really count. And not withstanding the phony pronouncements out of the bureau that only the top guys were going to Vietnam, the fact is that it just wasn't true.*

Q: Why not?

Captain Kerr: You would just have to probably ask some people who were back in the bureau. I can give you what my opinion on it was. First of all, there were a lot of top people in Vietnam. But what the bureau was advertising was that everyone that went to Vietnam was in the top 10%. Well, that was utter nonsense. It's not true. In fact, you know it was a joke among junior officers, "I just found out I was in the top 10% today; I got my orders to Vietnam."

One of the giveaways was that the detailers weren't ordering themselves to Vietnam, or each other to Vietnam. One exception to that was Captain Sam Orme who had been the captain detailer. He told me one night that he ordered himself to Vietnam, because he just couldn't live with himself having sent so many people to Vietnam that he felt that he had no choice but to order himself to Vietnam. I

---
*Bureau--Bureau of Naval Personnel.

think that was the exception in the bureau rather than the rule. Now I separate out once again what was happening in the Seventh Fleet; that was a different situation. I'm just talking about in country now. You had the Bob Salzers and you had the Sam Ormes and down the line you had an awful lot of talented JOs. But there were just an awful lot of people there that were not the best that was available at the time.

Q: And there were not incentives provided for people to go.

Captain Kerr: Well, no, there weren't any incentives to go, and there weren't any rewards for having done a good tour there. Admiral Zumwalt fought like hell to give some rewards to the lieutenant commander who had gone over to Vietnam and who had done exceptionally well, who had put his life on the line, who had been in a very threatening environment for a year, and who when he came out was getting zero credit for that from the bureau and wasn't even making the XO cut.* That was kind of the typical guy. He worked very hard trying to turn that around. He put his own personal involvement in it. We used to talk to the bureau almost every night from Saigon in an effort to

---

*XO cut—Typically, in order to continue on the promotion progression, a surface line lieutenant commander had to be picked to serve as executive officer of a destroyer-type ship.

impress upon them the fact that, "You may not agree with what the country is doing; you may not agree that this is the kind of training that a naval officer needs, but the fact is that this is national policy; the country is at war, and we are the warriors dedicated to fighting this country's battles. It's incumbent upon us to ensure that the very best people are sent over, because people's lives are at stake and the national honor and prestige are at stake in this particular war." And our ability to execute a very complicated sophisticated mission--namely, as I've said before, getting the Navy involved while at the same time trying to train the Vietnamese Navy and turn the damned thing over. It was a multifaceted operation that involved a lot of sophistication. It just required the best talent the Navy had. That's the way Admiral Zumwalt felt about it. The bureau simply was not supporting that up until that time.

Now, they responded to him, and you began to see a little turnaround. Pretty soon, after nine months or so, some people who were considered "front-runners" began to show up in country. But up until the time Admiral Zumwalt got there, that was simply not the pattern, not the case. I feel that in many cases the detailers were being driven by what they considered the right, quote, right career pattern for a surface guy, and it just didn't include a tour in Vietnam. It was more important to go off to destroyer school, or have a weapons officer tour on a DDG or something than it was to go to Vietnam.* Those guys were doing just what they basically were being told what the policy within the bureau is. So, in that sense, we weren't getting support even from our own personnel distribution system for the Vietnam war in country at that time. They supported us in the sense of putting in the numbers that had to be there. They were there. But they were not reaching down and looking for the top people and putting them over there. In a sense, it was inconsistent with the right career path to go over there.

You reflect upon that, and it's an extraordinarily hard thing to understand for me--how we could view that war as just another tour of duty; it turned out that it just didn't rank as high as other tours of duty. There are an awful lot of people who have remarked to me that at the time they didn't want to go to Vietnam--not that they were afraid to go to Vietnam, but they just didn't see how it was going to help their career.

Q: What did Admiral Zumwalt do to provide incentives for the Navy captains that were there?

Captain Kerr: Well, I think one of the biggest incentives

---

*DDG--guided missile destroyer.

right away was when Bob Salzer got selected for flag. There had never been a flag officer out of Vietnam. He got selected for flag. People tend to go to where people are being selected. If the water at this hole is a little bit sweeter, that's where everybody goes to drink. And the water in South Vietnam had been a little stale. So when Bob Salzer got selected, that sent out a signal through the Navy. Zumwalt was there. Zumwalt was building a reputation. It was becoming common knowledge that Zumwalt had taken charge, had taken hold. The Navy was turning its act around and on in South Vietnam. That some good people were beginning to go there, to get involved. Bob Salzer had been selected for flag.

Q: Well, I think he was selected after he left.

Captain Kerr: Well, he had left, but see, he only had a few months to do when Admiral Zumwalt arrived. It didn't make any difference when he got it. The fact is that it came right after his tour in Vietnam. So that was seen as a plus.

Q: My point is that the principal subordinates were still captains, whereas their counterparts, you were saying earlier, in the other services were generals.

Captain Kerr: Yes. That didn't change. The admiral never got those jobs upgraded to flag rank. But he began to write the kind of fitness reports that helped people. He got General Abrams to sign off fitness reports for some of those officers, which was very helpful. Those are the kinds of things that you do to begin to support your subordinates in the field. He went personally after people. He used to get on the phone at night and call them. He'd work the detailers at night. A lieutenant commander comes out of Saigon with a top record, and the bureau doesn't give that any merit. And instead of going to an XO's tour, he goes someplace else; that tells the lieutenant commander community something. The admiral understood that, and he tried to turn that around--not only to give the right image of what was happening in Vietnam, but because he believed that that person deserved that because of what he had done in country.

You know, the admiral once said that every fitness report you'd get in the Navy that's not under fire is just a guess. These guys were out in the field. They were getting shot at. They were running the war. The responsibility, the initiative, the sense of command and leadership that they were learning at this early age was remarkable. Plus, they were doing it in the battlefield. Those were traits and values and demonstrated performance things that are more important to a fighting man in many respects than being able to run an NTDS system on a guided missile destroyer.* In other words, you could learn to run an NTDS system, but you never know how the guy is going to react in battle unless he's been in it. And these guys had been in it. And our own system wasn't recognizing that. If the guy somehow hadn't been at the top of his performance ratings on his last ship, that's what they were paying more attention to than how well he was doing in country. I feel very strongly that the bureau let the Navy down in country. I think, as I said, it began to turn around after Admiral Zumwalt got there, but I don't think that the Bureau of Naval Personnel with regards to its detailing policies in the in-country effort, prior to 1968 certainly, can be very proud of its efforts to support the war. I mean they were more concerned about their own selfish policies of putting people in the right jobs and keeping them on the, quote, career path than they were with supporting the war effort in Vietnam.

Q: Well, did he work it from the other end also? There is a delayed reaction if you have to wait until the selection board results come out. Did he badger BuPers to send him brighter, better people earlier?

---

*NTDS--Navy tactical data system, a sophisticated combat information and threat-warning system installed in the newer ships of the fleet, primarily those ships armed with guided missiles.

Kerr/Zumwalt Staff - 65

Captain Kerr: Yes, absolutely. There were people that were going off to the war colleges. I hate to belabor this, and I'm probably a little cynical about it, but I had people tell me that their detailer told them, "Let me put you at the Naval War College. You don't want to go to Vietnam. That's not going to do your career any good. You might as well spend a year at the Naval War College." Can you imagine that? The goddamned country is at war! People are getting killed! And we're thinking in terms of what's best for promotion purposes. It's unreal. In many respects, while I have disdain for both, I have less disdain for the person who ran off to Canada than I have for the person who ran off in uniform to the Naval War College.

Q: What about handpicking people for the immediate staff? Did Admiral Zumwalt do any of that?

Captain Kerr: Yes, he did. Some he got and some he didn't. One that he didn't who comes to mind was Harry Train, who was on the Second Fleet staff at the time.* He tried to get him, and Harry Train had just been selected to go up to be Admiral Moorer's executive assistant.**

---
*Harry D. Train II retired as a four-star admiral in 1982, having served as Commander in Chief, U. S. Atlantic Fleet, among his various top-level billets.
**Admiral Thomas H. Moorer, USN, was then Chief of Naval Operations.

That was the level that he was after. He wanted nothing but the very best.

Q: You mentioned Captain Tidd; was this somebody he sought out?

Captain Kerr: No, Emmett Tidd had orders in, but he had orders into a different job. He brought him in to be his chief of staff. I'm sorry, the names don't come to me right now. I'd have to go back and take a look at the staff structure at that time. But he was certainly interested, not just in his own personal staff, but he was interested mostly in the operating forces. A lot of these people were at the lieutenant commander and commander level. Whereas the flag officers are kind of easy to remember, these were awfully good people, talented people, and people who as a group weren't necessarily being sent in country. But we eventually began to see a real turnaround in terms of the people who were coming in and the fact that he was able to do all these things that he did. To some extent it was a reflection of the fact that there was a solid base to begin with. But as these new people came in, they added a great deal of support and the kind of courage and intellectual aspects that was so necessary in that environment.

Q: We were talking about Vietnamization and the turnover. Did Captain Arbo run that, or did somebody else come in?

Captain Kerr: Captain Arbo left. And what happened was, Emmett Tidd was scheduled to relieve Arbo as the senior naval advisor. So it was decided that "Chick" Rauch would take over the job as senior naval advisor and move Emmett Tidd in as chief of staff. The chief of staff at that time was relieved early to make way for Emmett Tidd. He proved to be very solid.

Q: You mentioned that some problems cropped up in implementing the concept. What sorts of problems?

Captain Kerr: Oh, the problems were mostly cultural. Differences when you put U.S. sailors on the same boat with Vietnamese, you get two different cultures coming together in a very small space. We anticipated that there would be these problems. We found out that the Marine Corps had done some work in this area. So we called to find out who it was that they had got to assist them in what you might call cultural training or whatever.

Because there were a lot of, mostly instructors, Vietnamese who were going to be with the United States Navy. And then what we envisioned was on the boats was kind of a sequential turnover. In other words, you would put one Vietnamese on and take one American off and then put a second Vietnamese on and take off a second American sailor and finally the third, and eventually they would be in charge of that boat. The boat would be theirs, and they would have the assets as well as the mission. You know, there were certain Americanization overtones, I think you might put it, from the trainees, and the interface between the USN and the VNN, the Vietnamese Navy, we saw it as being very critical to the success of this whole effort.

We located a fellow by the name of Bob Humphrey who was over at Bangkok at the time, and he was under contract to Commander U.S. Military Advisory Command Thailand at the time. He had worked in Korea and in Turkey and with the Marines in I Corps. He had made a rather exhaustive study of the cross-cultural relationships and the resulting shocks and attitudinal barriers that developed when you bring two cultures together in an environment. So we asked him to come to Saigon and brief the admiral, which he did. He did a very convincing job. The thrust of it was how to take negative attitudes and turn them into positive attitudes so that you could speed up this whole process, and it doesn't get bogged down because of cultural differences and cultural misunderstandings and hangups.

So we came up with what was called the Personal Response Program--"PRP," I guess it was. We got a couple of pilot programs going by putting some Vietnamese sailors aboard LSTs that were down in the Delta. We also sent quite a few Vietnamese off to Guam. The purpose was for communications training as well as just to see how it would work out. The response, I think, was enthusiastic. But there were differing opinions about the whole thing--in the ability of the Vietnamese to absorb all this training and to understand it. But I think more than, you know, going into the details of it, more than anything else what's instructive is there is an understanding of the--you just can't go up to the Vietnamese Navy and strike a deal and say, "We're going to turn over these assets." You've got to understand that at that time that, although we'd been in the country in Vietnam since 1949, and we had been there in force since 1962 and we had a rear admiral in there as a senior advisor since, I guess, about '65, we really hadn't gotten on much with an effort to train the Vietnamese to assume the responsibilities for replacing us in country.

So, in an effort to implement the policy that the admiral wanted, an accelerated turnover to the Vietnamese, he recognized that the limitations and the effort to respond to those limitations, one was to understand the culture of the Vietnamese. Train the U.S. sailor before he came over about what to expect. You know, certain actions, certain mannerisms, their habits, et cetera, not to be hung up by those, and not to be surprised at how he reacts to things. You say you might expect one type of reaction and you get another, and you see that as negative. It might not be, because it's just in his culture how you react.

So a significant effort was made in this whole cultural area. I considered that to be also indicative of the type of commander Admiral Zumwalt was. He was willing to reach out and accept almost--or at least had an open mind to--almost any approach that had a chance of assisting us in working. You know, there are, I think, a lot of military people who would say, "Look, I'm not interested in a bunch of social scientists coming over here trying to tell me how to run this war."

Q: What was the initial staff reaction to the social scientists?

Captain Kerr: Well, some of the initial staff reaction was very negative. In fact, one of the interesting ironies was that "Chick" Rauch's reaction was very negative. In fact, he's the one who told me that we didn't need a bunch of social scientists who were going to come over and show us how to run this war. He was a nuclear submariner, had been a systems analyst and was thinking mostly in quantitative terms and quantitative analysis. But he became the guy who was directing the effort and began to see that there was some real value to it, and it was very helpful.

Q: One of the criticisms of the Vietnamese all along was that they were unwilling to fight their own war. Did you have to overcome this reluctance?

Captain Kerr: Well, I don't think that the Vietnamese as individuals or the Navy that I knew of as an organization was afraid to fight their own war. They certainly had a lot of personal courage. The people that I got to know personally, I had great admiration for their willingness to fight for their country and their own personal courage. But you had to put it all in the context of Vietnamese politics, the overpowering presence of the U.S. military there. I think the Vietnamese Navy was eager to assume the responsibility. Certainly Admiral Tran Van Chon, who was the admiral's counterpart, the CNO of the Vietnamese Navy-- there was certainly no reluctance, as I recall, on his part to work more with the Navy and to understand that this was basically their war and a willingness to assume the missions as well as the assets to fight that war with. I didn't see that on the Navy side and I think to accept that question, you really have to put it in the context of the total Vietnamese environment. There were a lot of things that were keeping some of those people from fighting for their own country.

Q: Anything else on the turnover that you want to say?

Captain Kerr: No, I don't think so. There are a lot of details about it which I've forgotten. Believe me, I worked with the admiral across the board, so once these decisions were made, the implementation of them we followed. I went to the briefings with him, but I never really got involved in the day-to-day details of it. Only in Charles Rauch, "Chick" Rauch, the admiral found a person that was as loyal and supportive as any person that he had in Vietnam. I have great admiration for that man and what he did. There was a guy that really had an open mind. Believe me, really a first-class person as well as a very talented naval officer.

Q: On SEA LORDS, who coined the acronym for that program or campaign?

Captain Kerr: Well, I believe it was Admiral Zumwalt. I remember he called me into his office one day. He was sitting there at his desk, and he had a single pad of paper he was writing things down. He had "SEA" and "LORDS." Underneath the "S" he had "South." Under the "E," East," and the "A," "Asia." And under the "L" was "Land," "Ocean," "River," "Delta," "Strategy."

I remember he really liked that acronym, because it allowed him to call Bob Salzer "First Sea Lord." That only got us in trouble once, because the message traffic that was generated as a result of this operation we wanted to separate it from message traffic that normally went to Bob Salzer as Commander Task Force 117. We went to the communictions systems and got his call sign "First Sea Lord" in the message traffic, so we could address traffic and it would go to that one portion of his staff that had been set up to deal with that message traffic. And one of them got routed to London sometime to the First Sea Lord.

Well, the SEA LORDS operation, as I recall, was an effort on the part of the admiral to bring together all of the task forces in Vietnam. He thought that we should be able to use the capability of the three different task forces--117, 116, and 115--to control a large part of the rivers and canals of the Delta. So, Bob Salzer and the staff worked together to put together this campaign which he called SEA LORDS.

Q: Was Salzer picked to head that because of the favorable impression he'd made during your tour?

Captain Kerr: Yes, plus Salzer had been more involved in the Delta effort. He had more experience. And he was just an impressive guy.

He was selected, and he and the members of the staff went together to put together what were the objectives and how to implement this. The objectives were, as I recall, to launch a campaign down the canal. It was called the

Long Xuyen Canal, which was between the Bassac River and the Gulf of Thailand. And, at the same time, a similar campaign down the canal running parallel to it from an area called Rach Soi and Thanh An. The purpose was to interdict two major VC supply routes coming down the western side of the Delta.*

This campaign was launched by the armored boats of 117, which was Salzer's Mobile Riverine Force. And it was successful in opening up the canal and killing a number of VC and seizing a number of caches of ammunition. After a few days of this effort, the Vietnamese Marine Corps troops who had operated with these boats moved in in their armored boats to what was called the Three Sisters area in the western part of the Delta while the regional force troops took over the bank security of the canals. Shortly thereafter, that area became safe enough that they were able to turn over the patrol of the waterways to the lighter PBRs. So, in a sense, as the admiral used to describe it, you go in first with your battleships, then you come in with your lighter ships, and you establish your control and presence.

So 117 went in and secured. Then 116, the lighter PBR boats, would come in and take over from them and establish the presence. And then these, in turn, would gradually be

---

*VC--Viet Cong.

replaced by boats of the Vietnamese Navy in order to free the U.S. Navy boats for other duties. That was the plan. We found that the refugee families who had not been in their homes along those canals since Tet had been returning.* That's probably as good an indicator of the degree to which the effort was successful as anything.

Another objective of SEA LORDS was to blockade several islands in the Bassac River which the VC had been using as crossing points. When they were once blockaded, we introduced the regional forces to sweep through and to take out the VC. These operations were equally successful.

Then, of course, along with these interdiction efforts operations along the river and the canals which parallel the Cambodian border in the northernmost section of the western Delta. And these patrols were initiated and became involved in an awful lot of firefights with VC infiltrating into Vietnam. We had reports back that the VC had stopped the tax extortions, and we believed that this interdiction could be further improved and that that barrier could serve as a very significant effort of interdicting the supplies in the IV Corps, as well as assisting in pacification through the presence, control, et cetera, and extracting a price from them.

The other thing, of course, was the use of the Swifts

---

*Tet was a vigorous North Vietnamese offensive against South Vietnam in early 1968, so named because it coincided with the Vietnamese Tet holiday.

in operating when we were out on the ocean in Market Time and bringing them in for incursions up the rivers. That was having a very significant impact in terms of the firefights that were being generated. I'll tell you the skippers on those boats, they loved that. It was probably the boldest action, really, of all the SEA LORDS efforts--the Swift boats coming up. There was some really remarkable episodes of heroism there. The admiral gave a direct order to Roy Hoffman, who was the commander, not to ride those boats in. He didn't want him killed. Roy Hoffman ignored the admiral's order and rode the first boat in every time his boats went in. He flat told the admiral that he couldn't order those young lieutenants in there without going in himself.

My recollections on the specifics of SEA LORDS are a little vague at this point, but, in general, you can see what it was. It was designed to take an aggressive posture in the Delta; to integrate all the forces; to apply pressure, presence; to extract a cost out of the enemy; to interdict his supply lines; to bring force to bear in areas and in a manner that hadn't been thought of and used before, i.e., the Navy presence. In the past, as I've said, we always thought of large troop movements. What Zumwalt basically did was say, "Abe, you haven't got a lot going in the Delta. Your troops are focused on other corps. I'm going to put the Navy and the Vietnamese Navy and the Vietnamese Marines in this war in the Delta." And that's what he did. And that was SEA LORDS, and it was very successful.

The next effort he swung on around then, you see; the next one was Giant Slingshot. That was to do basically the same thing in the Parrot's Beak area.

Q: How much involvement was there from the other U.S. services in this?

Captain Kerr: I can't really answer that. I know that there was some involvement from the Army that was stationed in the Delta, and we got some air support from the Air Force.

Q: It sounds like this would have been an idea thing for the use of the Marine Corps. Was there any sense of trying to get them more involved?

Captain Kerr: Well, yes. There has always been the thought that the Marines should have been out of I Corps and down in IV Corps. That was more ideally suited to their operations. But the way the thing evolved over a number of years is what really drove where the Marine Corps was, as opposed to where they probably would have been had we been able to sit down a few years later and say, "Now, how do we really want to go about this?" Because the Marines were fighting basically an Army kind of operation up in I Corps. Everybody had their rice bowl, and they weren't going to give that up.

Q: How much personal involvement did Admiral Zumwalt have with the boat skippers?

Captain Kerr: Quite a bit. The pattern that the admiral fell into was to get up in the morning and come down for breakfast, get briefed during breakfast on what had happened the night before, what were the significant firefights, what were the significant events. Then we would head for the helo pad and go visit them that morning. That had just an enormous impact on those guys, because they had been in a firefight at 10:00 o'clock or midnight, and here was the boss from Saigon heloing in to talk to them about it at 9:00 o'clock that morning. Plus the admiral debriefed them, and he had firsthand information on what had happened.

Q: Which was a sort of contrast to the way Admiral Veth had been.

Captain Kerr: That's what I'm told, yes. That had not been his pattern. His pattern had been to be briefed by his staff by the message traffic. Well, Admiral Zumwalt was also briefed by his staff from message traffic, but he also went out and made his presence felt and debriefed the people himself personally.

Q: Did he ever bring them to Saigon for any purpose?

Captain Kerr: Yes, he did. A lot of times they would be brought up to Saigon following a significant battle. We'd debrief them in Saigon.

Q: You talk about rewarding these people with fitness reports and trying to get them good subsequent tours; what about personal decorations?

Captain Kerr: Well, of course, we did that. I always carried at least half a dozen to a dozen medals in my briefcase. I'd an odd thing to carry a briefcase out in the battlefield, but I carried a .38 revolver in there and medals.

The admiral never wore a weapon at all, in contrast to General Abrams. When General Abrams would go out in the field, he would get in his helicopter. His aide would get on, and he would have his M-16 and 16 grenades hanging on him.* They would have two gunships running shotgun with

---
*M-16--the standard rifle used by the Army and Marine Corps in the Vietnam War.

him. We eventually had a helo running shotgun, but hell, I didn't know how to fire a rifle, and the admiral didn't know how to fire a rifle. I carried this .38 revolver in the briefcase. In fact, I always had the first chamber empty, because I was afraid I might pull off a round accidentally. So, I only had five bullets in it. The admiral used to always sit on his flak jacket rather than put it on his body. He felt the flak jacket was of more value to him sitting on it than it was wearing it. But, anyway, when we would get to these locales, the admiral would pin medals on these guys that morning. Within 12 hours of their engagement, they would be standing out with fatigues on. He would pin them on T-shirts, dirty fatigues, anything. Of course, then I'd go back to Saigon and send down a list of people who had just gotten medals to the awards board.

Q: It certainly circumvented the normal procedure.*

Captain Kerr: Yes, just completely. We were pinning medals on guys. Some we didn't even have the authority to pin on.

---

*The normal, official procedure calls for the proposed recipient's immediate superior in command to make award nominations, which are then evaluated and either approved or disapproved by those higher in the chain of command. Medals are customarily awarded after the evaluation and approval process has been completed, not before.

Q: Such as the Silver Star?

Captain Kerr: The Bronze Star. No, we never did that with a Silver Star. Eventually the admiral got Bronze Star authority. When we got over there, he had authority for the Navy Commendation Medal; that was as high as he could award. But I used to catch an awful lot of flak from these guys' bosses out in the field, because we'd go to the awards board and tell them that the admiral had just given this kid a Navy Commendation Medal that morning. And they would say, "What for?"

I'd say, "Contact his boss." They would contact his boss, and the first time his boss knew that the guy had gotten a Navy Commendation Medal was when the awards board called him from Saigon telling him that they needed the citation and all the supporting paperwork on it. But it had an enormous impact, an enormous impact. And, of course, you know, what you are after is the impact on the person in the field. You're not worried about how the bureaucracy reacts to it. So it was very favorable. These kids were involved. They were excited. They were scared. But they were taking the war to the enemy in the Delta, which they had never done before. And that's what SEA LORDS did.

Q: Who was in charge of tactics? This riverine warfare is essentially a new thing for the U.S. Navy, which has the blue sea tradition.

Captain Kerr: Well, it just grew up with the people who were in Vietnam. I don't think there was any office back in Washington that was in charge of riverine tactics. The amphibious command in San Diego, as I said, had--they were the sponsor and the owner of the assets. But, they hadn't done a lot of tactical thinking on it. There was a command up in Mare Island where they trained with the boats and probably did some tactical thinking there, but I think most of it just grew up with the people in Vietnam. Certainly Admiral Zumwalt's strategy for using them in the Delta in SEA LORDS was a significant and almost a watershed in terms of strategic use of riverine forces. Their presence had been there, but once again, as I said, they had become static. They had done that thing. Now we had to look for new ways to use those assets and make their presence felt. And that's what he did with SEA LORDS.

Q: Was Captain Salzer the man who ran it in the sense that he would say who would go when and where?

Captain Kerr: Yes. The admiral had named Salzer as the First Sea Lord. He was in charge of implementing that strategy. If there was a person in charge of the tactics, the day-to-day tactics, that was Bob Salzer.

Q: You mentioned one thing that had brought this up as the noninvolvement of the Navy was that there was a very low casualty rate. What was the result when the casualty rate jumped up?

Captain Kerr: Well, the casualty rate did go up. But, of course, the results were--we should put it the other way around, did the casualties go up when they became involved? Yes, they did. That was the price for involvement. But I think people understood that. If you're going to go out and engage the enemy, you're going to take casualties.

Q: Was there any reluctance on the part of some people to do this?

Captain Kerr: I can't recall anything of that. Throughout the year, I used to have some of the young lieutenants come to town. I say some of the young lieutenants, hell at that time, that's what I was. And they'd sit down and talk to me about some of the conflicts they were having over the war, some of the orders they were given, and the problems they had in executing those orders. So it was a very difficult war.

You give a kid an order to go out on the river and anything that moves on that river is presumed to be the enemy, and all of a sudden he sees something moving and it's nothing more than a family, but his orders are to shoot anything that moves on the river, and he knows that's not the enemy. He has a real conflict. He has his responsibility, his loyalty to his commander and his commander's orders and authority on the one hand and the moral question that arises between himself and the potential victims of carrying out that order.

Q: Who established the rules of engagement?

Captain Kerr: Well, the rules of engagement were established by CinCPac and established by MACV. I don't think we had any authority to establish rules of engagement. I can't recall now. There may have been some local authority that Admiral Zumwalt had. But, for the most part, the rules of engagement were more of national policies than they were local military rules. I may be wrong on that, but I believe most rules were established at the DoD level, almost, so there was civilian input and control.* They had a lot of political overtones.

Q: What about dealing with disciplinary problems, drug

---

*DoD--Department of Defense.

use, et cetera?

Captain Kerr: I don't recall that at all as being a problem. I just can't recall drugs ever coming up in the naval forces. I'm sure we had people using drugs, but it never was a problem. Discipline was not a problem with the forces. Now, there would be people who would argue that we had a disciplinary problem because of the way people looked and, you know, the way they kept their boats. They weren't always spic and span, and you would hit those fire bases and they weren't always dressed out in starched khakis ready to meet you, but we didn't see that--or at least I never did and I don't think the admiral saw it as a problem of discipline. It was just people who had fallen into a modus operandi that an outsider might see as a lack of discipline. But these guys were very disciplined when it came time to execute their mission and go out and face a pretty dangerous enemy.

Q: Well, this is the way Admiral Salzer put it--you make a guy work a 14-hour day for seven days a week, and you tell him he's got to do the spit and polish on top of that; it's unrealistic.

Captain Kerr: Yes, that's true.

Q: I was wondering if you had some kind of feedback on morale.

Captain Kerr: In my judgment, morale shot up tremendously within the first couple of months. You had two big things happen, as I said. You had SEA LORDS and the success of that involvement shot morale up. On the advisory side you had movement for the first time in terms of Vietnamization. We were going to get off dead center. We were going to turn this thing over to the Vietnamese. We had a lot of initiatives going. People felt engaged, they felt involved, they felt needed, they felt a sense of accomplishment. The personality and leadership style of the admiral. He gave credibility to the Navy in country. He gave us something to be proud of. He gave us status with our counterparts in the other services who now saw the Navy as an involved component of the whole effort in Vietnam. So morale went up enormously within the first couple of months of his taking command.

Q: I take it that General Abrams looked very favorably on these developments.

Captain Kerr: Absolutely. I think General Abrams was very, very pleased with Admiral Zumwalt and what he was doing.

Q: So he became sort of a fair-haired boy then?

Captain Kerr: Well, that's one way to put it. I think another way to put it is he became a very trusted and essential advisor to General Abrams and also a component commander whom the general looked to, not only for help in executing the admiral's mission, but also in supporting the general in executing his mission.

You know, a lot of people felt that once Zumwalt got over there, we finally had in country probably the best assortment--assortment is not the right word--but the best collection, the most distinguished, capable, competent, simpatico group that had been in Vietnam since the whole damned thing started. Well, Brown, Zumwalt, and Abrams all became chiefs of staff of their services.* So you had a very, very talented group, a dedicated group--a group that worked well together. Plus, Cushman was up in I Corps at the time.** At one point, all four of those guys were sitting on the Joint Chiefs of Staff together. So, we had awfully good people. And Admiral Zumwalt began to draw a

---

*General George S. Brown, USAF, served as Commander Seventh Air Force, with jurisdiction over all Air Force operations in Southeast Asia, 1968-1970; Air Force Chief of Staff, 1973-1974; Chairman of the Joint Chiefs of Staff, 1974-1978.
**General Robert E. Cushman, Jr., USMC, was Commanding General, Third Marine Amphibious Force in the I Corps area of South Vietnam, 1967-1969; Commandant of the Marine Corps, 1972-1975.

lot better group of people from the Navy. Plus, he began to get the Navy more interested in what was happening in country.

Q: So it sort of fed on itself, I would think, as far as positive momentum.

Captain Kerr: Oh yea, there is no question. The admiral had to work through the Navy system to get the support. We didn't have any budget. We didn't own any assets. It all came from the commanders in the Pacific. The admiral did everything he could to get these people to support him and to understand and to see what he considered to be an important dimension to the war in Vietnam. And some of them stalled on that and weren't willing to get on board, if you will.

So General Abrams merely shot those requests up through his channels to the JCS, and they'd get approved there, and they'd come back down the Navy side. So they would be sitting on Zumwalt's ideas or his requests or his initiatives or his recommendations, and they would come down as an order from the JCS. It didn't take long before people, as I said, people began to come to Saigon seeking out Admiral Zumwalt.

I remember one night Vice Admiral Smith got me aside and appealed to me to make sure the admiral understood that he was really on his team and wasn't fighting him.* That same admiral, a couple of months earlier, didn't even bother to come over to see Admiral Zumwalt when he was in country. I guess that's a fairly good indicator of how things were changing, and what sort of impact he was having on the war effort in Saigon.

---

*Vice Admiral John Victor Smith, USN, Commander Amphibious Force Pacific Fleet.

Interview Number 2 with Captain Howard J. Kerr, Jr.,
U.S. Navy (Retired)

Place: Captain Kerr's home in Vienna, Virginia

Date: Tuesday, November 9, 1982

Interviewer: Paul Stillwell

Q: Captain, let me begin this second session with an observation about the value of oral history, that it can provide explanations and insights and additional information that aren't contained in the official records. What can you say about the quality and completeness of the command histories for Commander Naval Forces Vietnam?

Captain Kerr: In late 1968, I began to read the command histories that were being compiled in Saigon and sent forward to the appropriate office in Washington which would, I assume, become the official history of the U.S. Navy effort in Vietnam. These command histories had been crossing my desk since I arrived there, and as an administrative role that I had, I'd put an initial on them and send them out for signature by someone to be forwarded on. But after we'd been in country for about two or three months and I had a much better feel for what was happening, I then began to look at these command histories with a little more critical eye. First of all, we didn't have a historian in the sense of someone who even had a background in that field. An officer was assigned to that billet like any other billet in Vietnam. I don't recall who it was, but I remember having a discussion with him one night, and he basically saw his job as just collecting and collating messages that came into the headquarters, and putting them in the right chronological order and sending them forward. Also, he was not a substantive player in the NavForV arena, nor was he expected to be. But it seemed to me that--based on my personal knowledge of what was going on, the role that Admiral Zumwalt was playing, the shaping of the new strategy for employing forces, the increasing strong relationship with the Vietnamese Navy, an effort to reshape them to begin to assume more and more duties, and also because I had an understanding of the background and the framework in which Admiral Zumwalt was working--I thought that the official histories that were being sent in were wholly inadequate for someone 20, 30 years from now to sit down and read and try to understand what was really happening. It's not that the material that was being sent in didn't have some value and wasn't accurate and wasn't correct. It's simply that it did not give you the full flavor of what and why things were happening. They were just as I said, a collection of messages, official message traffic, reports of incidents on the river, reports of firefights. There was no analytical effort, and there was no serious effort to put it together in some meaningful way so it tied together. So I was concerned about that, because I felt that there was an awful lot happening in those three or four months since Admiral Zumwalt had arrived, and I couldn't see any of that being reflected in the official history. So I went to see the admiral and told him of my concern for this and suggested that we try to find someone who could bring a little more discipline, a little more analytical ability to this job so that the story could be told a little bit better than what it was. An officer who had just gotten his doctorate degree from the Fletcher School of Law and Diplomacy was under orders to come to Saigon to work in the MSTS office, of all places.* This is a good example of the kind of detailing that was going on in Vietnam. Here you had a fellow that the Navy had just spent X number of dollars and three years of his life to get a doctorate degree in the discipline of international relations, of which history is a big part of that discipline, and he was being sent to be an administrative officer in the MSTS office. You know, that's the container ships, the merchant arm that was supporting us. So I had our personnel people have him report to our office when he came in, and I knew who he was. I had gone to school with him at Fletcher, a fellow

---

*MSTS—Military Sea Transportation Service, which has since been renamed Military Sealift Command. This is an arm of the Navy which provides logistic support through its own ships and chartered merchant vessels. It had a very active role in hauling war materials to Vietnam.

by the name of Dick Schreadley.* Dick is now out of the Navy and a newspaper editor in Charleston, South Carolina. And he's a very intelligent, very capable guy, and I explained to him what was my assessment of the official history of the war in Vietnam that was being put together. I asked him if he would be interested in a reassignment out of the MSTS office over to the NavForV staff to take on this job of trying to put a little more meaningful history together. Dick indicated that he would be, so we had him go up to the office and take a look at what was being done. Admiral Zumwalt wanted some confirmation that my own assessment was accurate. Dick came back and said that the situation was far worse in his judgment than what I had indicated to him, and he would be delighted to take on the job. So I went to see the admiral and cleared it with him and Dick got assigned to that job. By the way, he'd be someone that might be of interest to you people in terms of putting this oral history together, because he did that for the next year, I believe, while he was in Vietnam.

Q: Fortunately, part of the output of that was published in the Proceedings, so it's available already.**

---
*Commander Richard L. Schreadley, USN.
**Schreadley wrote the following articles: "SEA LORDS," U.S. Naval Institute Proceedings, August 1970, pages 22-31; "'Nothing to Report' A Day on the Vam Co Tay," Proceedings, December 1970, pages 23-27; "The Naval War in Vietnam, 1950-1970," Proceedings (Naval Review Issue), 1971,

Kerr/Zumwalt Staff - 94

Captain Kerr: Okay. Good. Well, it goes to show you I don't read the <u>Proceedings</u> as closely as I should.

Q: Well, was this something of the old school tie at work? How well had you known him at Fletcher?

Captain Kerr: Well, Dick and I had gone to school there together for a year. It was a little bit of the old tie, but, hell, the important thing is to get somebody in who could begin to put together a little better history. Had I gone back to the bureau and requested that, we would have gotten the same kind of bureaucratic response, "We'll look for somebody," and then next summer somebody would have come out. And I saw Dick rolling in. Had he been going to an operational unit or to a job down in the Delta supporting the war effort, I wouldn't have made any effort to try to pull Dick into the headquarters staff. But he was going to be an administrative officer at the MSTS. So I thought that he could be better used in the NavForV headquarters than over there.

Q: Was it being treated as a collateral duty before that?

Captain Kerr: No, there was a fellow up there full-time.

Kerr/Zumwalt Staff - 95

But, as I recall, he had been a first lieutenant on an LST or something, and he just took the messages that came in each day and put them in a pile, and at the end of each month put grommets through them and mailed them off to Washington, and that was the history of the Vietnam War.

Q: The old philosophy that a line officer can do anything.

Captain Kerr: Well, line officers are certainly educated to put grommet holes in messages and compile them.

Q: One of the observations that has been made about Admiral Zumwalt is that he could accomplish much more than most people can. Do you have an explanation for that?

Captain Kerr: Well, yes, I think number one he was more intelligent than most people. He was very perceptive, very analytical, a man who was capable of taking in enormous amounts of material, synthesizing that material very quickly, shedding the irrelevant aspects of it. You know, the kind of guy that gets right to the heart of the matter. He's also somebody who worked more than anybody else. His day generally started about 6:00 o'clock, and he'd go running in the morning. I'd go with him. In fact, I'd never done any jogging in my life, and one morning he came in to my bedroom at 6:00 o'clock and rolled me out on the floor and said I had five minutes to be downstairs in my tennis shoes, and my jogging career started. And I still do it today.

He worked harder, plus he had a capacity to deal with routine things very quickly. The staff would work for hours putting together the paperwork for him and, you know, a guy with a more bureaucratic view of things would spend the whole day reviewing it, and Zumwalt literally would go through it in 15 or 20 minutes. In other words, the things that he focused on were the things that he considered to be essentially important, and particularly essentially important for the commander to focus on. And those things that other people should be focusing on, he let them focus on them. He didn't sit there and review what they did and cross the "T's" and re-dot the "I's" and change the syntax and the wording, unless it was something that was very important to him. So he had a tremendous capability to set priorities and sift through the things that were unimportant and give them the sort of casual attention that was necessary. Plus, he didn't spend much time each day, like a lot of us do, with mundane things, like, "What are we going to wear today? What's my schedule today?" Those things were taken care of for him. For example, he had a lot of support from his staff, which allowed him to focus on other things. Most of us got up in the morning and wondered if we had enough clean clothes to wear. The admiral had things laid out for him. The reason I'm getting at this is not to point out that it takes so much time to lay things out, but the admiral was always thinking about the next event, analyzing things, preparing himself for the important things that were coming up to the point where he didn't even pay any attention to what he was putting on. I remember one morning, the steward was gone, and the Vietnamese houseboy went up and laid out some clothes for him. They laid out a set of green fatigues. They laid out white socks and white shoes, and a khaki combination cap, and that's what he came down in. And as he walked into the dining room for breakfast, we all looked up at him. Suddenly I started laughing. He looked down at me and said, "What's the matter with you this morning, Howard?"

And I said, "Admiral, have you looked at yourself in the mirror?"

There is no doubt that he had looked at himself in the mirror, totally missed the fact that he had three different uniforms on. And I suggested that he return, and since we were going out in the field that morning in a helo, that he might want to take his white shoes and socks off and replace his combination cap with the appropriate fatigue hat that generally was worn with that and put his boots on. That's what he did. Then he raised hell with me because the wrong things had been set out for him.

Well, I guess the point of this thing is that his mind was always occupied with what I considered to be the important things that he was focusing on, and to the point where he could just literally set aside in his mind this horrendous plethora, I guess, if you will, of mundane things that all of us deal with each day, trying to match a tie with a shirt, making sure we've got the right socks on, et cetera. He never focused on or paid any attention on those things at all. So he was able to exclude all those things and focus on the things that had his attention. So I think for all those reasons he was a guy who crammed, oh, hell, sometimes a week into one day. I used to always feel that I'd get up at 6:00 in the morning and I'd go to bed at 12:00 at night, and I still felt like I was ten miles behind, trying to catch up.

Q: Well, there's the lesson in that story in a larger sense--that it's very important what is brought to him in the sense of paperwork too. And that puts a tremendous obligation on the officer who performs the filtering function.

Captain Kerr: Well, that's true and that tells you a little bit about how he did business. He always liked to have an alter ego, generally a junior officer like myself, Bob Powers, somebody who was with him all the time, who understood what was on his mind, what his priorities were, and it was to serve this filtering purpose so that you got to him the things that he was concerned with.* And for another purpose--to make sure that the people who he had talked to, and wanted to get something from, understood exactly what it was he wanted, so that there was an efficiency in what they were doing. In other words, by having this alter ego, he saw it as a mechanism that created enormous efficiencies in his day as well as in the days of the people that were supporting him. I think it worked very well. It did put a burden on the person who was in that role. And a lot of times, it was not always understood, particularly by more senior officers who basically saw things in the more classic organization chart. In other words, the flow of things should be in accordance with that organizational chart. But, as I think I've mentioned earlier, Admiral Zumwalt had an essential distrust of a bureaucracy. He understood that there were things that the bureaucracy had to do and only they could do. But when it came to the formation of policy and the setting of the priorities and the implementation of that policy, he always liked to have an alternate means to succeeding in those areas other than having to deal with the staff.

---

*Lieutenant Commander Robert C. Powers, USN, who served on the staff as logistics plans officer and requirements officer and then flag lieutenant. His Professional Note, "Beans and Bullets for Sea Lords," was published in the Proceedings, December 1970, pages 95-97.

Q: One of your many roles on his behalf was as his eyes and ears to go places he couldn't go. Could you discuss some of these situations in an operational sense?

Captain Kerr: There were a number of occasions when the admiral wanted to get some feedback on conditions out in the field, either based on something he'd heard, that he wanted confirmed, or some concern he may have had. It wasn't that he didn't have total confidence in the commanders whom these people worked for to report to him. But he understood that there were times when, well, like the captain of a ship, he just doesn't always know what's going on in the engineering department, and sometimes it's good to know. I could go out. I was a lieutenant. I was the same age and vintage of the people that were out there. I could sit down and talk to them, and I was able to kind of put together the flavor, the content of what was happening, what wasn't happening, what was on their minds, what were they happy with, what were they unhappy with, what would they like to see changed. And also we could get some data points on whether or not the policies that were being set in Saigon were actually filtering down to the level that they had to be implemented. I guess some people would say I was a spy for the commander. They would see it in that light. I never saw it that way. I never came back to Saigon and put anyone on report with the admiral. My job was to go out and not only assess what the circumstances were, but also I think I served a purpose, a lot of times, in defining for them what this policy coming out of Saigon was when sometimes their immediate commander hadn't defined it for them in the terms that they fully understood. So I don't think it ever created any problems. I think it irritated a few people, but, well, that's just one of the collateral costs of implementing a lot of change. And that's really what Admiral Zumwalt was doing. He was changing things all the time, and I don't mean that he was changing his policy constantly, but he was changing the role of the Navy in Vietnam, and he wanted to make sure that people understood and sensed the direction that he was moving, and why these things were happening. He was out constantly telling them, and so I went out like a pollster or something to test the pulse and see what it was. I took on quite a few jobs of that nature and, I think they were helpful not only to us in Saigon and to the admiral, but also to the people in the field in that when I left, I think, they had generally a clear understanding of what it was the admiral was doing.

Q: Was there also a sense of transferring information the other way, that you could act as a conduit for these junior officers to get things to the admiral they might not want to send through the chain?

Captain Kerr: Well, that's true. There's no question about that. That was part of it. I tried to be as discreet as possible with that. Some of the information I just never took back. Yes, I had to make a judgment call. Was this a disgruntled young officer who was trying to put his boss on report, or was this a young officer who was bringing to my attention a matter, an issue that was of such importance and moment that it should be brought to the admiral's attention? A lot of times the commanders had already brought these to his attention, and this served to confirm what they had told him. So, I think, once again here, I'm trying to point out here that we were trying to do this in a very concerned, positive, measured way to ensure that there was a flow of communications from the commander down to the lowest guy, and from the lowest guy back to the commander without interfering unduly with the chain of command.

Q: Did you find any cases in which the junior officers wanted to be more aggressive than they were being allowed to?

Captain Kerr: No, I didn't find that that was a problem. If anything, I found just the opposite to be the problem, that a lot of times they were overly aggressive in a situation that had political overtones, and, therefore, in retrospect being too aggressive is the wrong way to go. I remember one case in particular where a young officer took a boat up, I forget the name of the waterway, but it separated Cambodia from South Vietnam. He saw some VC collecting taxes and went after them, and they shot at him. He opened fire and shot at them and jumped out of his boat and chased them with a shotgun, and was in Cambodia. This resulted in an official protest from Prince Sihanouk at the time.* So, here was a case where the fellow had been a little too aggressive. On the other hand, the guy was being shot at. He didn't understand the political sensitivities of the situation. That was a dimension that probably pervaded this war. You know, it was the political dimension, and we couldn't expect all the officers to understand that, and certainly it shouldn't take priority when you're getting shot at if you're the guy that's on the scene. There were also instances where the officers were caught in this enormous dilemma of whether or not to open fire on something that was moving at night in the water, or not to fire on something that was moving. I remember one lieutenant getting me aside one evening and in a very emotional, tearful way telling me that he had been told that he was to waste anything that moved on the water after midnight. He said he just couldn't do it, because he knew

---

*Prince Norodom Sihanouk, Cambodian head of state at the time. This incident is discussed in the Proceedings, August 1970, page 26.

that a lot of these movements on the water were just locals who were out at night for very routine, peaceful, domestic reasons, and if we started opening fire at everything that moved we were going to end up by killing a lot of innocent people. Yet he was under direct orders from his immediate superior to do that, and he found himself in a very difficult situation where he didn't want to disobey his orders, yet on the other hand, his conscience wouldn't let him do what he had been directed to do.

Q: How was it resolved?

Captain Kerr: Well, these things aren't really resolved. We listened to them. I expressed the fact that I certainly understood his dilemma and would take it back and discuss it with the admiral, and I did. And, whenever the admiral had an opportunity to visit, he would raise these issues with the commanders. But, you couldn't start tying the immediate commanders' hands. You start laying down too many criteria and, as you know, it becomes no policy at all. I don't think we ever resolved that kind of thing. I don't think we ever resolved it in the whole war. It was just something that every young man that was over there and out in a boat at night had to deal with almost individually. There just wasn't any way, because, hell, the reason the order had been put out by the commander in the first place was that there were too many examples where that peaceful family is coming home and the mother takes out a grenade and throws it in the back of the boat as they're waving at the sailors. So, viewed from that context, it was the right order to put out. Viewed from the context of the kid who had to execute it, it is a very difficult thing to do. So we had a lot of that. As I said, there was no real way to resolve those things.

Q: Did you encounter areas in which junior officers were ordered to do dangerous things in which they felt their immediate superiors didn't have a proper appreciation of the risk involved?

Captain Kerr: Oh, I think so, but I don't recall anything specific where somebody brought that to my attention. I think there were cases where some of the junior officers thought that some of their immediate superiors were missing the action while they sat back at headquarters on the radios demanding more information on how the fight was going. As far as they were concerned, if they wanted to know, they could come out and find out. But I guess that happens in any conflict. It wasn't one of these issues that was brought to my attention too often.

Kerr/Zumwalt Staff - 106

Q: We've talked about the three primary task forces that conducted Operation SEA LORDS. What about Admiral Zumwalt's role in connection with covert operations, the SEALs and so forth?*

Captain Kerr: Well, SEALs, of course, were in country, as you know. They were in the Delta. They were headquartered there. There were, of course, SEALs who were brought covertly into the country. These were SEALs who were assigned, I believe, from the Navy to a civilian agency for temporary additional duty. Then they were sent in country and were assigned to be an advisor to a Vietnamese district official. An individual's identity as a Navy enlisted man, as a Navy SEAL, was never disclosed, either to that Vietnamese official or to his military counterpart who was generally an Army lieutenant colonel or colonel who was on the advisory side. This sometimes presented some problems, and I know that General Abrams did discuss that with Admiral Zumwalt once. And I went out and spent five days once down in the Delta getting around and talking to a lot of these individuals and finding out what particular problems they were having. Other than the fact that generally the colonel, once he found out, was enraged by the fact that this civilian advisor that he assumed was a

---

*SEALs--(sea-air-land) are a group of navymen who undergo very rigorous physical training and weapons training. They act as sort of a guerrilla force that can be inserted from the sea in order to perform covert operations on land.

member of the CIA, or some other civilian agency, found out he was an enlisted Navy man, and that disturbed him greatly. There really weren't any other serious problems with it. From what I could see, they did the job that they were sent in to do.

Q: What was that job?

Captain Kerr: Well, their job was to advise the Vietnamese official and to assist him in counterinsurgency operations in his district. And the manner of those counterinsurgency operations was sometimes very gruesome.

I went out on a couple of night missions with these guys. I had no idea what it was they were going to do when we went out. It's the kind of level of warfare that, you know, is essential in that kind of environment, but it's very gruesome, I guess, is the word and untraditional in the sense that the kinds of things that naval officers are trained for; even with myself I had no background, understanding, or concept of what these guys did and what they were doing until I went out and watched them in the field.

Q: What did you do on these missions?

Captain Kerr: I stayed alive. That's what I did. I basically stayed in the background by their orders. They didn't want me involved at all. They were willing to take me along to observe and see what was going on, but they didn't want me involved. I wasn't trained to do that at all.

I remember one night we went out with a group of Vietnamese SEALs, and this fellow that I was with was an advisor to these people, assisting them in their counterinsurgency operations. They came upon a Vietnamese camp. There must have been seven VC in that camp. They were sitting around, some were eating, some were smoking. They came from three different directions, took them by surprise. The American and myself--I was off in the shadows of the trees. The Navy man did not participate. The Vietnamese SEALs moved in quickly. They lined these VC up. They tied them, blindfolded them, and they started querying the first one, and all of a sudden this guy pulled a knife out and cut open his stomach, took his liver out, and then went across and wiped it in the faces of the other guys. They got all the information they wanted after that.

Q: Gruesome, as you say.

Captain Kerr: Very gruesome, yes.

Q: But effective.

Captain Kerr: Well, I can only assume it was effective, because I saw an awful lot of dialogue taking place after that first one resisted the questions. I didn't understand; it was all in Vietnamese, of course. But it was very gruesome and a level of warfare that I had never been trained in or understood. One reads about it. You see movies about this, but until you're actually out there in the field and see it firsthand, you can't really appreciate it.

Q: Did Admiral Zumwalt have any specific doctrine to try to prevent atrocities against innocent civilians?

Captain Kerr: I don't recall. I do know that we had rules of engagement that covered this. The admiral was responsible for vigorously enforcing the rules of engagement. I don't recall many lapses in those rules of engagement, other than the one I mentioned up in Cambodia, and that one got resolved fairly quickly and easily.

I remember the lieutenant when he got called up to Saigon for an interview that same day to find out what the hell he had done. He was told that Sihanouk had accused him of firing into Cambodia and killing innocent civilians. And this kid, with much aplomb and not the least bit of hesitation or deference, turned to whoever it was that mentioned that to him and said, "Well, you tell Sihanouk he's a lying son-of-a-bitch."

That's basically what the State Department did, but they did it in the usual diplomatic language.

Q: I was reading in Commander Schreadley's article about a JG named Bernique.*

Captain Kerr: That's the same guy, yes. In fact, we renamed, in Vietnam that body of water he went up as "Bernique's Creek." It probably is still in the maps of Southeast Asia.

Q: We started in a little bit on the admiral's day and life around the enclave. If you could pick it up there, the sorts of accommodations that he and you had, and the admiral's mess and so forth.

Captain Kerr: Well, we lived very comfortably. The house that the admiral had was right next to the headquarters. It had been the home of the head of the military advisory assistance group through the Fifties, and then it was General Westmoreland's quarters when he was the commander of the Military Advisory Group, Vietnam.

---
*Lieutenant (junior grade) Michael Bernique, USNR. See Proceedings, August 1970, page 26.

When General Abrams relieved General Westmoreland, he wanted to live out at the MACV headquarters.* He didn't want the time added to his day of transiting back and forth. Plus, there was a security risk also; every time you were in a car driving around Saigon you were a target.

So this house was made available to Admiral Zumwalt about two months after he arrived in Vietnam, and we moved in. It came complete with two Vietnamese families that had been there for two decades--took care of the house and grounds. We had four or five stewards that were assigned to the admiral. And myself and another aide by the name of Lew Glenn, and the chief of staff, and the admiral lived in the house.** It was just traditional Southeast Asia opulent living, I guess you could call it. A big house, big ceiling fans. It was very nice. But, you know, it wouldn't have made any difference to Admiral Zumwalt whether he was living in that house or something much smaller than that, and much less opulent. He never cared about those things. He didn't want that house because of the size or anything. It was the convenience; it was right next door. It was offered and we took it; that's all. In all the time I worked for Admiral Zumwalt, he in comparison to all the flag officers I've ever known in the Navy, he

---
*General Creighton W. Abrams, Jr., AUS, relieved General William C. Westmoreland, AUS, as Commander U.S. Military Assistance Command Vietnam in 1968, shortly before the arrival of Admiral Zumwalt.
**Lieutenant W. Lewis Glenn, Jr., USN

was the least concerned with and insistent upon perquisites. He just never cared about them at all. They just weren't a part of his makeup.

Q: Was the South Vietnamese cuisine included in the regular diet?

Captain Kerr: Yes, and much to our--well, we liked it, but let me tell you--we all paid a price for it at one time or another. In fact, I became, myself, very, very ill after one meal and almost had to be medevaced to Clark Air Force Base.* I passed out up in my room from illness, and I was so sick I couldn't even crawl to a telephone to get help. The admiral came back from some function that night and walked into my bedroom and saw me laying on the floor and got me out to the hospital at Tan Son Nhut. Yes, we enjoyed the Vietnamese food, but the conditions under which it was prepared sometimes demanded a price. We tried to have the Navy stewards do most of the cooking, but occasionally the Vietnamese would insist upon preparing something for us.

Q: Did you ever have any concern that you might be poisoned or whatever?

---
*Medevac--an evacuation for medical reasons.

Captain Kerr: No, I don't think we ever thought in those terms. I don't recall that I did. The stewards used to watch the Vietnamese when they would be preparing the food. No, we never really thought that we were targets, although I don't know whether I mentioned on the last one the effort to . . .

Q: Please do.

Captain Kerr: We used to play volleyball every day after lunch, and obviously someone was watching our schedule, because one day the admiral went out in the field, and I didn't go with him that day. I stayed behind, and all of a sudden I heard this enormous thunderclap. I went outside, and someone had thrown a satchel charge over the fence onto the volleyball court where we played. So they were watching us, and there was an attempt on the admiral's life, although he wasn't present and they didn't know it.

One thing that we did try to do was to prepare ourselves to defend the compound in the event there was another Tet, although we didn't do a very good job at that. I don't think naval officers are very good at that kind of thing. The only people we had to help us were the stewards. I was always concerned that somebody was going to get shot every time we tried to practice. Plus one of our predecessors had, a fellow by the name of Kerrey, who's now the new governor of Nebraska, had been the aide in Saigon.* He kept enough ammunition and hand grenades in the closets to blow the whole house up if it took a hit. And I had all that removed. I was afraid that somebody would pull off a stray round and we'd all go up. We weren't nearly as well trained as you'd see the Army. When General Abrams would go through Saigon, God, he had gun jeeps fore and aft. His aides all decked out in M-16s and grenades. We just never did that. I think it goes to the lack of training that you have.

Q: Did you have Marine guards?

Captain Kerr: Well, we did eventually. We did when we got concerned about the admiral's--well, when we first got there we were just driving through the streets of Saigon. I used to carry this .38 pistol in my briefcase--a big warrior, you know, with a .38 pistol in his briefcase, and that was it. It was all we had. We got a little concerned that that wasn't enough if somebody decided to shoot at us. So we got a jeep and we got a couple of Marines. I even had some second thoughts about that, because whereas those

---

*Lieutenant (junior grade) Joseph R. Kerrey, USNR, who served as governor of Nebraska from 1983 to 1987. Lieutenant Kerrey was sent to Vietnam as a SEAL team leader in January 1969. On 14 March, he was severely wounded during action near Nha Trang Bay, for which he was awarded the Medal of Honor.

guys could protect you if somebody is tracking you, they also tend to attract the attention of people who may not know who you are. So it had its pluses, but it also had its risks involved.

Q: What about domestic enemies? Was there any effect from U.S. war protestors on the effort there?

Captain Kerr: No, no. I don't recall any U.S. protestors in Saigon. Is that what you mean?

Q: Well, I mean more people, such as Jane Fonda and Ramsey Clark, who were speaking against the American war effort.* Did this have any effect in weakening the influence of what Admiral Zumwalt was trying to do?

Captain Kerr: No, none whatsoever, none whatsoever. Clearly, their impact was on the people in this country. I say this, the radio-television networks in Saigon would play everything these people were saying. They never kept it from the soldiers and sailors. You know, like the effect of Tokyo Rose, I don't know that it ever had that much effect. You always see in the movies where people were sitting around listening to her and laughing and

---

*Jane Fonda is a movie actress; Ramsey Clark served as U.S. Attorney General from 1967 to 1969.

joking about her. That's basically how it came across in Saigon. They'd put Jane Fonda on television; everybody would clap and jeer. No, I don't think it ever had any impact at all.

Q: To what extent did you in the compound have the ability to keep up with news?

Captain Kerr: Well, we had daily news summaries that came in by messages that the Navy did. We had the <u>Stars and Stripes</u>.* We had newspapers from home. We had the evening newscasts in Saigon. Plus, once a week the radio-television office in the Pentagon would send us all the television networks' news programs for the week. They were generally edited, so we just got that that had to do with Vietnam. But, then, of course, that was 80% of what was on the air each night. The domestic stories here in the country that were unrelated to the war, they generally edited out. We had a pretty good picture of what the news was reporting. Then the admiral made a habit of meeting with a lot of the in-country news people on a routine basis at least once a month. We'd have them in for dinner or for a lunch or for a briefing. We had a chance to talk to all the news broadcasters, as well as the writers from major

---

*A daily newspaper with separate editions in Europe and the Far East, published by the U.S. armed forces for a readership comprised of service personnel.

newspapers and news magazines that were in country. In fact, I remember one evening having a long discussion with a fellow from Time magazine, and I told him that--he had written something about the Navy's efforts in the Delta. I got him aside and I said, "Look, you just know that's not true."

And, he said, "Look, and I'm ashamed of that." He said, "I'm ashamed of my magazine and my editors." He said, "The story that came out in Time magazine bears no resemblance to the one that I sent to New York."

We wouldn't go to the point of condemning his editors for slanting his story, or redoing his story to conform to an editorial position they had taken, but it was clear that that's what was happening.

Q: In what sense was it slanted?

Captain Kerr: Well, I forget the specifics now, but the point is that it was slanted in a sense that it came across in a very negative way about the war effort in Vietnam, when it should have been a very positive story, should have supported the things that the administration and the President were saying, as opposed to chinking away at their credibility. We'd see the same thing in the television news stories. We'd sit there and watch five days of news in one hour. I mean the general drift and theme and bias and the position that they were taking, and then using interviews and statements and other things out of context to support that was very obvious. I remember the case where they were going into Cambodia. This newsman jumped up on this tank and asked this kid what he thought about the President's thrust into Cambodia. And, this kid says, "Hell, I don't even know where we're going. Nobody ever tells me anything."

Then the newsman turns around and he said, "And here we have another example of the failure of the commanders to tell the troops what is going on."

He'd probably asked half a dozen other people who all might have said something, "Yes, we know we're going in and we understand that it's going to be dangerous, but we consider this to be an important thing to do." That wouldn't be used. What would be used was the kid who had said something negative.

Q: Well, that may have been one of the reasons that in my reading of Admiral Veth's oral history he had a very negative view toward the news media.* Was there that kind of negative view on Admiral Zumwalt's part?

Captain Kerr: No, not at all, not at all, I don't think

---
*Rear Admiral Kenneth L. Veth, USN, who was Admiral Zumwalt's predecessor as Commander U.S. Naval Forces Vietnam. He is the subject of a Naval Institute oral history.

so. You know, the admiral worked very well with the news media. He had a very good press fellow, a guy by the name of Jack Davey.* I think, one of the things, of course, was that the admiral was very honest, very forward, very candid with the news media in telling them his story, and they always appreciated that. No, I don't recall him ever having a problem along those lines. Nor do I think he developed overall--he'd be unhappy about a given story, the way it was written, but in general, no, I don't think he had that negative feeling about the press.

Q: Well, a smart, ambitious guy on the way up can use the media to enhance his own cause.

Captain Kerr: Yes, that's true, but also Admiral Zumwalt was something, had something that the people were interested in reporting on. He was young, he was new, he was articulate, he was charismatic, if you will, and he had a story to tell. And, that story always supported General Abrams' efforts and the administration's efforts. So in that sense the admiral never slanted anything to assist himself. But, yes, I think the press that came out on Admiral Zumwalt in Vietnam was very helpful to him.

---
*Commander John R. Davey, Jr., USN.

Kerr/Zumwalt Staff - 120

Q: Well, many times that is a result of the factor of cooperation. You're more inclined to go along with somebody who helps you.

Captain Kerr: No question about it.

You're asking me did Admiral Zumwalt know how to use the press? Sure, he did. He understood the importance of it and understood that the press could be helpful to him. I wouldn't say that he overly courted the press, but he certainly was cooperative with the press, and the press were cooperative with him.

Q: Did General Abrams issue any guidelines for dealings with the media, things that could not be talked about?

Captain Kerr: I'm sure he did, but I just can't recall right now. There had to be guidelines out. But I just don't remember now any of the specifics other than the fact there were guidelines.

Q: Certainly, though, it was much more open than the censorship that had been a standard, say, in World War II.

Captain Kerr: Well, I don't think there's any question about that. My God, we had television cameras all over the country, and they were basically interviewing people on the field and putting them on the evening television news. So, yes, in that sense that's very true.

Q: So the nature of the times contributed to the openness.

Captain Kerr: Oh, yes, sure. But I think the fact that the news media were able to insist upon so much access to people and to events suggests that it was a whole new set of circumstances surrounding the reporting of Vietnam than in any other war that this country had ever been in.

Q: To what extent did the admiral bring in officers from the field to his compound to meet with them there?

Captain Kerr: Well, he did this on a fairly routine basis. He'd bring his commanders in quite often to discuss things with them. But a lot of the officers who were leaving Vietnam would come by, and they'd spend the night, have dinner with him, and discuss their views of the war, their views of the Navy's effort. Unfortunately, it seemed like most of these were leaving the Navy. Most of these young officers were leaving the Navy. I think these officers had an enormous impact on Admiral Zumwalt, not just those who came through to say goodbye, but those that he would see out in the field. I think they shaped his thinking a great deal in what he did when he became CNO. He had great admiration and respect for what these young officers were doing, and I think they influenced him tremendously.

Q: In what sense?

Captain Kerr: Well, in the sense that--look at some of the early things he did as CNO. They wanted to get rid of what we know as "Mickey Mouse." They couldn't understand why the Navy would still impose that type of thing. They couldn't understand why a person that had a neatly trimmed beard couldn't retain that beard. You know, they'd go out in the field and you'd have kids out there living under miserable conditions, under fire each night. It's hot. They'd have these torrential rains. Eating out of tin cans. Living in boats. Miserable conditions! They never complained about those. What they complained about was why they couldn't have a beard. What they complained about was the "Mickey Mouse." And, it made a lot of sense, it seemed to me, and what the admiral picked up on immediately was, "My God, if these guys aren't complaining about the conditions under which we're asking them to fight, the least we can do is remove from them those things that are bothering them." So I think in that sense they had a great impact on him. Plus, he felt that these officers, young officers were being tested in the real arena that mattered for a military person, in that the types of stress and strain that they were under would serve them throughout their Navy careers and their civilian lives in ways that people who had never been put in that situation would be able to match them. And so, I think, when he became CNO, he basically saw that as his constituency, as his natural constituency, and that the future of the Navy rested more with these young people, what they had learned and brought with them out of that Vietnam experience than with a lot of traditions and regulations that long since should have been removed from the system.

Q: Was there any concern that these people coming from the harsh living conditions you have described might feel some resentment when they saw how the admiral lived?

Captain Kerr: No, no, not at all. We've exaggerated how the admiral--I mean, we lived well, but let me tell you, Admiral Zumwalt was in that helicopter every morning. He spent more time in the field, exposed to enemy fire, meeting with, talking to, examining, understanding what was going on than any military commander in Vietnam, and they understood that.

Q: That would prevent the resentment.

Captain Kerr: Well, sure. You know, if he would have just

been sitting in Saigon in that big house holding dinners each night, no, nobody is going to respect a military commander in wartime living like that. But, you know, we were in the air almost every day. Wherever the fight was, that's where he went. Wherever the difficult situation was the night before, he got reports on, that's where he was the next morning, and they knew that and they understood that.

Q: To what extent did logistics support and supply support concern the admiral?

Captain Kerr: Well, I don't think there were any real logistics problems, but the mentality sometimes of the people who were supplying it was a problem. I can remember that we got a message one day from the type commander back in San Diego telling us that the preventive maintenance reports of PBRs in the Delta were coming in too slow. You know, after we laughed about it, we all got angry, because some of those boats had been sunk by the Viet Cong. I guess those things always happen in wartime where you have people who are totally removed from the scene of action, and their universe is the same whether it's wartime or peacetime. We found that sometimes the distance between San Diego and Saigon was far greater than just the mileage distance. I think that probably the biggest problem was trying to get people to understand what was really happening. When the admiral put those ships in dangerous waters, they started getting shot at and the guys weren't doing their PMS and sending back their reports to San Diego anymore.* They were out trying to find VC ammunition and supplies that were infiltrating into the Delta, notwithstanding the fact that that was being articulated back to the States, not everyone understood it.

Q: Well, if you're going to have stepped-up contact with the enemy, you're going to shoot a lot more. Were you able to adjust in terms of ammunition supply?

Captain Kerr: Oh, yes, yes. I don't recall that there were problems like that. There may have been. Well, it's been so many years now some of these things I just can't recall that well, Paul, but I don't recall shortages of ammunition or food. There certain was never any shortage of beer; I can assure you of that. I can still see these giant helicopters bringing great pallets full of Schlitz and Budweiser beer out. You'd look up in the sky, and there would be this great big helicopter, and there would be about 50 cases of beer on this pallet heading out for fire stations. There was never any shortage.

---
*PMS--Planned Maintenance System, a Navy-wide system whereby various preventive maintenance actions are required to be performed on weapons and other pieces of equipment at specified intervals. Obviously, when one is actively engaged in fighting a war, there is some difficulty in doing the required PMS checks on a timely basis.

Q: Moving to another staff function, do you recall any particular problems or situations regarding intelligence?

Captain Kerr: Well, I think there was concern on the intelligence, on the part of the intelligence people about the--what was really happening in the Delta, as I recall. That was one of the big issues, and how were the VC really infiltrating in the Delta, and how were they supplying them? And the admiral's intelligence officer, Captain Rectanus, had, as I recall, a thesis that they were being supplied through Sihanoukville and bringing it overland, infiltrating into the Delta.* And I think this proved to be accurate and correct. The admiral had tremendous intelligence support in Vietnam. I'd have to say the strongest section in the NavForV staff was in the intelligence section. It was the best collection overall of talented people. It had a real simpatico, too. It was a good team; they worked well together, and they were just superbly led by a captain and now retired Vice Admiral Rectanus, who kept a real good handle on his intelligence officers, and demanded of them the most rigorous analytical standards. The admiral came to rely on them very, very much.

----
*Captain Earl F. Rectanus, USN.

Q: Well, one of the big controversies of the Vietnam War is the question of body counts. Was there pressure on the Navy in that direction?

Captain Kerr: I don't know that there was any pressure of body count. It was a part of every after-action report that came in. I don't recall that there was a lot of emphasis in the Navy side put on body count. I don't think that the admiral saw it as a highly significant data point in trying to determine how well we were doing in the war effort. Certainly, killing VC was an important part of what the Navy effort was. It was just a by-product of that effort, but I don't think that all of a sudden we thought we had taken a step closer to winning the war because on Thursday the body count had gone up. It just wasn't that significant a data point.

Q: What were the measures of effectiveness that were used in assessing how well the Navy did?

Captain Kerr: One of the measures of effectiveness that we were looking for was were we halting the infiltration into the South. What the admiral wanted to do, and what he was trying to assess was the impact of putting presence there. Can you make the enemy react and expend his resources? Which he wasn't doing, wasn't having to do, because there was no Navy, no presence there, no one trying to interdict his efforts. Make him have to change his modus operandi. Make it expensive for him. These are harder things to quantify. But, when we arrived in Saigon, the things we were measuring, which were easy to quantify, didn't tell us a damned thing about how well we were doing.

Q: So this goes back to Captain Rectanus's organization, really, to see how well you're doing in terms of what they turn up.

Captain Kerr: Yes. Well, in terms of the hard data points that we were looking for, numbers of tons of supplies that were captured, uncovered, destroyed--that's really what we were trying to do, more so than how many bodies were counted as dead.

Q: How good was the relationship between intelligence and operations?

Captain Kerr: Oh, I think it was very good, and I think the operations were really driven by the intelligence assessments. The admiral, as I say, had great confidence in what he was told by Rectanus. He'd move on that very quickly, and I think it proved to be correct.

Q: How much did Admiral Zumwalt act as his own operations officer?

Captain Kerr: Quite a bit. I don't mean in a sense of implementing things, but in terms of the conceptualizing and the broad organization and, you know, putting together that calculus that is necessary to bring the thing off, bring the forces to bear at the right time with the right people, he did a lot of that. He worked very closely with the operations people. I won't say he was his own operations officer, because he had a very poor one, but if you just sat outside his office and watched who was going in and out of his office all day long, it was generally Rectanus and the operations guy.

Q: Who was the operations officer?

Captain Kerr: A fellow by the name of Dick Nicholson, who was a commander at the time and now a retired rear admiral, whom the admiral had tremendous confidence in, great respect for, and who eventually left that job and went on down to be the commander of Market Time operations.*

Q: Had he been in the slot, or was he one like Tidd that

---

*Commander Richard E. Nicholson, USN.

got put in by Zumwalt?*

Captain Kerr: He was put in. The admiral's first operations officer was fired. I forget his name now, but he just wasn't on the same wavelength with the admiral. Every time the admiral asked him to do something, it either didn't get done or got done half-assed or way behind schedule. So, one night, the admiral told him he had to have something done by 10:00 o'clock that evening. He and I came back, and he told me to go over and find out if it was done. I went over and it wasn't done. I went back and told the admiral that it wasn't, and he wrote out a little note, relieved him. He handed me the note and told me to take it over and give it to him. I did. And this guy asked me when this was effective. And I said, "Immediately." I contacted Dick Nicholson right away and told him that the admiral had asked me to advise him that he was the new operations officer as of that moment.

Q: Where had he been up to then?

Captain Kerr: He'd been working in the front office doing some special projects for the admiral.

Q: That's a pretty abrupt change of assignment.

---

*Captain Emmett H. Tidd, USN, Zumwalt's chief of staff.

Captain Kerr: Well, it's not peacetime operation. The admiral saw it in terms of not only the need to support the overall objectives, but in terms of lives and resources.

Q: Were the Vietnamized units essentially interchangeable afterwards with U.S. units in operations?

Captain Kerr: Not as long as I was in Saigon. That may have come a little bit later, but I left in the summer, August-September of 1969, and the Vietnamization problem was just beginning to roll at that time. We had integrated some operations, but in terms of replacing the Vietnamese unit with a U.S. unit, I don't think we'd arrived at that state of training in the Vietnamese Navy or integration of our efforts.

Q: What changes, if any, came about when the Nixon Administration took office?

Captain Kerr: Well, I think the big thing and most important thing was Nixon had bought time that Johnson didn't have and Humphrey wouldn't have had. In other words, the biggest change was that we saw that even if we accepted the fact of the inevitability of having to leave Vietnam and turn things over, the time frame had been changed. We were no longer under pressure to make it happen in, say, six months. We saw that we were going to have some time to do it. I guess one other way to respond to your question is to recall some discussions I overheard. It was in March when Secretary of Defense Laird made his first trip out to Saigon.* In this meeting Laird basically stated that the U.S. objective was to assure the Vietnamese of their right to self-determination, which was a continuation of policy as we had known it. Laird made the observation, as I had just previously, that the administration had bought time that the Johnson Administration would not have had. As I recall, Abrams was talking to Laird about not even commenting on troop reductions, even though there was great political pressure to do that. And, as you recall, one of the first things the Nixon Administration did was to announce a troop reduction. Now, what that really amounted to was a reduction in the authorized ceiling. Nobody went home. We just hadn't filled all the billets that were authorized. We just reduced that ceiling. But Abrams was basically taking the position that we shouldn't do that until, and that we should be using that as a lever with the North Vietnamese. Also, at that time, Abrams commented on that he'd like to go into the Laos and Cambodian sanctuaries that were being used against them. They suggested that

---

*Melvin R. Laird became U.S. Secretary of Defense with the advent of the Nixon Administration in January 1969.

they wait and take a look at it the following summer, and Abrams responded that we wouldn't be any better off.

General Brown, who was the commander of the Air Force, was there. He said he thought that what the North Vietnamese wanted is for us to start bombing in the North again so they could trap Nixon like they had trapped Johnson.* And General Brown said at that meeting that what we needed to do right now was to mine Haiphong.

And Abrams continued to push for permission to raid the sanctuaries of Laos and Cambodia. And I remember he specifically requested the May time frame for doing that.

Q: Which happened one year later about May.

Captain Kerr: Yes, 1970, wasn't it?

Q: And the mining of Haiphong came two years after that.

Captain Kerr: Two years after that. So you can see that's, I guess, confirmation that the military was thinking what needed to be done militarily at that time to apply the maximum pressure. But politically they never got permission to do it. So they were thinking in those terms as soon as Nixon took over. I guess, to answer your

---
*General George S. Brown, USAF, Commander Seventh Air Force.

question, to wrap it up was that two things, I guess, number one, the first thing we noticed was the reduction in the sense of we were going to try to scale down our presence, in the sense of turning more over to the Vietnamese, and the sense of relief that we had bought some additional time that we wouldn't have had.

Q: How much voice did Admiral Zumwalt have in the strategic considerations?

Captain Kerr: Well, at that time he still was not a key player in the circles that involved the civilian people from Washington. He was clearly growing in his influence on Abrams. But when Laird came to town and the other senior people out of Washington, Zumwalt was not called in to be a party to the discussions yet. Where he was having his influence was with General Abrams and with his continued efforts to influence decisions on the Navy side by his messages back to Washington, his trips back to Washington to brief people, and basically by the success he was having in Saigon.

Q: Did Admiral Zumwalt get back to Washington any?

Captain Kerr: Yes, he went there twice during my tour.

Q: Did you make any of the trips with him?

Captain Kerr: I never made a trip with him back to Washington. I always stayed in Saigon and was the point of contact back at headquarters.

Q: Was this Laird's first trip to Vietnam?

Captain Kerr: Yes, this was Laird's first trip to Vietnam. I think it was one of the most important events for Zumwalt. Laird did not schedule any visit to see the Navy at all, but he was visiting the Army units in the Delta that the Navy supported. And Admiral Zumwalt got permission from the Army commander who was his host to come down and brief on that aspect of it. Well, the admiral went down there. I went with him. He made his pitch. He expanded the pitch outside the planned scope. He saw it as an opportunity to put his total Navy efforts before the Secretary of Defense, which he did. I'll never forget the Army commander afterwards commenting on the fact that it's the last time he'd ever invite Zumwalt to participate in a briefing--that he had been scalped, that Zumwalt had usurped the visit of the Secretary of Defense. Zumwalt just outdid him, that's all. He did it in a friendly way, but he hadn't done nearly as good a briefing as Zumwalt did. Zumwalt came across as a very intelligent, balanced battle commander in the field. And Laird liked it very, very much. I think from that moment on Laird always remembered Zumwalt and remembered that particular day. And I think it had a very important impact on Zumwalt's efforts in Vietnam--and his career.

Q: From the list of items you've recited, it sounds as if MACV had a shopping list of things they were trying to sell they hadn't been able to sell to the previous administration.

Captain Kerr: Yes, I think that's probably true, Paul. Johnson's political position in this country could hardly have allowed him to step up--I mean he had halted the bombing just before the election in an effort to help Humphrey. It's clear that he was in no position to politically go in and mine Haiphong. And I'm sure that General Brown didn't just come up with this idea when Laird came in. So, sure, all these things had been presented to the President as options and as recommendations from the military, and they had been denied permission to do those things.

Q: And Nixon wound up being clobbered when he did go into Cambodia.

Captain Kerr: That's right. He was clobbered politically, but militarily it made a lot of sense. But remember, at that point, people were less interested in what was happening militarily than they were in the political fallout from a given military move. People weren't viewing this in a strictly military context. They were viewing it more in a political context. So nobody would assess whether or not anything made any military sense alone. Every time you would make a recommendation, they had to see it the context of did it make political sense. And I'm referring to domestic politics, necessarily the politics between ourselves, the North Vietnamese, the Russians, and the Chinese.

Q: How well attuned was Admiral Zumwalt to the political considerations?

Captain Kerr: Paul, I think that was one of the real strengths that Admiral Zumwalt brought to the decision-making process in Saigon. He was extremely sensitive to the political dimension.

I recall in May, I think it was, 1969 when General Abrams was asking for a reassessment from his commanders of policy options. This was probably triggered by a similar request from Washington on an assessment of things. And the admiral got us together, and we discussed these. It was generally the case after we'd discussed them, he would sit down and do the first draft himself. Then he would pass that draft out to a few members of his staff and then we would retool that, and then come back to him and go through however many iterations it took before we finally hammered out a final position. But in this particular draft, I remember that the admiral commented on the fact that Hanoi's strategy at the time was based on their recognition of their strengths and our weaknesses, the United States weaknesses, and in exploiting both. He told General Abrams that he didn't believe that Hanoi doubted for a moment the military superiority of the U.S. forces in the field vis-a-vis Hanoi's. I think the statistics showed that militarily he was taking a hell of a beating at that time. And, in fact, as the admiral pointed out, it was the enemy's fear of military defeat that caused him to shape his field strategy for its political impact. The admiral pointed out that Hanoi could sustain critically high losses in the face of overwhelming superiority pointed to Hanoi's strengths and the U.S. weaknesses, which was basically the political stability that Hanoi maintained, and that lack of political stability which threatened the U.S. And he went on to state very clearly that there was no doubt that should the divisiveness of U.S. public opinion continue, that the results in the country were going to be very serious, and that if the popular support for the U.S.

involvement in Vietnam continued to dwindle, it could have the disastrous result of reducing the President's options and forcing him to take positions that the admiral believed would be far-reaching in regards to the world order and the U.S. position in that world order. In this particular letter Admiral Zumwalt demonstrated enormous sensitivity to the political dimension and to the issues that the political leaders were facing in the country. He commented that the military people in the field simply could not ignore the extent of the pressure on the President that was coming from the political unrest in the United States. The U.S. system and its people, its traditions he commented, had always supported its military involvements, and he felt to a great extent that support continued at this time. However, the people and the whole political process were being tested and tried and, frankly, were found strained in what was then a very unconventional environment. He believed that if we were to realize an acceptable settlement, we must provide some relief for the pressure-cooker atmosphere that the political process was straining under at that time. He didn't believe that the U.S. domestic opinion had forced the President's hand as late as '69. President Nixon still had some time before he had to take action. But he went on to conclude that one assumes that Hanoi does nothing to precipitate U.S. escalation, he now seems to have effectively foreclosed from major military initiatives such as, by foreclose I mean the President foreclosed the resumption of bombing North Vietnam, the quarantine of Cambodia, and the blockade. It seemed clear to him that the policy options were open to them were basically two at that time, and one was to negotiate a mutual withdrawal, or two was to initiate some form of unilateral reduction of forces.

I think this particular period, the admiral had been in Saigon for nine months now. He was, I think, recognizing the political situation in the States. And of all the senior military people that I met, listened to, participated in discussions with, or just sat and listened, I never met anyone that had the political sensitivity that he had. Now, I think this particular options paper that I'm referring to, that I remember him writing, really tells us three things. One, it tells us about the political dimension that the admiral was able to bring to his judgment-making. It tells us a little bit about the relationships between Admiral Zumwalt and General Abrams, and that General Abrams sought his counsel, sought his advice. It tells us also that the admiral felt comfortable enough with General Abrams, as a military commander, to opine on political issues. And, also, I think, it tells us that there was a military commander in Vietnam who was able to put forth basically political options. In other words, can see political options while he was at the same time managing a war. So the answer to your question is, I think he had an enormous sensitivity and understanding of the political dimensions to the war in Vietnam, as well as the relationship between that and our political system and process at home and the whole situation that was evolving in the States.

Q: Were you part of the sort of mini-staff on political and strategic considerations?

Captain Kerr: Yes.

Q: Who else was on that?

Captain Kerr: Well, there was Captain "Chick" Rauch, Captain Dick Nicholson, Captain Rectanus.* That was the group. I know in this particular paper, we were the ones that worked on that. But, once again, just the fact that the admiral would sit down and draft these papers himself gives you some idea of how he worked; it tells you a little bit about himself. He found that if he did it himself the first time, he wanted to force the discipline of writing it, because it forced the intellectual processes in himself. He could think through it a lot better if he had to sit down and write it as opposed to simply talking about

---
*Captain Charles F. Rauch, Jr., USN.

it and asking someone else to do it.

Q: Was that a typical pattern for him?

Captain Kerr: Yes, it was on something like this. Anything that was of this importance that was going to General Abrams and up the chain, he would generally do that.

Q: Is there anything else to say about wrapping up the Vietnam duty?

Captain Kerr: I don't think so, Paul. I think I've probably talked too much. Let me caution future readers that it's been 13, 14 years and my memory isn't all that good, and I've probably shaded some things and exaggerated others. I think essentially the facts are correct. There's probably a lot more left out than has been included, and that's unfortunate, but I think basically what I've tried to do here is less tell the story about Vietnam than tell the story about Admiral Zumwalt in Vietnam. Well, anything to repeat now would just reiterate what I've already said. So, I think we can go on to another subject.

Q: When was your next contact with him after you had left

Vietnam?

Captain Kerr: Well, the next time I saw him was in North Carolina in 1970 when he came back to the States following his relief as commander in Vietnam and his assignment as Chief of Naval Operations. The significance of that lies in two things that happened that day. Number one is that Admiral Zumwalt, who had led all the naval forces in Vietnam, who by every right should have returned to this country with at least some fanfare and acknowledgement, landed in Raleigh-Durham airport in North Carolina, and his entire welcoming committee was myself, my wife, and his son. So here was the returning commander from Vietnam, and he was met by no one, except his son and two old friends.

Q: Why did he happen to fly into North Carolina?

Captain Kerr: Well, he flew into North Carolina because his son was graduating from ROTC, and he was going to speak at the graduation.

Q: And why were you there?

Captain Kerr: Well, I was there because his son had contacted me up in Norfolk where I was stationed and invited me to come down to his graduation and see the admiral. And there was going to be a party that they were giving for him. We were just invited down for that.

The second significance was that night at the party, the admiral revealed to me that he had written a number of directives that he intended to put out when he became CNO. And I queried him about what these directives were. I was thinking in terms of kind of traditional Navy instructions and directives that go down. He said no, he didn't intend to do that. He thought the situation required his communicating completely up and down the chain of command. Reenlistment rates were so bad and the racial tensions and other problems in the Navy were of such a nature that he felt that things needed to be turned around quickly. He felt he needed to try a host of new initiatives to try to recapture morale in the Navy and turn enlistments around. He thought that one of the problems may be that some of the Navy skippers just couldn't relate to the young officers. And, here again, remember I mentioned earlier about his literally having been captured by these young officers in Vietnam, and he didn't want to lose them. He saw the future of the Navy in these guys. But, yet they weren't staying in the Navy, and every indicator we had was they were very dissatisfied with the leadership in the Navy. They were unhappy in their jobs. Basically the fun and zest had gone out of going to sea. The admiral wanted to put both fun and zest back into going to sea. So he told me that one of the things he was going to attempt was to put together a special squadron that would reduce every billet one rank. And this eventually became known as the "Mod Squad," DesRon 26 in Norfolk.* He told me that evening in North Carolina that whereas he would have to turn over the assignments to the Bureau of Naval Personnel, he intended to see me as one of the skippers of those ships, and that his intention was to show that with younger commanding officers who could relate more to the crew and the junior officers, that enlistment rates would come up. Plus, he wanted to show those younger officers that they could aspire to reach command a lot sooner than was previously the case.

So I went back to my ship in Norfolk. That was in May, I guess, or June of '70, and I eventually got orders in January of '71 to command the USS Hawkins. And the squadron was formed in the summer of '71. Dick Nicholson, who had been in Vietnam with us was the squadron commander.** I had command of the Hawkins. There were six other ships and six other COs, each of whom were one rank junior to that normally assigned to that ship. For example, I had ten years in the Navy the day I relieved, and the guy I relieved had 20 years in the Navy. So that's

---
*Destroyer Squadron 26.
**Nicholson held the rank of captain at the time he commanded Destroyer Squadron 26. His Naval Institute oral history includes a section on his tour with the "Mod Squad."

some indication of it. I was the junior person in the squadron in terms of rank and time in service. Everybody that came into that squadron had very fine Navy records, very fine Navy careers, and they're still doing very well in the Navy. But the squadron did very, very well. We had great success in our ships, but, also within ourselves. We're still all very good friends. I attribute the fact that there wasn't a lot of bitter competition to Dick Nicholson, who was the squadron commander. He did just a super job of making everybody understand that their own personal success was tied to the success of the squadron, and not necessarily to the success of their ship.

Q: Did it achieve the objectives that Admiral Zumwalt had established?

Captain Kerr: Well, not really. I don't know that anyone's ever really tried to measure those objectives. Certainly it did within that squadron. He wasn't just trying to show that it could be done within that squadron. He wanted to show that it could be done Navy-wide. The fact is that it could not be done Navy-wide. And, so, as I say, it just proved that if you want to form a mod squad in the Navy, you can do it. You go out and pick yourself seven number-one COs and you're going to have seven number-one ships. That's basically what happened.

Q: Were there problems involved with this?

Captain Kerr: Well, the problems--we didn't have any problems. I never had a problem on board the ship. None of the other ships had any problems. The only problem that we had was, you know, the kind of attitude throughout the Navy originally. A lot of people were bitter about it and unhappy. Some of those were displaced off their ships, and understandably so. Then there were a lot of old people-- they weren't necessarily all old, but people that were just sitting around waiting for us to fall on our ass, and that never happened. And they wanted to point the finger at us, and they wanted to point the finger at Zumwalt, and they never got that opportunity. The squadron did absolutely outstanding. It held every record that a squadron could establish in the Atlantic Fleet. It was the number-one squadron in the Atlantic Fleet. But in terms of did it make people reenlist because they sensed that they could get command early? Did it make them stay in the Navy because they could relate to the COs? I don't know. I never had a very good reenlistment rate in my wardroom on the Hawkins. And I think the general feeling was, "Well, we know it's working here, but we just don't see that it can be applied Navy-wide."

Q: Did you get a chance to see the impact of Z-grams among your crew?

Captain Kerr: I sure did. Yes. The Z-grams were coming out almost daily there for a while.* It wasn't the best way to establish policy, and I think Admiral Zumwalt knew that. It's one of those things that he likes to say where he had to select the least-worst choice of doing something. He knew that if he sent the policy down to his fleet commanders and they in turn sent it on down--number one, it would never come out the way he intended it to, and it wouldn't have the impact, and would take too long. So he had to trade that off against the impact that these Z-grams had on the chain of command. He was assuming that people were going to get behind him on these things and they were going to explain it to the crew. I've often said that Zumwalt assumed a more enlightened constituency than what he had. I can remember walking aboard the ship in the morning and the XO meeting me and saying, "Captain, we've got a real problem. Z-gram 57 came in and it's already been interpreted on the mess decks before I got here this morning."** So you are always put in the situation where you read it and you saw what he meant, and the crew had already put the most liberal interpretation on it they

---
*Z-grams were special messages by which Admiral Zumwalt informed the Navy of dozens of policy changes during his tenure as CNO.
**XO--executive officer.

could. So you were always sort of restraining them, and they saw your reinterpretation of it as somehow denying them something that Zumwalt had given them. So that was a problem that every commanding officer had to deal with. And some dealt with it effectively. Some wrestled with it less effectively, and some just said, "Screw it, if that's what the guy wants, let him have it." So they didn't support him at all in this.

Q: Well, you're obviously not the best guy to talk to on this, because you were not a typical skipper.

Captain Kerr: Well, I was typical in the sense that I had to deal with the same kind of crew, the same pressures, the same everything, though I understood where he was coming from on these things. I think I was able to accept these in the spirit in which--well, I knew, that he'd intended it. But I'll tell you, I had some problems with the crew, because there were many things that I said, no, that's not what Admiral Zumwalt--or I would put it in the context that this is how this will be implemented on this ship, and sure as not, some kid would stand up and say, "But that's not how Admiral Zumwalt wants it."

And I'd say, "Well, how do you know?"

"Well, Charley Ravenaugh at breakfast this morning

said, Captain, that this is the way it was."

So I remember calling the admiral's office one day and saying, "Look, could you do us at least a favor; don't send these things out in the middle of the night. Let the captains get their hands on them before the crew." But if the captains got their hands on them before the crew, why shouldn't the admirals have them before the crew? You know, it really was a situation where the admiral had to have the support of the commanding officers to deal with this situation. Some of us dealt with it effectively. Some less effectively. The ones that I could never admire were those who just ignored it, and basically they used it to cover up their own poor leadership and management aboard ship.

Q: That was a time when there was a great deal of racial tension in the Navy. Was that manifested in your ship?

Captain Kerr: Oh, we all had it. First of all, let me say that I was one of those "dumb bastards" who didn't think he had a racial problem. I use that phrase because a black once told me, "If you as a commanding officer stand up today and say that you don't have a racial problem on board your ship, you're a dumb bastard."

And I stood up and said, "I don't have a racial problem on my ship." And, sure enough, I did. And I didn't know it. I didn't recognize it. I didn't know how to recognize it. I never had been trained to recognize it. I wasn't sensitive to it. And there were no institutional procedures for blacks to bring forward particular problems, the peculiar problems to them that they had. And eventually Zumwalt, in his Z-grams, institutionalized these things, and we found that method and that vehicle. And I think that if there's one thing that Admiral Zumwalt did that I think he deserves the credit of every person in the Navy, then as well as now, and that's he led the Navy basically out of the dark ages of racial injustice. He moved us all to a higher form of interpersonal relations, to greater sensitivity, to problems that were peculiar to blacks aboard ship. He made us understand concepts like social justice and meaningful human relations. People say that blacks were in the pantry--hell, that's a little exaggerated, but the point is made that they were in the pantry. We didn't understand them and we didn't make any attempt to.

Q: Well, how did you come to the perception personally that you did have a racial problem on your ship?

Captain Kerr: I came back to the ship one night and there was a race riot on the fantail.

Q: That would enforce the idea.

Captain Kerr: Yes, yes. And, I say race riot, that's kind of an exaggerated term, but there was a fight going on on the fantail of the ship that had been precipitated by a racial incident on board the ship where a white officer had said a very unfortunate and dumb thing to a black enlisted man. That spread throughout the ship. And, as a result of that, I sat down and had a lot of sessions with blacks on board the ship, brought together white and black groups. And I basically had to teach myself things that I had never learned before.

Q: Anything else about that tour of duty that is relevant to the Zumwalt experience?

Captain Kerr: Well, not really. I think that, as I said, the Mod Squad was a great success for those who participated in it. I think that it probably, in the long run, was something that the admiral probably shouldn't have done. It irritated too many people. It was one of those things where the payoff just wasn't that big for him, for the Navy. The negatives kind of outweighed the positives in that sense. We all benefited from it personally, not only the experience of being there, but professionally we benefited from it. But I don't think it helped that much.

Kerr/Zumwalt Staff - 153

I guess the most important thing that I learned in that period that I was there was the issue of race relations, if you will, within the Navy. We just had to deal with the situation. It was a time bomb ready to go off. People blamed Zumwalt for it when it went off a year later. My position on that is that if Zumwalt hadn't been CNO for a year, if he hadn't already provided these safety valves, we'd have had an explosion in the Navy that was far greater than the one we had. Because at least the blacks knew there was somebody at the top that understood and was trying to do something. If they hadn't had that; if we hadn't already put in place certain things, the explosion aboard some of our ships would have been far worse than it was.

Q: We got into the Mod Squad discussion as an item that you were discussing when you met him in North Carolina. Did he have any sense of reflection on what had been accomplished in Vietnam during those discussions?

Captain Kerr: No. No, and that's something we've never talked about to this day. I think Zumwalt came home like a lot of people did. Of course, he had been promoted to four stars and been made CNO, so there was a sense of personal achievement, but there was no sense of coming home as a successful conquering military hero. As I said, he almost snuck into the country.

Q: Was it typical of him that he would be looking forward in his discussions?

Captain Kerr: Yes, absolutely. That's a good point, Paul. He was the kind of guy that was always looking forward and very seldom reflecting on the past.

Q: That's what I was trying to draw out of you.

Captain Kerr: Well, you brought that out very well now that I think about it. Zumwalt's mind-set is always on tomorrow and not yesterday.

Q: Where then did you go after the <u>Hawkins</u>?

Captain Kerr: Well, I came up and worked on his personal staff for about a year, and then I went over to the White House. I was Spiro Agnew's aide until he resigned, and then stayed on with Vice President Ford.* And when Ford assumed the Presidency, I became the deputy to John Marsh, who was named counselor to President Ford. I stayed in that position until December of '75, and then I left the White House and went back to sea.

---

*When Spiro Agnew resigned in October 1973, he was replaced as Vice President by Gerald R. Ford.

I kept in touch with Zumwalt while I was at the White House. I was a source of some information. I never violated any trust or loyalties in the White House by passing information to Zumwalt. I was not Zumwalt's man in the White House in that sense. But in terms of describing the atmosphere, the flavor of things, the pressure points, who was on the rise, who was on the fall. Really the kinds of things that a close White House watcher can pick up on his own. I would pass those things on to the admiral.

I guess the most significant thing that happened while I was there that involved Zumwalt took place in June of '74. Zumwalt had sent a letter to President Nixon about mid-June of '74 having to do with the SALT issues.* It was a letter that he had tried to get the support of the Joint Staff, Joint Chiefs of Staff, which they would not support him on, I understood they agreed with him generally, they felt he had taken it too far, the letter. And essentially what he did was be very critical of the President and the President's handling of the whole nuclear balance issue. He felt that the President was not getting the advice of his military chiefs, he was not seeking it, that national security policy in this area had been captured by a small group at the White House led by Kissinger. And, by implication, he basically said that the President wasn't executing his responsibilities under the

---
*SALT--Strategic Arms Limitation Talks.

Constitution, which requires the President, by law, seek the input of these people.

Nixon took this letter before the National Security Council. Ford, as Vice President, was then a member of the National Security Council. Ford had not seen the letter, but that's not unusual. The NSC staff under Kissinger never let Ford see anything. So Zumwalt had gotten a copy to me, and I sent it into the Vice President. And the Vice President called Mr. Marsh and me together and asked us if the other Joint Chiefs agreed with this. I told the Vice President what I've already said here, that essentially I understood that the chiefs, they in principle had agreed, but they felt that the letter was a little too strident, that it had too much of a cutting edge on it, and it overstated the situation. Put your own interpretation on that kind of language.

So Nixon's reaction to that was, as I was told, to consider firing Zumwalt. But at the time he had all the problems he needed. This was June of '74. He was just two months from resignation. The last thing he needed was another fight over firing the CNO. And Zumwalt would have had a lot of backing up on the Hill, of course. So, given the fact that Zumwalt eventually got into political life, you can speculate on your own whether or not that would have been good for him or bad. My guess is that Zumwalt probably would have dearly loved to have been fired by Richard Nixon. It's like finding your name on the enemies list; it turned into a real political plus. I think that's true, it probably would have helped him politically.

But Zumwalt was scheduled to be relieved on the 29th of June. Ford had accepted an invitation to speak at the change of command in Annapolis. I had drafted a speech, and it had been approved by the Ford staff; Ford had approved it. It was all set to go. I had complimented Zumwalt too much, so the speechwriters had scrubbed a little bit of that out of there, but essentially the speech was intact. And when it was announced that Zumwalt was going on "Meet The Press" the day after he'd been relieved, and that word had leaked out that he was going to discuss SALT.* And at that very moment Nixon was in Moscow. Word came back that Zumwalt was asked not to appear on "Meet The Press." He said that he would appear on "Meet The Press." He was then asked not to discuss SALT, and he said he intended to discuss SALT. Well, as it turned out, Zumwalt turned over command of the Navy on the 29th of June, but he didn't retire until midnight the following night, and he was to go on television on Sunday when he was still on active duty. Well, finally the order came back from Moscow that Zumwalt was <u>ordered</u> by the President not

---

*"Meet the Press" is a weekly television program in which public figures are interviewed by a panel of news media representatives.

to discuss SALT. And they went back and they found a directive that went back to the preceding March where military commanders had been told not to discuss the subject, and there was such language floating around as the threat of a court-martial. So this created some real problems for the change of command, because Schlesinger, who was then Secretary of Defense, wasn't sure whether he was going to go.* Every retiring chief since the end of the Second World War had received the Distinguished Service Medal. None had been authorized for Zumwalt. He didn't know what the hell his role was going to be there at Annapolis. The Vice President had called me in and wanted to know what he should say now in light of all--in other words, my speech was out the window. To his credit, Ford could have very easily stepped away from that change of command, but he did not do so. Ford always had great respect and admiration for Zumwalt, and he was a man that once he committed himself to something, he lived up to it. So I credit Ford tremendously with his determination and guts to see this thing through, because there were a lot of people who were ready to desert on this one. Well, anyway, we all went up to the change of command, everybody showed up, and Ford made a rather bland speech.

Q: Did you write that second speech?

---
*James R. Schlesinger.

Captain Kerr: Yes. We wrote it in the helicopter going up to Annapolis. I remember I got up to Annapolis and went over to the Superintendent's house, and Moorer was there and the other Joint Chiefs.* They were all gathered around in little groups, and standing all by himself over in a corner was Zumwalt, the outsider, the guy who had ended his brilliant, spectacular Navy career with no one talking to him. I went over, and he asked me if Ford was still going to speak, and I said, "Absolutely."

He said, "Well, it's to his credit that he came."

And I said, "Yes, it is."

Schlesinger signed his Distinguished Service Medal, the only one not signed by a President since the Second World War is Zumwalt's. Schlesinger finally sent out a message that said, "If I don't hear back from you within three hours, I will go ahead and give this Distinguished Service Medal to Zumwalt." He never heard back. You go back and you'll note that Schlesinger's name isn't even on the program at the Naval Academy, because they couldn't get confirmation that he was coming, so they left it off when they went to the printers. Anyway, that's how Zumwalt ended his Navy career--full of controversy, a person who was challenging the establishment, a person who was, through his actions, putting himself in the limelight of

---
*Admiral Thomas H. Moorer, USN, Chairman of the Joint Chiefs of Staff.

Kerr/Zumwalt Staff - 160

the news and the vortex in the center of controversy, and it was very typical of him. To have gone out in some sort of traditional fashion, you know, and retired in Annapolis and lectured and taking spring reviews is just not the man at all. He's a brilliant, controversial high-energy guy, who's always going to be involved in controversial issues, and he will create those. But he does it because he's very committed to what he believes and feels very strongly about it. So I always see his exit from the Navy as being almost a good description of one element of the man, one characteristic, one part of his personality, which is controversy.

Q: We've talked of his political sensitivity, do you think that knowing that President Nixon was vulnerable on Watergate, that he was using that to get something in SALT?

Captain Kerr: No, no, no. No, I don't think so. I think he just felt very strongly about an issue, and he felt, well, he had gone through the procedures of trying to get the Joint Chiefs of Staff to take a position on this. And had they, it would have just gone forward signed by Joint Chiefs. So, I think, it was only after they had failed to agree to that that Zumwalt felt he still had to do that. No, I don't think he was necessarily creating this specifically to leverage off of Nixon's position. But, as I said, I think it would have, given the fact that he eventually went into political life, I think that having been fired by Richard Nixon would have helped him politically, but I don't think he sought that.

Q: Was he already harboring the notion at that point of challenging Kissinger?

Captain Kerr: Well, I think he was already harboring political thoughts. As we know, a group of people had tried to get him to run in California when Reagan won election. So he saw himself as a political person, and I think he had hoped to be one of the first political people, successful political people since the Second World War, to have left the military a very senior rank and go into politics. It just doesn't happen. We've seen a couple of POWs do that, but basically Eisenhower, I guess, is the last. And I don't think there were any limits to Zumwalt's ambition. He always thought very big.

Q: Going back to that time just after you left the Hawkins, what were your duties on his staff after that?

Captain Kerr: Oh, I worked on a group called the CNO Executive Panel staff. We were his alter ego.

Q: What issues did you deal with?

Captain Kerr: Well, just about all the issues that he wanted you to get involved with. Most of them were political-military issues. I can remember I got called in one Saturday and told to write a defense plank for the Republican Party platform.

Q: Any other duties that you had at that point? Were they mostly of this political nature as opposed to Navy-type business?

Captain Kerr: Well, most of the things were Navy business, but cast in a political context. Sometimes that political context was international, sometimes it was domestic. That's what I essentially did until I went over to the White House.

Q: Well, any final observations on this man you served with?

Captain Kerr: Well, I think one can see in this six hours or seven hours, however long I've been talking about him, the great admiration have for him and respect I have for him. I think he's clearly one of the premier military men of the post-World War II period. Certainly a man of great accomplishment, in my judgment, while at the same time great controversy. But accomplishment sometimes has its birth in controversy. I think Zumwalt is seen by the general public as the guy who got rid of the "Mickey Mouse," who put beer in the barracks and allowed the sailors to have beards. But he was far more than that. As I said, he--to me, the most significant thing Zumwalt did was he redrafted and reshaped the social contract of the Navy. He cast it in a more humane, just way and that can never be changed, you just cannot roll that back. The Navy was grossly behind the country, certainly our other services in that regard. He was, at the same time, a man of enormous intellectual powers which he brought to bear in the strategic world. But that capacity is known to a small elite of people in this country that follow those issues. I think his legacy to the Navy is the new social contract that the Navy has, that it's operating under today, and so, to me, that will be his legacy to the Navy, that which he'll be remembered for the most, and I think it is the most significant contribution that he made, and it was a contribution that probably he was uniquely capable of making at that time. And I think in that sense he was probably chosen for that reason, and so he ended up being the right choice at the right time and did what was necessary for the Navy during that period. He did a lot of other things, but essentially he had to do that. The Navy just had to have somebody that was going to be the facilitator of this change, and he did that. He had the courage and the strength and the morality and the leadership to lead the Navy in that regard, and also the courage and the strength to take all the heat from those who didn't want to see that contract rewritten.

Q: Thank you very much.

Glenn/Zumwalt Staff - 165

Interview Number 1 with Captain W. Lewis Glenn, Jr.,
U. S. Navy

Place: Office of the Deputy Chief of Naval Operations (Surface Warfare), the Pentagon, Arlington, Virginia

Date: Wednesday, 16 May 1984

Interviewer: Paul Stillwell

Q: Captain, before we get to your service in Vietnam, I wonder if you could sketch briefly your background in the Navy, prior to reporting there.

Captain Glenn: I started out in destroyers. My first destroyer was DDR-878, Vesole, in Charleston, South Carolina. I was the first lieutenant and then the fire control officer on Vesole, and after about a year on Vesole, they were recruiting for DDG-23, the Richard E. Byrd's commissioning crew. I was given orders to report to Richard E. Byrd in Seattle, Washington, as the commissioning ASW officer.* We commissioned Richard E. Byrd in March 1964. I stayed with her as ASW officer, and then in the Med our CIC officer got emergency orders back to the States.** I had an assistant ASW officer, moved him into the ASW officer position, and I took CIC.*** After my tour on Richard E. Byrd, I went to PG School and

---
*ASW--antisubmarine warfare.
**Mediterranean Sea.
***CIC--combat information center.

got a master's degree in physics.* When the detailer came out to discuss our orders, I assumed that I would be going to destroyer school prior to my department head tour. I was told instead that I was going to go to Vietnam.

At that time, the detailer had no idea what the assignment was going to be, but my name was put in a hat with others for the flag lieutenant job at ComNavForV.** I was selected for that job and started out working for Admiral Veth in July 1968.***

Q: Did you welcome that assignment to Vietnam?

Captain Glenn: I had mixed emotions, not so much about going in-country Vietnam, but at that time, there was a lot of talk from the bureau about the first team going to Vietnam, but the perception was that the first team did not go to Vietnam.**** You never saw anybody detailed out of BuPers into Vietnam. So I thought that having done very well in the Navy thus far, why was I being given a second-team assignment? But I felt that the country was at war,

---

*PG--postgraduate.
**ComNavForV--Commander U.S. Naval Forces Vietnam.
***Rear Admiral Kenneth L. Veth, USN, Commander U.S. Naval Forces Vietnam and Chief of the U.S. Naval Advisory Group, U.S. Military Assistance Command Vietnam. He held these two posts from April 1967 to September 1968. Admiral Veth's oral history is in the Naval Institute collection.
****In country refers to the forces operating in small craft in the rivers and coastal waters of Vietnam, as opposed to the Fleet ships supporting the war effort from at sea. The bureau indicated here is the Bureau of Naval Personnel (BuPers).

and we were paid to fight wars, and I guess I looked forward to finding out what it was all about. You know, it was the only war that I had ever had the opportunity to participate in. So, once again, I was enthusiastic about it from that point of view, but concerned whether the Navy was leveling with me. Was I really doing well or was somebody telling me something?

Q: Did you have a concern that it might have a negative effect on your overall career?

Captain Glenn: Yes, I was a little bit concerned, because I was anxious to get my destroyer department head tour behind me, and I felt that this was delaying it. Was I going to get behind my contemporaries? I'd spent time in PG School getting a master's degree, and was I going to be behind? So from that point, yes, I was a little concerned.

Q: Were you a lieutenant at that point?

Captain Glenn: Yes, I was a lieutenant at that point.

Q: Describe your arrival in country and meeting up with Adnmiral Veth, please.

Captain Glenn: Well, I don't remember too much about that.

We just flew into Tan Sohn Nhut Air Force Base.* As I recall, I checked in through a doorway. The guy I was relieving, a guy named Sam Meese, was there. Sam Meese was a gross sight. He had a .357 Magnum in a clamshell holster and was suited out in green fatigues. We drove back to the quarters, and about a week before, they had taken a rocket in the front yard. Sam, who had been a PBR commander in the Delta and had gotten a Silver Star before coming to this job in Saigon, had not been wounded in Vietnam until they took that rocket in the front yard, and he was apparently cut from some debris.** We went from the quarters, and Sam showed me around and I got settled in. Then I went over and met Admiral Veth.

Admiral Veth was a real gentleman. I went into a routine of intelligence briefs and things with a little travel around the country. Frankly, it was not quite as exciting as I expected it to be, except that the rocket attacks on Saigon were pretty intense, and they were throwing them around at random. Having caught one in the front yard, I didn't know whether they'd be using any kind of targeting, so you worried about a random rocket coming in on you. You heard them hitting all over the place. But

---
*Tan Sohn Nhut was the principal airport and airbase serving Saigon.
**The Delta refers to the network of waterways at the mouth of the Mekong River in South Vietnam; PBRs were river patrol boats operating on these waterways. The Silver Star is a medal for heroism in action.

Glenn/Zumwalt Staff - 169

other than that, it was a fairly quiet situation for the first six or seven weeks.

Q: How would you describe the daily routine under Admiral Veth?

Captain Glenn: Well, the quarters were not co-located with the headquarters at that time, and so it was breakfast at 7:15 or so, arriving headquarters 7:45 or 8:00 o'clock, intelligence brief, through the various message traffics, briefings, a fairly substantial social schedule in the evenings, but usually left the office at 5:30 or thereabouts. I did not find the pace particularly demanding at that point.

Q: Who were involved in these social gatherings?

Captain Glenn: Well, the military plus the various Vietnamese dignitaries. The staff was included, of course, Captain Sam Orme, for instance, was the chief of staff, and at most of the gatherings, the CNO of the Vietnamese Navy, Commodore Chon, would have something, and you'd usually have three or four staff members and the admiral at these various things.* Also a number of visiting firemen from the U.S., various admirals and congressional delegations

---

*Captain Samuel T. Orme, USN; Commodore Tran Van Chon, Vietnamese Navy.

and things like that coming through.

Q: Did the admiral go out into the field very much?

Captain Glenn: No. We flew up to Danang a few times, and I think maybe we flew up to Nha Trang to the Vietnamese Naval Academy. But I remember little field activity at that time.

Q: What was Admiral Veth's role as a commander then? What kinds of things was he doing, trying to implement, trying to achieve?

Captain Glenn: Well, I think that Admiral Veth had forces in place. We had the Market Time operation going off the coast of Vietnam with the PCFs, and then, the PBRs were closer in to the coast.* But it was a strategy, kind of a defensive strategy. The armored boats down in the Delta were supporting the Army's 9th Infantry Division and getting into some firefights. But, in general, the Navy's role appeared to be interdiction at sea of supplies coming in from sea and generally on the high seas. Not much of a role inside the country of Vietnam, except some firefights

---
*Market Time, conducted by the Navy's Task Force 115, consisted of offshore surveillance forces aimed at cutting off the waterborne flow of supplies to enemy forces in South Vietnam. PCFs are fast patrol craft, frequently known as Swift boats.

in the Delta where the heavy boats were. But as I looked at it, generally we were on a defense mission.

Q: How would you characterize the relationship between Admiral Veth and Captain Orme, chief of staff? Did they work well together?

Captain Glenn: I think that they worked well together. Admiral Veth let Captain Orme run the staff. Captain Orme was a very capable individual. But, again, there were just not a lot of new initiatives, and things seemed to be rolling along in a firm, fixed pattern, and one day seemed to follow another without any peaks or valleys as far as excitement goes.

Q: Did you have a sense that you weren't really in the war, after this anticipation you'd had?

Captain Glenn: Yes. I was a little disappointed. I had come over thinking that we were really going to do our part, and I guess I felt that the surface Navy was kind of offshore, etc., but the aviators on the carriers were doing some bombing, etc., but we weren't--it seemed to me that the surface Navy was not participating enough in this effort.

I remember Commodore Hoffman sent a couple of his PCFs inshore and got into some firefights and took some hits, and the atmosphere around headquarters was not one of jubilation.* It was kind of, "Well, we have limited forces. Let's not take a chance on losing those limited forces." So I guess I was anticipating more action, and I was a little disappointed at what I thought was the level of activity, but again, I was not familiar enough with the situation to assess what could be done.

Things changed dramatically when Admiral Zumwalt arrived. When he first got there, he took about a five-day tour coming into office for about half a day, and then he took a trip covering I, II, III, IV Corps, seeing all the operating bases, to try to get a picture of what was going on.** Immediately after the change of command, he started formulating his idea for what later became Giant Slingshot. He looked at the map, and he saw the Parrot's Beak coming out of Cambodia, here was the Vam Co Dong and Vam Co Tay rivers running along Parrot's Beak, and he saw the potential for interdicting the Viet Cong supplies there.*** He started talking about that almost immediately, and then started laying the basis for it by talking to General

---
*Captain Roy F. Hoffman, USN, Commander Task Force 115.
**South Vietnam was divided into four geographic sectors with I Corps (pronounced "eye corps") the farthest to the north and IV Corps farthest south.
***When viewed on a map, the rivers dividing Cambodia from Vietnam are in the shape of a parrot's beak jutting into the territory of Vietnam.

Goodpaster and General Abrams.* They had a meeting every Saturday, and previously these meetings had not been very long, and there hadn't been a lot of preparation for them. He started going with presentations and suggested operations and trying to get support for his ideas, and he very rapidly built up a very fine rapport with General Abrams.

As soon as he got General Abrams's support, then he could start putting his various plans into action. He saw that the Viet Cong were bringing their supplies down through Cambodia and that the Parrot's Beak was the closest point to Saigon. He reasoned that they were bringing those supplies down the Parrot's Beak, and then waterborne into Saigon and into the Delta, and everywhere else. A tremendous quantity of supplies flowing through there, essentially unhindered. And, of course, as we know, being a maritime nation, the way to move supplies, if you want to move large quantities of supplies easily, then waterborne hulls is the way to do it. And the VC saw this readily, so every night they were moving tremendous quantities of materials in their boats along those rivers.**

---

*General Andrew J. Goodpaster, USA, Deputy Commander U.S. Military Assistance Command Vietnam; General Creighton W. Abrams, USA, Commander U.S. Military Assistance Command Vietnam.
**VC--Viet Cong, a Communist guerrilla organization which had infiltrated South Vietnam and was fighting against U.S. and South Vietnamese forces.

Glenn/Zumwalt Staff - 174

Q: Had this been ignored under Admiral Veth, do you think?

Captain Glenn: No, I'm not sure it had been ignored as much as it had been not recognized. Admiral Zumwalt looked at the chart, and his mind immediately saw the opportunity for this waterborne interdiction. As soon as he put his fingers up and pointed to the V along the Parrot's Beak and said, "We can interdict it here, and then there's a canal running along the other border of Cambodia, where we can put those Florida boats. The outboards with the airplane motors on the back of them and use them in the areas where it's too shallow for the PBRs. We can interdict that whole border between Cambodia and South Vietnam." He immediately saw that. Since the PBRs were being used as backups for the PCFs offshore, he said, "We'll bring the PBRs inland, and use the PCFs along the coast." Commodore Hoffman had seen some of this and had already used his PCFs for a couple of raids that I referred to earlier.

Q: But that Commodore Hoffman had been sort of discouraged from following up on.

Captain Glenn: Yes, in the past that had been discouraged. However, Admiral Zumwalt put these boats in place, and we took pretty heavy casualties for the first few weeks of Giant Slingshot, about 68%, I think, and it was starting to look like even though we were stopping the flow of supplies, maybe the cost would be too high. But as is usually the case when you put your young men into combat and they are given an opportunity, Lieutenant George Stefencavage came up with the idea of a waterborne ambush.* The PBRs in the past had been going out at night and patrolling the rivers. You can hear a PBR for ten miles in Vietnam because it's just a very quiet rural area. They had been taking rocket fire and small arms fire and substantial casualties.

Stefencavage decided that rather than them moving along the rivers at night, that they would position themselves. The squadron of about six boats would head up the river at about sunset and one by one they would cut their engines and drift over to the riverbank. They would then wait there until the VC came along the rivers, initially in their boats, and they'd open up on them with machine guns, etc., and stop them. The VC soon saw that they couldn't move on the rivers, so they started moving along the banks. Well, that didn't make a lot of difference either, because Stefencavage and his guys were in place, and they would take them out.

Q: Would they move ashore from the boats and wait for these people to walk by?

---
*Lieutenant George Stefencavage, USN.

Captain Glenn: They did it both ways. They sometimes stayed on the boats, and other times they would move ashore with shotguns, which at close range were the best weapons, and ambush the VC with shotguns. I think one very interesting point and an important part of this was the fact that Stefencavage put his boats in place, and within a week it was being used throughout the Delta. The link of communications was Admiral Zumwalt. Our daily routine with Admiral Zumwalt was to get up at 5:30 and run two miles, then breakfast at 6:00, and at about 6:15, we would leave for the airport. He wanted to fly to the two spots in country, usually in the Delta, that had been hit the hardest the night before and had taken the heaviest casualties. So they'd bring me a pouch early in the morning to take a look at right after our run and before breakfast, and I'd figure out where the two places were that the VC had hit hardest the night before, or where our most successful firefights had been. We had helos at the heliports, and we would leave after breakfast, about 6:30, and fly to the Delta. Normally, we'd spend all morning in the Delta, perhaps an hour at one fire base and an hour at the other base. You must realize that the fire bases along the banks of the river for the PBRs had a perimeter that was a couple of hundred yards--I mean, it was a pretty small fire base. Again, though, because Admiral Zumwalt had worked with Abrams to get support from the Army, we had pretty good helo gunships available for our troops and also Army artillery support. Additionally, the Army did some probes to keep the VC from overrunning our bases, but even so, the VC did hit these bases.

We would also try to put our guys in where there was already a Vietnamese Army outpost of some kind close by. Admiral Zumwalt flew into these various places; we'd get to all of them within a week, so when he heard about Stefencavage's, then he moved the information quickly around to the other PBR commanders, and it became the standard routine over there, the waterborne ambush. It was a very successful idea.

Q: Was there any official communication system to promulgate these tactical ideas?

Captain Glenn: No. I think that things moved so fast over there, and Admiral Zumwalt moved around the country so fast, that before you could get a message written down, the word was out. He talked to Commodore Hoffman, Commodore Price, who was 116, and to Salzer, 117, on a daily basis.* So things were going out instantaneously, and it

---

*Captain Roy F. Hoffman, USN, Commander Task Force 115; Captain Arthur W. Price, Jr., USN, Commander Task Force 116; Captain Robert S. Salzer, USN, Commander Task Force 117. The oral histories of Price and Salzer are in the Naval Institute collection.

wasn't really a necessity for a lessons-learned type message to go out. And you know with Admiral Zumwalt moving from PBR base to PBR base, like all good subordinate commanders, you don't want the boss to find out something that you don't know about. So Commodore Price would get to his PBRs more frequently than Admiral Zumwalt did to be sure that he didn't get caught up short. And, of course, he was often there when Zumwalt would fly into these places. Our operations were fairly small, and with a gent as active as Zumwalt, you rapidly moved from place to place.

Q: How would you characterize these give-and-take sessions between the admiral and the people in the field?

Captain Glenn: Well, I think at that point you saw Admiral Zumwalt's true humanity come out. We all recognized his brilliance and the depth of his intellectual capability and his ability to quickly take these intellectual capabilities and move them into practical battlefield plans. And he was respected for that, but he brought a human side into these visits to the field. He would find out what the guys really needed down there, from the third class boatswain's mate to the ensign, to the j.g., he would find out their needs. And then if they said that they wanted a bag of charcoal or a case of beer or something like that, then when we got back at the end of the thing, on the way back in the car to the officer, he would go over what had occurred, and he said, "Let's make sure that we don't return to that base without providing the things they wanted." So when we left, I always had a little list of things, and we'd go out with a couple of cases of beer and charcoal or whatever the guys asked for. It caused the guys to recognize that this was an individual who really cared about them on an individual basis and not just as a unit or a piece of equipment that he could move about.

And once again, we all loved him and still do, and I think that that great humanitarian part of him was a tremendous part of drawing people to him and drawing out the very best in all of us. You know, you would do anything for him. I mean, the days over there, once again, started out at 5:30 and then in the field 'til noon, or if we were going somewhere other than the Delta, it might be in the field 'til 3:00 or 4:00 o'clock, and then it was over to the headquarters and briefings and papers and things like that. You know, you left the office at 6:30 or 7:00 o'clock, I can't remember, something like that, back over to the quarters for the dinner, and then either more paperwork, and then at 11:00 o'clock or 11:30, you were done for the day, and this continued seven days a week. The only difference was on Sunday we had a church service at 10:00 o'clock in the headquarters. But that was only one hour, and that was the only change. So seven days a week, things went exactly the same.

Q: The social life, I take it, had been completely dispensed with?

Captain Glenn: No, but it was very, very limited, and the social life was really more of a working social life. It was bringing people in who had good ideas, flying the commanders in from the field, and things like that. So there would be a working dinner at night with Commodore Hoffman or Commodore Price or Commodore Salzer or some Army general or something like that. The social life was a working social life. I guess the thing that you have to say about him is that when you can work with somebody seven days a week, 16, 18 hours, and you love that guy, he's got to be something special, because a situation like that where you never get away, could really grate on you if you weren't working for a very special human being.

Q: How did the rest of the staff adjust to this dramatic change in pace?

Captain Glenn: Some adjusted very, very well; and some just couldn't handle it. One thing, though, about Admiral Zumwalt, he had his team that he brought with him and so he was really moving when he got there. He brought Dick Nicholson in with him, who was a commander, I believe, at the time, and Chick Rauch, who was a commander at the time, and, of course, Howard Kerr, who was a lieutenant.* He worked particularly with those guys to do special things for him, but Sam Orme, who was the chief of staff, was responsive to Admiral Zumwalt's requirements, and, I think, was very effective, but he was due to rotate and was relieved soon after the change of command.

Joe Rizza came in as the new chief of staff. A very, very dedicated naval officer, but he had some difficulty prioritizing. He worked 20 hours a day, but he had a hard time telling the things that were critical from the things that were fairly inconsequential.** For that reason, he was not very effective. A smart man with a Ph.D., and Admiral Zumwalt got him a job at the National War College as an instructor, and moved Captain Tidd in as the chief of staff.***

But I think it was a breath of fresh air to the staff, frankly, to get active, to get energized, to start moving, and I think there was good support in the headquarters. Those elements who did not support him, it wasn't an intentional lack of support, but it was proof of the fact that, as I said earlier, I didn't feel the first team was

---
*Commander Richard E. Nicholson, USN; Commander Charles F. Rauch, Jr., USN; Lieutenant Howard J. Kerr, Jr., USN.
**Captain Joseph P. Rizza, USN.
***Captain Emmett H. Tidd, USN.

being ordered to Vietnam. Therefore, some of the assistant chiefs of staff weren't capable of responding to the level of demand that Admiral Zumwalt suddenly put on them, because they weren't first team naval officers. They were dedicated individuals but not the Navy's best. And so when Admiral Zumwalt needed them to respond at a higher level, they weren't capable of it. So it wasn't disagreement or intransigence; it was lack of ability. Fortunately, that situation did not exist in the field. Salzer, Price, and Hoffman were extremely capable field commanders, and they immediately understood what Zumwalt was telling them and were able to move out. So he had the leadership in the field; it was just headquarters, in some cases, that were not able to keep up with Admiral Zumwalt's moves. And when he said something, he had thought it out, and he really meant it. And he wanted you to move out on it, and some people just couldn't respond to that.

Q: Did he take steps to replace these people who couldn't respond?

Captain Glenn: Yes. He moved rapidly to replace people who couldn't respond. First, he moved Dick Nicholson from his special assistant into the N-3, the ops jobs, and then he had Chick Rauch working on a turnover to the Vietnamese type situation, and Paul Arbo was the adviser to the Vietnamese.* Paul Arbo was a very, very capable gent, but Paul Arbo disagreed with Admiral Zumwalt's approach to turning over to the Vietnamese, and again, Admiral Zumwalt had thought this plan out. He knew what the situation was in Washington and that we had to really move out on turning over to the Vietnamese. Again, Paul Arbo wanted the Vietnamese better trained before we turned things over to them. Admiral Zumwalt saw the window closing, and he saw that we were either going to have to get things turned over and get them trained to a certain level, or there was going to be no opportunity for them at all to have an opportunity to fight for themselves. Paul Arbo did not recognize that political window was closing, tended to resist, and Chick Rauch relieved Paul Arbo as the senior naval adviser to the Vietnamese.

Another effort of Admiral Zumwalt was to phone the captain detailer every night at 11:00 o'clock, which was about 11:00 in the morning here in Washington, asking for people by name that he wanted for the staff.**

Q: Where did he get these names?

---

*Captain Paul E. Arbo, USN.
**A detailer was an officer in the Bureau of Naval Personnel who worked on the assignment of personnel to billets. A captain detailer then was an individual responsible for fitting available captains into jobs.

Captain Glenn: He got names from other members of the staff. I remember Tom Emery, who was later on the staff of CTF 115 and became the commander of Operation Silver Mace down in the lower part of the Delta.* Tom was my weapons officer on <u>Richard E. Byrd</u>, and I happened to know that Tom was a bachelor, so he could move quickly. So I mentioned his name, and within a couple of weeks, Tom was in country, and very successful. Tom's a commodore now. But he got the names from people around him, recommendations. Admiral Zumwalt very much believed in people, his team. Once he saw that somebody could do a job for him, he would tend to keep that individual and move him from place to place, very much a team-type thing. And that's true of all of us, when we see somebody that can do a job for us, we have a tendency to glom on to that individual.

Q: How did he respond to you? You were a holdover from the old regime and not one of the people he had brought with him.

Captain Glenn: Well, that was a thought that I had when he got there. You know, what was he going to do? Was he going to replace me, or was he going to keep me? And I guess he didn't know what he was going to do either, since he didn't fire me, I assume that I met the mark. We have

---

*Lieutenant Commander Thomas R.M. Emery, USN.

been very close ever since. But for me it was an interesting position to be in, because I did not come as one of the team.

Q: Did there seem to be the insiders and outsiders on the staff, those that were with him and those who weren't?

Captain Glenn: Well, I felt that, yes, there were the insiders and the outsiders. Since you could say that I was one of the outsiders, I felt that by working hard and responding, I became an insider. So my feeling is there weren't insiders and outsiders; there were guys that either could respond to his fast pace on things, or you couldn't. I'm sure that there were those who genuinely disagreed, too, and there were some of those around. But I think, in general, you were either fast on the uptake and could move with him, or you just weren't capable of moving at the motion and at the level that he wanted you to move. Captain Rectanus, for example, was an outsider, but Captain Rectanus was a brilliant intelligence officer.* He was able to respond, understood what Admiral Zumwalt wanted, produced it, and so he stayed as the intelligence officer on the staff. I think that was generally the way it was.

Let me ramble a little bit, though, because I think I have some unusual insights into Admiral Zumwalt from a

---
*Captain Earl F. Rectanus, USN, was, like Lieutenant Glenn, a holdover from ADmiral Veth's staff.

personal point of view. Let me relate those, and then we'll go on. We used to go over and see his family on the Philippines once a month, and with Admiral Zumwalt, you were immediately totally accepted. It wasn't an aide-admiral relationship with him; it was more a father-son or a confident-friend, and you'd go over, and you would just naturally do the things that you would do at home. We'd go meet with the family, and they had somebody help with the cooking, but I'd fix drinks, because at home with my family, I mean, I'm around, I fix a drink; you do things like that. When he had guests over, you made drinks and things just like you would for your mother and dad, anyway, but it was that kind of atmosphere. You were never in a driven mode with him; it was just a very, very natural relationship. He did more than his share; he expected you to respond, and you did.

Again, he had that same humane streak in him. He would go visit our battle casualties. I never recalled his predecessor going to the hospital. I remember whenever a planeload of Navy casualties came in, we were always at the hospital. I remember one particular young man who died almost as he was talking to Zumwalt. It was a j.g. who had been hit by a mine in Nha Trang. And it just broke Admiral Zumwalt's heart to have that promising young man shattered. He's just a compassionate, caring individual. He'd never forget to get letters off to the relatives of these people. Once again, in the field, he was always anxious to make sure that awards were presented to these guys, and we had few awards before that, but his feeling was these guys were getting shot at. The rest of the Navy was doing a good job, but these guys were laying it all on the line. And if a guy did something heroic in combat, that's what awards were for. So we almost always went into the field with awards that were written up immediately for these individuals who had been in firefights, who had done something substantial the night before. He just really cared and he cared about every detail, and he just kind of set the example for you, and you just rolled with it, and filled your 18-hour days with enthusiasm.

Soon after he came, we moved to quarters that were just next to the headquarters. We had a volleyball game every noon we could, rather than eating lunch. That was to keep the weight down and get a little exercise. The whole staff would get out there and have a very spirited contest. I remember one day we flew to the Delta at noon, and the VC threw a satchel charge into the volleyball court, the day we weren't playing so I guess God's hand was in that. But he was just a natural, inspirational leader, and he knew that the little bit of athletic activity at lunch helped dispel the tensions, and he was very much a participator in that, and just a super, super human. I'll come back to this later.

Q: Did he seem concerned by the almost certain knowledge that stepping up the pace would cause more people to get wounded and killed?

Captain Glenn: Yes, he was very concerned by that, but he was more concerned--or not more concerned, because that's not a fair statement, but he recognized that we had a job to do over there, and he felt that by stepping up the pace, which might cause more casualties in the short run, that we might terminate this situation sooner. Personally, I think we lost the war in Vietnam because we failed to play with a full deck. It's kind of like going out in a football game, and you pull your fullback and a couple of tackles and one end, and you just take kind of a half a team, and you can't win a game that way. I think he thought that if we could interdict those supplies coming out of Cambodia, cause them to dry up, then he could slow the war down in the Delta for the Army and for the other troops down there. If we could bring the Delta under control, because that was the rice bowl, and really what the North Vietnamese wanted, because it was the food supply. The Delta was really the rich prize. He felt if we could slow the flow down and basically secure the Delta, that maybe the North Vietnamese might decide it's just not worth doing.

Q: You described him walking over to the chart and conceptualizing the Giant Slingshot and so forth. To what extent was he his own operations officer, so that he eclipsed the N-3?

Captain Glenn: He was his own operations officer. He moved so rapidly intellectually in his assessments of what was going on, and because he was in the field every day getting on-scene assessments of what was going on, that he could quickly adjust his forces, and he would move the lines of the troops or the boats or the bases, or whatever, to account for this. Captain Nicholson went with us on a number of our first excursions and then went into the N-3 job, and I think that really what Captain Nicholson did was reflect Admiral Zumwalt's immediate desires. But Admiral Zumwalt was his operations officer. The Vietnamese theater was not large enough to absorb him. I mean, he could easily follow that entire tactical field and run the operation and also do other things. You would have to have a far larger scope of battle than Vietnam offered to saturate him; he was using perhaps 10 to 20% of his capacity. I expect that had he come along in the Second World War or something like that, that he would have been a fleet commander of the Nimitz status, because he had that intellectual depth and ability.

Glenn/Zumwalt Staff - 190

Q: How much interchange did he have with Admiral Chon of the Vietnamese Navy?

Captain Glenn: Well, he was instrumental in Commodore Chon becoming Admiral Chon, and he had a great deal of interchange. He had Chick Rauch as his special assistant on that turnover to the Vietnamese, and he recognized that he had to get Commodore Chon to take the responsibilities as commander in chief of his forces. He had to find out what the Vietnamese would accept, because it did no good to try to impose U.S. standards on the Vietnamese if the Vietnamese could not accommodate them. He examined how the Vietnamese Navy would survive when the U.S. Navy pulled out. One thing that the Vietnamese were capable of doing was building a concrete mesh boat, so he set up a facility for the Vietnamese. Rather than putting in very complex machinery, which the Vietnamese couldn't handle, not because they weren't smart enough, but because they hadn't been brought up in the U.S. environment where a kid starts tinkering with a Ford when he's 16, and so immediately has some mechanical know-how and this is not true of a guy who's been in a rice paddy all his life. Admiral Zumwalt looked for things that these people with their agrarian background could handle, and started to turn things over and for them to start building and developing equipment so that they could survive. I believe had he had five years or had he been there sooner, he probably could have done some more dramatic things. But there was not enough time. We gave the Vietnamese our machinery and said, "Why can't the Vietnamese handle this? Why can't a Vietnamese quickly learn to disassemble a U.S. rifle or something? Why do these guys take so long?"

Interview Number 2 with Captain W. Lewis Glenn, Jr.,
U. S. Navy

Place: Captain Glenn's home in Vienna, Virginia

Date: Tuesday, 22 May 1984

Interviewer: Paul Stillwell

Q: Captain, last time, as we finished up, we were talking about the business of turning over U.S. assets to the Vietnamese, and you discussed the admiral's relationship with Commodore Chon. Did he have relationships with Vietnamese officers more junior to Chon?

Captain Glenn: He had relationships with officers more junior than Chon, but the opportunities to nurture these relationships really weren't there, probably somewhat to Chon's plan, because I think that Commodore Chon had some concern for his position. He was the CNO of the Vietnamese Navy, but he had been fighting all his life, and he jealously guarded his prerogative to meet with his counterpart.

Q: Did Admiral Zumwalt get out into the boats himself to see how well the turnover was working firsthand?

Captain Glenn: Yes. Again, as I related last time, we went to see the firefights, but we made other trips also. During Christmas of 1968, we flew fixed wing to an area in the Delta where there was a combined Vietnamese-U.S. operation going on to clean up the lower reaches of the Delta. We flew into this relatively desolate airport, landed on Christmas Day, and there were only Vietnamese around the airport. We were supposed to have two helos spotted at the airport. There were no helos, but there was a company or battalion of Vietnamese guarding the strip. We started asking around, and we finally came up with two U.S. advisers working with those Vietnamese. They were a part of this combined operation, and they agreed that they could give us a jeep and driver to us about 20 miles away. There the combined Vietnamese-U.S. armored boat operation was headquartered. So that Christmas morning, we hopped in the jeep and went roaring off through the countryside, much of it controlled by the VC. I did convince the admiral to take his cap off, fatigue hat, which had three silver stars on it. I thought it was prudent, driving through VC country, not to be flashing a three-star hat.

We went over to this operation where the Vietnamese and the U.S. were working together, the Vietnamese being transported on the boats; the Vietnamese working alongside our coxswains and various other positions. Once again, he had only been in country about four months at that time, but already he was pushing to get more combined operations, more experience side by side, because he recognized that we were going to have to leave the country, and the only way the Vietnamese could pick up the load was by observing their U.S. counterparts as much as possible.

We went often to the Vietnamese Naval Academy at Nha Trang to visit the midshipmen, professors, etc. That was up in II Corps. There was a combined operations center down at Vung Tau, and we went to that combined operations center fairly frequently to try to accelerate things, to see what kind of progress was being made. So he made a lot of firsthand observations. Again, one nice thing about war is that there's not as much paperwork. There's too much but still not as much, and so we were able to take those mornings and go out into the field and still finish the paperwork by 6:30 or 7:00 in the evening, or finish up whatever had to be done after dinner. Again you only needed sleep, and there was nothing else to do but work, so 16, 17, 18 hours really didn't make much difference.

Q: Did he make an effort to learn the Vietnamese language so he could discuss things personally with these people?

Captain Glenn: I don't remember him making any attempt to learn the Vietnamese language, and I don't know whether that was by design or not. I'm a very poor linguist. I'm tone deaf, as you can tell from my accent. I've been away from the South 20 years, and my accent doesn't change. A cause of that to a certain extent is my tone deafness, and

I have a very difficult time with languages. So I probably wouldn't have been focusing on that, but I don't recall any particular attempts on his part to learn the Vietnamese language.

Q: Did Admiral Zumwalt work through interpreters, or did the Vietnamese generally speak English?

Captain Glenn: The Vietnamese generally spoke English. Once again, the French had been in Vietnam forever, and many of the Vietnamese had had their children educated in the United States or perhaps had been educated in the United States themselves at our naval war colleges and Army war colleges. It would have been a nice thing to do, because it always makes people comfortable, but it wasn't essential.

Q: You talk about this trip, going out into dangerous territory. How much concern was there for the admiral's personal safety?

Captain Glenn: I had a lot of concern; he had none. He was just totally devoid of any fear or worry or anything like that, and so he was always willing to go anywhere at any time, doing anything, and we did. The only thing I tried to do was just common sense things like, "Take your three-star hat off, boss." And when he wanted to go down the river in an open boat or something like that, I'd just tell him, "That doesn't make much sense. There's no way you can get those sewn three-star things off your lapels. You also are older, you know, you're going to be a prime target. Don't do it." And things like that. But the places we went, rockets had been through the wardroom the night before; the rockets could have come in the wardroom at that time. There was never any attempt not to go into a place because the security was not good. He felt that if his lieutenants could be there, he could be there. And the only thing I tried to do was to at least not make him an obvious target. So we went.

I would say that I knew the Delta and probably flew over more of South Vietnam in my year than anybody else in country. I had a lot of my hours. I think I had something like 378 hours in a helo and numerous hours in fixed wing. You got where you knew every river. You could tell where the B-52s had been a couple of weeks before, because when you'd flown through there prior to it, there weren't the big marks in the landscape that looked like craters in the moon. We went everywhere, and on occasions, we were fired upon. One such occasion was at the very tip of the Delta, I think Ca Mau is the name.

Q: Ca Mau Peninsula.

Captain Glenn: Ca Mau Peninsula. There's a river that runs behind the Ca Mau Peninsula, and we were sure that the Vietnamese were darting into the Ca Mau, and moving supplies into the lower part of the Delta. So we went down one day in fixed wing to reconnoiter the place to see if it was possible to put a fire base or something in down there. We flew low, and as we flew low, we could see tracers coming up at us. That made it pretty obvious that the Viet Cong were there. So we put a fire base in there. As I recall, the operation was Silver Mace. I may be wrong on that, but I think it was Silver Mace. We sent an LST in and used it to support PCFs based there.* We had already cut them in the northern part of the Delta with the Parrot's Beak operation, and coming across the other river from the Parrot's Beak operation, and coming across the other river from the Parrot's Beak to the Gulf of Thailand. Having cut them along there, we figured if we could take the Ca Mau away from them, then we could also cut any opportunity for them to have a base on the southern end. The supplies just went to nothing.

Q: Did Admiral Zumwalt make any Swift boat and PBR patrols himself just to get a feel for what they were like?

---

*LST--tank landing ship, an oceangoing amphibious warfare vessel with a shallow draft that also suited her for work in the rivers of Vietnam.

Captain Glenn: He wanted to make numerous Swift boats and PBR patrols, but I always managed to keep him out of those things. Once again because he was making such a tremendous contribution over there, and if some chance rocket hit, and we lost him, we'd lose such a valuable asset that it shouldn't be done. He kept pressing me, and I kept pushing the issue aside. I still think I did the right thing. As everyone knows, he made a tremendous contribution over there and to the Navy, to the nation, and I think sometimes you have to just step in and help people like that, because they don't worry about their own personal safety.

Q: How did you do that, just avoid scheduling any such things?

Captain Glenn: Yes. He would say, "Put such-and-such on the schedule," and I just wouldn't schedule it. We'd finish up one thing at a fire base and he'd say, "I'm going down the river with these guys."

I'd say, "No, we've already set you up to go to that other fire base that got hit last night and took a lot of casualties, and those guys are counting on you coming. We don't have time." And he would go. He was easy to schedule, because he didn't like to worry about that stuff, and so I would lay it on. He was easy to keep on a schedule. He recognized that his time was limited, so when you told him, "We've got to go," he would go. He seldom kept people waiting. Once again, he's a very, very considerate, kind person.

On a personal note, a good example of his consideration was shown to my roommate, Howard Kerr, and me. Howard was the flag secretary. We got food poisoning while we were over there, and both of us got pretty sick. At 1:00 o'clock at night, the boss was in trying to find out how we were getting along, and did we need a doctor? I mean, he was thoughtful, concerned. For that reason, he was easy to keep on schedule, because you'd tell him, "Hey, you're keeping somebody waiting," and he would give you a little annoyed look, but he didn't want to inconvenience people. You could keep him moving.

One other personal insight I'd like to offer. He worked, once again, very hard, six, seven days a week, but he tried to go home once a month. I used to fly home with him. And when he got home, he dropped away all his papers and everything else and spent all his time with his family. He was either sitting around talking with them or trying to get a tennis game with them, or strolling with them, or whatever, but just as he concentrated 100% of his time on the war when he was in Vietnam, when he got home, he thrust everything aside and concentrated 100% of his time on his family. He was very, very devoted to his family. He has unbounded energy, and he'd focus his energies in one direction and then another. So his time with his family was all quality time. I guess I learned a good lesson then, and I think it's important in the Navy, because you are away a lot, but you can be away even when you're home if you don't spend quality time with your family. He showed me a lot about focusing on the family and spending quality time with them.

Q: Did he go in for any recreational type things like going to Baguio or what have you during these trips to the Philippines?

Captain Glenn: I don't recall us doing that at all. It was basically at home with the family, maybe some people in for dinner, maybe not. Generally since he only saw his children once a month, he tended to spend that time with the children. Mouzetta and Ann were the two who were home at that time, and, of course, Elmo and Jim were not. Jim flew into Vietnam once just to see us and kind of toured around the country with us for about three days, but Jim was in school, and Elmo, of course, later transferred to Vietnam, but he was, I think, deployed previously to the Mediterranean. He was a j.g. in the Navy. But the two girls were at home, and Mouza, and he would spend time with the family; once again, good, quality time.

Glenn/Zumwalt Staff - 201

Q: Did you ever see him fatigued by this great pace he was setting?

Captain Glenn: No. He was also intelligent in his pace, in that he would get a measured amount of sleep at night--not much, but he would try to get six hours or so, and tried to keep it pretty steady. He was also careful in his diet and careful in his alcohol intake. As a matter of fact, in his alcohol intake, he liked to have a martini before dinner. He said, "You know, sometimes I'm tired at night and I'll order a second martini, but when I'm really bushed, I might want a third. Make sure that the third is water with olives." So any time he ordered a third martini, he got water with olives, and he would give me a terrible, withering look, because it was one of those times when he was just exhausted. I could tell he wanted it, another martini, but water and olives he would drink.

Q: When you say he was careful about his diet, what do you mean by that?

Captain Glenn: Well, he was careful. He didn't eat eggs. Cholesterol--he was concerned about cholesterol, and so he didn't eat eggs. In the morning, he would have honey and wheat germs, fresh fruit. And, once again, we played volleyball and had a light salad and tea at lunch, or just tea. He was careful to keep his weight under control and careful to eat a good diet.

Q: Was there a doctor there to look after this physical condition pretty closely?

Captain Glenn: Well, we had a doctor on ComNavForV staff, Dr. Wenger, I believe, and he did, but once again, I could never remember him missing a day. I mean, seven days a week, and I never remember that he would sleep when he got home, you know, eight or nine hours, but once again, usually it was to bed at 11:00, 11:30, up at 5:30 to run. So he maxed, got the max out of life--still does, I guess.

Q: Did you ever see him emotionally fatigued or drained or depressed?

Captain Glenn: Yes, but the times I saw him emotionally fatigued generally came after some firefight and some guys had gotten killed. It was pretty upsetting to him. He had ordered the operation and it hadn't gone well. You know, they turned a bend in the river, and the VC were there with rockets and machine guns, and a number of guys killed and wounded. He felt a great personal responsibility for each individual in Vietnam. So that would weigh heavily on him.

Even if you took out a number of the VC, he still felt a personal responsibility for each individual that was there, and he couldn't remove that burden from himself. So he would be emotionally fatigued sometimes. He was upset sometimes when he didn't feel he was getting enough support, air support or whatever.

There was an interesting dichotomy in the Vietnamese War, because you had the brown-water Navy fighting in the Delta, and then you had the Seventh Fleet offshore, and there was very little interplay between the two. He would try to sometimes get more air support for our troops inshore, and those targets just didn't have the priority that the targets in Hanoi or in the north had. He, at times, felt that maybe we should put more priority on protecting our own troops, helping our own troops and less priority on North Vietnam, I think, particularly when we were in some of the very, very tough areas down in the Delta. I remember the Rung Sat Special Zone. They had been working that for years, and then finally tried to clear it out. He thought he could use air support in there, and we couldn't get it. So there were some problems there, but he didn't get emotionally worn out. He is a very gentle man, and he very seldom goes up an octave, though occasionally he would if he didn't feel his guys in the field were getting everything they should. It upset him.

Glenn/Zumwalt Staff - 204

Q: Would that be the thing that would make him most angry?

Captain Glenn: Yes, yes, absolutely.

Q: Did he make presentations to General Abrams for more of this kind of support and get thwarted?

Captain Glenn: No, he was singularly successful with General Abrams. He and General Abrams probably ended up with as close a personal relationship as two flag officers can have, and I think it was because they were kindred spirits. Both were real warfighters and both wanted to get in there and win. For that reason, he would bend over backwards to give the admiral Army support. I remember fairly early on, there was a meeting which set the tone of things. There were meetings every Saturday morning at MACV, and one Saturday the Air Force and the Navy were scheduled to brief General Abrams on how they were going to turn over things to the Vietnamese.* The only people in the room were flag officers, chief of staff out at MACV, and General Abrams and General Brown, and presenters and a couple of aides, and some other flag officers, maybe Ambassador Colby, I can't remember, but not a large

---

*MACV--U.S. Military Assistance Command Vietnam, which was headed by General Abrams.

group.* The Air Force briefer got up and started making his pitch. General Abrams turned on General Brown after about three minutes and said, "Look, when I ask you to present something to me, I want it presented to me. I don't want that kind of trash," and a few other choice words.

At that point, Major General Corcoran, who was chief of staff at MACV, came racing back to Admiral Zumwalt and said, "You want your briefing officer to go on after this? You can have another day or two if you want to."**

Admiral Zumwalt said, "No, we're ready." So after they finished with that, Major General Corcoran announced that the Navy next would give its brief. Admiral Zumwalt walked forward. He was the briefing officer, and he briefed this thing. I mean, Abrams started out with a countenance that looked like granite, ready to eat nails, and as the logic flowed for the Navy's turnover and their program, you could see Abrams just start to glow. At the end of the thing, he turned to Brown, and he said, "Now you understand what I want." And I think that set the stage for the future. Zumwalt was an action officer. He let his staff officers work, but he stayed on top of things. He came back to brief the Navy hierarchy, and he didn't bring

---
*General George S. Brown, USAF, Commander Seventh Air Force. He was later Air Force Chief of Staff and then Chairman of the Joint Chiefs of Staff. William E. Colby, who later served as Director of the Central Intelligence Agency.
**Major General Charles A. Corcoran, USA.

back a briefing officer. I mean, he was the briefing officer. He liked to get where the action was, and he felt if he did it, then he would know it better than others, and was eminently successful. He has a very soft voice, but the power of his arguments--I mean, you just couldn't top him. It's incredible.

Q: How would you compare the relationship between Admiral Zumwalt and General Abrams with the Veth-Abrams relationship?

Captain Glenn: It was entirely different. There really was no Veth-Abrams relationship. I don't remember any real personal meetings between Veth and Abrams or any real requests for equipment or anything else from Veth. So really there wasn't any relationship. And that was one of the first priorities Admiral Zumwalt saw, because the Army was the top dog in Vietnam, and if we were going to do some substantial operations, we had to have their support and cooperation. We also had to make them believe that we were fighters, which General Abrams was. So until you convinced General Abrams that you really were there to kill VC, to make some offensive moves, to try to get them out of the country, you weren't going to have cooperation from MACV. He did that, and he was very successful.

Q: Part of an aide's job is to make life easier for the admiral. How did you perform that? What things did you do for them?

Captain Glenn: Well, I guess I tried to make sure that I took all the trivia away, tried to make sure that he didn't ever have to worry about anything but concentrating on the major issues. And that started from quickly finding out what he wanted to eat, so that breakfast, lunch, and dinner were something that he could ingest and it was done. Get the stewards to lay out his uniforms and other items so that he didn't have to worry about those. Get an itinerary that would click and allow him to see everybody he wanted to see. At the same time, to give him periods of quiet time so he could think. To act as a barricade at the door sometimes and to be abused, because you wouldn't let someone go in during these quiet times. I tried to learn enough about him personally and professionally so that I could just take every item that he didn't have to do away from him. And either I did it or get somebody else to do it. I'd take adequate notes on a trip so he didn't ever have to worry about what was covered. I tried to make sure that there was never any slipup. The time for cars to arrive, the time for guests to arrive, the time for all those million and one things that happen during the day. I tried to stay ahead of the power curve on all of those so that he knew they were going to happen, and he didn't have to worry about it. You know, just everything from the white wines at a formal dinner to the right color socks.

Q: Did you have any slipups, despite your best efforts?

Captain Glenn: Well, I guess the slipup that I remember most was at dinner one night at the quarters. The guests at the dinner were General Abrams, Admiral McCain, who was CinCPac at the time, the ambassador, General Brown, etc.* It was a very nice dinner and one of the larger ones Admiral Zumwalt had hosted. In Vietnam, nobody dressed formally. It was hot, no airconditioning, so it was an open-shirt gathering. We had roast beef au jus, and as the steward was serving Admiral McCain, he tipped the platter, and the juice came down over his hair. Admiral McCain had a beautiful shock of white hair, and this juice came down his face onto his shirt. I mean, not a tremendous amount, but enough to get through his hair, down his face, onto his shirt. I got up in great embarrassment to try to help Admiral McCain. He got up, and I showed him the bathroom and he got himself cleaned up. I offered him a shirt of mine and he turned to me and said, "Ah, no, if I use your shirt, you'll just frame it and tell everybody that this is

---
*Admiral John S. McCain, Jr., USN, Commander in Chief, Pacific.

a four-star admiral's shirt that you've been wearing." So he said, "I can wear my own."

The next morning, when Admiral McCain was leaving the country, he called the quarters at 6:30 to talk to Admiral Zumwalt. (I monitored Admiral Zumwalt's calls.) His comments were short and to the point, "I just wanted to tell you to please ensure that nothing happens to that steward. That was an accident last night and absolutely no fault of his. But, I know that you won't let anything happen, but I just want to affirm my intent in this matter." I must admit, that was something that I'll never forget about Admiral McCain. It seems to me it takes a very large man to remember something that small at 6:30 the next morning and to make a call to make sure that people did not overreact. I was impressed.

Q: What was the purpose of you monitoring the calls?

Captain Glenn: I believe that is done by all flag officers. I was in Admiral Hayward's office as his administrative assistant three years ago, and we monitored those too.* There are two reasons. One the same reason they take an aide on a trip, that is they're very, very busy, and if you can take a little bit of the pressure off, they can concentrate on bigger things. So in monitoring a

---

*Admiral Thomas B. Hayward, USN, Chief of Naval Operations from 1978 to 1982.

call, for example, if someone asks a question concerning a piece of correspondence, you can remember where the paper is or you can retrieve the paper for the boss. The boss has read it, but this refreshes his memory. He doesn't have to tell you, "Go get it." If you are monitoring the call and are on top of things, within about 60 seconds, you'll have that paper on your boss's desk. I do that even in my job today.* So it's just a help to your boss so that he can do his job more efficiently. These guys work terribly long hours with very demanding schedules. They've got reasonable staffs, but running a 70 or 80 or 100 billion dollar corporation is so great that you've got to help streamline operations in every way possible.

Q: Did you tape-record these calls?

Captain Glenn: No. No, we never tape-recorded anything.

Q: I would think that this would save time, that the admiral wouldn't then have to tell you what he wanted, because you had picked it up during the call yourself.

Captain Glenn: Yes, if phone taskings come in, and you're a good aide, the boss doesn't worry. He'll put the phone

---

*At the time of the interview Captain Glenn was serving as executive assistant to Vice Admiral Robert L. Walters, USN, Deputy Chief of Naval Operations (Surface Warfare).

down, go back to what he's doing, and in ten minutes, you'll show up with whatever things were needed. So it works both ways. It's a tremendous time saver, and that's what you're there for.

Q: Did you learn to read his handwriting?

Captain Glenn: Yes. Yes, I was able to read his handwriting very well, but probably not as well as Howard Kerr.

Q: Captain Kerr was talking about a time when Admiral Zumwalt came down to breakfast wearing pieces of three different uniforms. He had part khaki, part white, and part green. Did you see other examples of absent-mindedness?

Captain Glenn: Oh, yes. He totally concentrated on the job. When we'd go home to Clark, he would come out with the worst-looking outfit you've ever seen.* He just didn't worry about that stuff. Those things weren't important to him, so somebody else worried about them for him. Incredible man.

Q: How long did these trips to the Philippines last,

---

*Clark Air Force Base in the Philippines, where Admiral Zumwalt's family was living while he was in Vietnam.

typically?

Captain Glenn: We would go over Friday night, and we would leave early Monday morning (0200) so we could start the working day in Saigon.

Q: So essentially it was one weekend a month.

Captain Glenn: One weekend a month, yes.

Q: Who minded the store back in Vietnam during those trips?

Captain Glenn: The deputy commander. Admiral Zumwalt made some changes though. When he arrived, the commander and the deputy were both in the same office. Soon after that, he moved his deputy into the Delta, so that he'd be closer to where the action was, so they could both find out what was going on rather than both sitting up at headquarters.

Q: Who was the deputy during most of this time?

Captain Glenn: Admiral House for a short time, and then Admiral Flanagan was there for most of the time.*

---

*Rear Admiral William H. House, USN; Rear Admiral William R. Flanagan, USN.

Q: How close was his working relationship with those two?

Captain Glenn: Not real close. He had definite ideas and needed to implement them. I'm not sure he felt that there was a need for a deputy. He felt more like it was a position created rather than one needed. There weren't enough representative functions or other items to require a deputy.

Q: I would think that would be especially so in someone like Admiral Zumwalt, who was not a slave to the normal chain of command.

Captain Glenn: Yes, it would be, and it was obvious. That's why he moved him out of the headquarters, because he was wasting their time. And that's another thing--he would not waste anybody's time. He didn't like that. So he put them where they could get involved in the action of directing the field commanders.

Q: What can you say about the admiral's ability to absorb information and concepts?

Captain Glenn: It was phenomenal. Immediately upon arrival, he took a trip, six days, through Vietnam, and by the time he got to headquarters and relieved, he already knew what he needed to do. He looked at the map, saw the Vam Co Tay and Vam Co Dong Rivers running along the Parrot's Beak of Cambodia, and immediately saw how to interdict the supplies coming down from North Vietnam. When they went to I Corps, they had to go into Cambodia because they couldn't bring them down through Vietnam and the natural infiltration point was the Parrot's Beak. In six days, having traveled around the country, wham, he was able to then figure out, "Okay, I have forces in place, I've got those guys who are too far offshore. I'll just bring everything in one more notch, put the LSTs where the Swifts were, the Swifts in closer, and then put the PBRs up the rivers." It was like a computer. He could see it all; the logistics, every end of things. It was brilliant. He conceived on a grand scale, but he was also able to worry about all the fallout and what you had to do to make this happen. So it was fascinating seeing him at work. And, once again, for a 26 or 27 year old, it was an absolutely wonderful experience, one I'll never forget and one that's been very useful.

Q: Did he have a good memory for details?

Captain Glenn: Yes. I can't recall him forgetting anything, but I must be careful, because I also worked for Admiral Hayward; he didn't forget either. There must be a

Glenn/Zumwalt Staff - 215

common trait that runs through these individuals. Their capacity for recall is almost mystic. You stop a briefing in mid-sentence and pick it up a month later and if you start that sentence, they say, "Don't give me the trivia. Let's start where you were."

Q: It makes them good for oral history.

Captain Glenn: Yes, yes, it would. It could occupy you for 50 years.

Q: Did Admiral Zumwalt use murder boards when he was going to give a briefing?*

Captain Glenn: Yes, he would. He would give the briefings and let his staff murder him. He was very, very easy to criticize. He took criticism well and would change things. If he didn't feel that what you told him made sense, he would work it around so you thought you had made your contribution. When there was a flaring error and you pointed it out to him, he immediately fixed it. People liked to murder board him, because they knew that he wanted the truth. They didn't have to tell him just what they thought he would like to hear. They told him what he

---

*Murder boards are used when someone has to make a speech or briefing. Beforehand he will try it out with his staff and other advisers who point out shortcomings and raise the sort of questions that listeners might be expected to bring up.

needed to hear, and even if they were wrong, he never unloaded on them. So you were always willing to speak up, and you always felt free to give him your very best advice. Great men sometimes are not willing to let others have a piece of the action, but he was not that way at all. He absolutely would listen, and take aboard what was good.

Q: You talked last time about the insiders and outsiders on the staff, the ones who really got with the program. Would he include some of these outsiders in his murder boards to get their viewpoints, also?

Captain Glenn: Oh, yes. When people talk about Admiral Zumwalt's "kitchen cabinet" or his small staff, they haven't really studied the problem. I remember I was an XO when one of his Z-grams came out, and it was talking about Mickey Mouse or something like that.* Of course, the XO on a ship is the guy who enforces all the rules and regulations. When that Z-gram came out, it didn't change things on my ship one speck. If a guy looked neat in his haircut, then I let him wear that haircut. I didn't go out and measure a guy's hair to see whether it was a quarter-inch or an eighth-inch. Some guys looked scruffy with a quarter-inch of hair, some guys look scruffy with a half-inch. I would not allow any excessive hair, but I felt

---

*XO--executive officer of a ship. Z-grams were messages sent to the fleet by Admiral Zumwalt when he was Chief of Naval Operations; for the most part, Z-grams published information on changes in personnel policies.

that what he was telling us was, "Use your judgment. You're mature guys; use your judgment."

Some people felt that because he formed a "kitchen cabinet," it was because he was unwilling to listen. I think it was just the opposite. I think it was done because others were unwilling to "tell it like it is," and maybe an unwillingness to explore the unknown, because he was not a man who was willing to stick with the status quo. He was going to try things. He would rather shoot 1,000 arrows at the target and have ten hit than only shoot two and the two hit. So he tended to try new things. And if you were unwilling to explore new things, then he tended to reject you, not because your advice wasn't sound, but because you were unwilling to look at new avenues and opportunities, and he felt that we should do that. He had a natural curiosity. People who were willing to explore new things, came up with bright ideas and were willing to work, got his support.

At the same time, I must say that I think Admiral Zumwalt's greatest failing was that once he had decided that you could make a contribution, he always kept you on board, even when others might be moving ahead faster in their width of vision. I would have to say that his greatest failure was once he embraced a man, he never dropped him by the wayside. He always kept that guy with him, and I think at times to his personal detriment.

Q: Are there any examples you could use to demonstrate what you mean by that, that he wasn't moving ahead as much as he might, perhaps?

Captain Glenn: I'd rather not. Sorry.

Q: You talk about people who are unwilling to offer things. Is that because they don't have anything to offer, or they think he might not be receptive?

Captain Glenn: Well, I think it probably works both ways. They probably think that he would not be receptive. At the same time, they're so locked in their traditional ways that they don't want to step to one side to make sure that the straight and narrow path they're walking on is really the yellow brick road. And I think there was a lot of that. The Navy is a conservative outfit, and he was so different that it was disturbing. I thought he was a breath of fresh air. I still think he's a breath of fresh air. He has a lot of brilliant ideas that I think should have been implemented, and I think that some strategies he tried to implement in the Seventies would make us be better in the Eighties.

Q: Were there things in Vietnam that he tried to do but

did not succeed?

Captain Glenn: Yes. He tried to use many different techniques. He was successful in getting the PBRs up the river, and he was successful in moving the Swift boats into other places. He wanted to get the surface effects vehicles working in Vietnam. He thought that they would be very useful. However, because of the noise they made, they really weren't adaptive for that type of warfare, and so some effort and money was wasted in that area. However, I would suspect that a good deal of the data base for our decision to go with these vehicles for the Marine Corps comes from that research in Vietnam.

Q: How much concern and latitude did Admiral Zumwalt have on rules of engagement?

Captain Glenn: He felt that his commanders in the field had good judgment. He told them basic rules of engagement. He always felt that his subordinates were as capable as he and that he had responsible young men. They weren't going to kill civilians or innocents, but they had to be given a reasonable opportunity to protect themselves, because once again, when some guy rises up out of the rice paddy with a B-40 rocket and shoots it at you, you've got to return the fire or die. He was not hung up on rules of engagement.

He was hung up on the fact that he had good people in the field and that those guys were willing to give their lives for their country and for what they thought was right, and therefore, they deserved to have delegated to them the authority to make decisions in the field. And that's why many of these tactics such as the waterborne ambush were developed. It made ingenuity go up a hundredfold because of his approach to things, and it saved lives, and it got the VC, so it did the job.

Q: Do you have any other examples of that kind of ingenuity?

Captain Glenn: Paul, you know, there were hundreds, I guess. The Stefencavage one sticks in my mind so clearly, because it was such a tremendous boost to us at a time when we really needed the boost. Before he got there, his commanders were on very short leashes. And after he got there and talked to them and got them rolling, they were trying all kinds of operations. They were moving out in different directions.

Q: What impressions do you have of the principal subordinates. That is, Salzer, Price, and Hoffman?

Captain Glenn: It's incredible that the luck of the draw

could have put three men in their positions, and Zumwalt did not know them when he arrived. A very, very mixed breed. Roy Hoffman, you know, was a seaman-to-admiral type. He was a captain over there. He was a rough, tough, do-anything, action-oriented guy who went on every firefight himself, wanted to be there, a fascinating individual.

Salzer, on the other hand, was, I think, an economist out of Yale. He was very, very bright, good mind and a tremendous ability to plan. He quickly rose to the forefront of the commanders, because he could see beyond his heavy boats. He could see ways to put things together, ways to pinch the VC with combined operations between the Swifts and the heavy boats and the PBRs. He was a terrific wartime strategist and activist.

Art Price, on the other hand, was the only aviator in the group, and he brought a good insight into how aviation can be used, and he got more air support, and used air support in clever ways.

Q: I take it from what you say, there was a lot of give and take between them and the admiral, not just him putting things out.

Captain Glenn: Oh, absolutely. Absolutely. He met with them, and he would just cull their good ideas. There were times when he had what he thought was a good idea and his field commander said, "You know, sounds great here in headquarters, but let me tell you, I've been there, and that just won't work, boss. That may look right on the map, but let me tell you, they've built such-and-such there, and you can't get a boat from there to there, and you can't get support from there to there. There are no supplies." So he'd back off. Good sessions, though.

Q: How frequently would he talk to the task force commanders?

Captain Glenn: A monthly meeting in Saigon, and then he'd talk to them on a daily basis. Either they met him when he was in the field, or he would fly to their headquarters for a briefing once a week or so. Good interface.

Q: In all of the descriptions of Vietnam, there is great emphasis on the body count as a means of measuring success. Was that emphasized at all with Admiral Zumwalt?

Captain Glenn: No, he didn't emphasize body count. He was interested, though, in arms and supply caches, how many guns or how much food or whatever. He just felt the body count didn't tell you too much, but if you were getting to their supply lines, then eventually they would run out of bullets. They might be able to find food, but you can't find bullets, and you can't make guns in a rice paddy.

Q: How good was our intelligence on that sort of thing?

Captain Glenn: You mean, how much we got?

Q: In being able to measure what they probably had overall and how much of that we were getting.

Captain Glenn: I really don't know how good the intelligence was. I just know that supply stocks that were intercepted in the riverboats were pretty dramatic and effective. You figure what a sampan can carry and cut off the sampan, then they have to carry the materials on someone's back. Then you really do limit how much can be carried. If you find ten tons of ammunition and rifles and it's 50 miles down the Delta and you know somebody's got to bring that on their back, then you're talking a lot of man-days and months and years to move that material.

Q: In an offensive scheme like this that depends on tactical surprise, what steps were taken to try to ensure communications security?

Captain Glenn: As I recall, there was no real concern

about communications security because the PBRs were six boats in the middle of nowhere. I don't remember concern about communications. The Army, I'm sure, had some because of big sweeps but we were small potatoes compared with the Army. We ended up doing a lot by cutting supply lines, and that's something the Army really couldn't do. The supplies were moving by water or along the riverbanks, because you can't move supplies over rice paddies. So the Army wasn't stopping the movement of supplies. It took the Navy to do that.

Q: Did he get involved any in the psychological warfare operations?

Captain Glenn: You know, I don't know, because that effort, I believe, was in a special category, and I didn't go to any briefings outside the headquarters on it, so I really don't know.

Q: What about the pigs and chickens operation. Do you recall that?

Captain Glenn: I know what you're talking about, but I just don't have a good recollection of it.

Q: In his oral history, Admiral Veth had a negative

impression of the news media. How would you describe Admiral Zumwalt's relationship with the Media?

Captain Glenn: Well, he was careful. You know, a good relationship, but he was always careful. He felt as long as you knew your newspaper person and knew he was a professional, that if you said, "This is for the record," or "This is background," or "This is deep background," that the individual would respect that.* He did not particularly trust the newsperson whom he did not know. I believe he felt that some of the news people would do anything to sell a newspaper. So I would say that he didn't have a great trust of the media. However, he trusted the media that he had worked with before.

Q: Did you then monitor the things that were coming back, newspapers and TV, to see how these things were used once he had interchange with them?

Captain Glenn: Yes, and it seems to me they were pretty fair. I don't recall any instances where they abused him. But I don't remember us spending a lot of time worrying about feeding the press the right information. If he felt

---

*Background material is that which can be used for publication but not quoted directly or attributed to a specific individual. Deep background is that which cannot be used for publication at all but which is provided to a reporter so that he will have a better understanding of the subject and not inadvertently make mistakes in his stories.

he could talk about something, then he talked about it for the record. If he didn't feel he could talk about it, he either would know the individual and give it to him as background, deep background, or he wouldn't. So it wasn't an attempt to feed the press information that they should get, it was, "Can we tell them about this operation? Is it over? Is anybody's life going to be in danger if we tell them?" But we never tried to manufacture or tailor information going to the news media. Always we were straight with them: "I can't tell you anything about that. The reason I can't tell you is because the guys are still down there; they're still working; it's a tactic that we're trying. If it gets in the news, some of my guys may get killed, and I will not take that chance."

Q: What can you say about Admiral Zumwalt's political awareness and capability?

Captain Glenn: Well, he was very politically astute. He recognized the political pressures that the nation was bringing to bear long before they hit their fever point, and he knew that the politicians would, of necessity, have to bow to this public opinion. So he recognized the realities of politics. If a guy wants to stay in office, he's got to do something for his district, or he's got to do something for his state. The American people were sick of Vietnam. They didn't appreciate it. I must admit, I fault the media a little bit for that, but can you really fault the media? I mean, the big problem was that every night when you sat down at your TV set, they saw either a young American guy getting killed or somebody else getting killed, and frankly, you get tired of it. So the American people got tired of people getting killed. It's not something that you enjoy, and you had ten minutes in color, in living color, every night. He recognized those problems, those difficulties. I wonder how World War II would have gone if every night it meant 15 minutes of color photographs of our guys hitting the beaches and getting blown away in the Pacific or some of the terrible battles in Germany.

Q: In that sense, you would say that the media was a hindrance to the war effort?

Captain Glenn: Yes, the media was a hindrance to the war effort, but once again, we've got a free country, and you've got to make a living if you're a media person, and so you bring forward what will sell.

Q: I think the big difference between Vietnam and World War II is what technology permitted to be happening.

Captain Glenn: Absolutely. In Vietnam, you've got people who were shattered, in terrible situations physically, and a helicopter would arrive on the scene almost immediately and move this person away, and he'd live. In the Second World War, the guy died, bled to death.

Q: Did you perceive any difference in the conduct of the war after the new administration came in in January '69, the Nixon Administration?

Captain Glenn: I saw an acceleration in the turnover to the Vietnamese, but Admiral Zumwalt had previously been aware of that need. He arrived knowing what Nixon's plan was going to be. So from our point, I don't think things changed a bit. Yes, they changed in Vietnam, because others came to realize what Zumwalt already knew. We were a year ahead, or six months ahead of our time. He was very astute. He stayed ahead of the power curve all the way. We saw others falling in line with what we already knew, or what Admiral Zumwalt already knew was going to be the need to turn things over or the ACTOV--Accelerated Turnover to the Vietnamese. He implemented that from the beginning. He knew what was coming, so no change for us, but yes, the rest of Vietnam, the Air Force and Army realized that the Navy was really on board and far out in front.

Q: You said your objective had been to get home when you wound up the tour. Did you have any misgivings about leaving an operation that you had gotten so intensely involved in?

Captain Glenn: I have never had a job in the Navy that I wanted to leave. Again, though, the Navy causes you to have to set some priorities. If you want to have a family, you've got to have some time with the family, so you've got to move from one thing to another. I left it with great misgivings or disappointments that everything that I had seen rolling along wasn't complete. Disappointment that I was leaving the friends that I had made. I hated to leave those. But I can say the same thing about my XO's tour, my command tours, you know. You don't want to leave those things, because you are involved and you're excited and you're engrossed. At the same time, life moves on, and I guess that's one of the things that I enjoy about the Navy. It gives you new and different challenges time after time after time.

Q: Did Admiral Zumwalt ask you to extend your tour any?

Captain Glenn: No. I had a son who was six months old when I left and he was going to be a year and a half when I got home. And he would not have asked me to extend. I guess I was at that young, tender point where you just know better than to ask that type thing. I probably would have done it out of loyalty to him, so he would never have put me in that position.

Q: Many of the people who have served closely with Admiral Zumwalt wound up with subsequent tours near him. Why didn't you?

Captain Glenn: Well, I left and went immediately back to a sea tour. By the time I completed my sea tour, he was in a position where he was concerned about some of the criticism that he was getting, and I think that he recognized that I wanted to stay in the Navy and was in for the long haul. He did not want me to be tarnished by his brush. The people he kept around him were the commanders and the captains that he could make flag officers out of, and he could reward those individuals. I was a lieutenant, and I think he felt that in my case that it would be counterproductive to me to get too close. And I think there's probably some truth in that. There's still a backlash in the Navy. I am never embarrassed to express my admiration for Admiral Zumwalt. But there are a lot of people who disagree with me. So I think that he did me a favor. We've been close friends ever since.

Q: To wrap this up, is there anything else you want to say about him that I haven't asked about?

Captain Glenn: I'm sure there are millions of things that after you leave, I'll say, "Why didn't I think of this?" But I really don't. Once again, he's a wonderful man. I admired him, I still admire him. I call him a friend to this day, and if he called me right now and asked me to go do something, whatever it was, I would put down what I was doing and do it. He's that kind of guy. He would do the same for me.

Q: I'm grateful to you for spending this time and sharing your thoughts about him.

Captain Glenn: I enjoyed it. Thank you much. Thank you.

Interview with Admiral Worth H. Bagley,
U. S. Navy (Retired)

Place: Admiral Bagley's home in La Jolla, California

Date: Monday, 16 May 1983

Interviewer: Paul Stillwell

Q: Admiral, could you begin, please, by telling me how your association with Admiral Zumwalt began?

Admiral Bagley: I saw him infrequently through the years. He was a friend of my brother's in their earlier youth. And professionally I really had no contact with him until the late 1960s. At the time, he was a cruiser-destroyer flotilla commander in San Diego, and I was on the local staff. We had recurring contact then through the Sixties. And I was in command of a cruiser-destroyer group in WestPac in 1969 when he was in Vietnam. I saw him a couple of times during that period.

And then the next time--and really the first time--that I knew him in any intimate fashion was during the time when he was the CNO, and I went back there early in that regime.

Q: In his book he said that he specifically picked you to come back from your tour as the flotilla commander so you could work on his Project 60.*

Admiral Bagley: I arrived back in OpNav after the Project 60 operation had gone along for some time under Stan Turner.** And I took over when Stan left to go to another job. I went on with what hadn't been completed and oversaw a large part of the implementation of what had been recommended after it was once approved. I was involved in the briefing of SecDef and others in order to get general concurrence on how to proceed.***

Q: Why had he picked you for that position?

Admiral Bagley: I guess you'd have to ask him.

Q: It would seem from his book that he was asking for you specifically.

Admiral Bagley: I guess he felt I could do it. He knew that I believed in the general idea of what Project 60 was intended to do: take a look at the world in a fresh way; see what our current and prospective strategic requirements were; judge that against where the Navy stood, what the Navy could do uniquely for national defense, and also take

---

*See Elmo R. Zumwalt, Jr., On Watch (New York: Quadrangle/The New York Times Book Co., 1976), pages 66-67.
**Captain Stansfield Turner, USN, who later became a four-star admiral and served as Director of the Central Intelligence Agency during the Carter Administration.
***SecDef--Secretary of Defense Melvin R. Laird.

into account what the Navy had gone through (that's worth some separate comment), and then decide on the proper course over the next four years to match those two categories--one, the strategy and two, the Navy. Of course, coordinating with what the other services could do. And, as it turned out, Project 60 saw that there was a need for some Navy missions to be augmented by capabilities that existed in the other forces, and that was one of the recommendations for economical use of sea power--particularly the use of the Air Force for mining and some sea control work.

Q: You said some additional comment could be called for.

Admiral Bagley: I'd say that it is important to remember the general environment at the time that Zumwalt became CNO. We were ending a war--or shortly would end the war in Vietnam--which had been very strenuous in terms of the demands it made on the Navy and on resources. There was a lot of attrition, particularly of aircraft, and they were being barely replaced. Ships were being worn down, maintenance was falling behind, and people were getting very tired. That had followed the McNamara period, in which there was a great effort to justify not modernizing.* So the coincidence of the McNamara non-

---
*Robert S. McNamara was Secretary of Defense from 1961 to 1968.

modernizing, low-production, holding-forces-generally-as-they-were period, followed by a period in which the services--and the Navy in particular--were worn down, meant that when he came in, this wasn't much of a Navy. I mean, it was a good Navy, but it was not the kind of a Navy that people were used to, and it wasn't the kind of Navy that would meet the sorts of strategic challenges that Zumwalt thought were either existing or looming.

And among the strategic things that he thought were important: he was the first to recognize that there was a growing defense mismatch between the increasing oil supplies the United States imports and our growing strategic interest in the Middle East. That existed against a background of growing instability in the Middle East. The '67 war between Israel and the Arabs still locally generated a great deal of argument, regional disputes that remain to this day not settled. The civil war in Lebanon disrupted conditions on the Mediterranean coast and had implications down into the Persian Gulf. And also for the first time, in about 1968, a real Soviet presence in the Indian Ocean was established, making it more important for us to realize that our interests were growing there, that strategically we had to do something with power which was more counteractive or at least balancing, so that people could see our interest as well as that of the Soviets.

During that same 1960s period, things hadn't gone too well in Europe; the allies were not terribly happy with what we were doing in Vietnam. We hadn't been able to do as much in Europe during that time as we had wanted to do; they as a consequence hadn't done very much. The Soviets had taken advantage of that alliance neglect to build up both their manpower and their forces, even more than they had done in the previous five to ten years.

In the Far East there was already discussion which took later form of changing our relationships with Taiwan in favor of a relationship with the Republic of China, which would have a number of effects. If done right, and if the Chinese were strong enough and had the proper sort of will in fashioning their own policy, a friendlier China would tend to take some of the pressure off Europe by the Russians having to worry more about the Far East.

So those several things in conjunction meant that we had to think more about energizing sea power. We had to think about how we would deter war and protect our interests in more areas than we had thought about prior to that time, and we had to do it with a lesser Navy than we'd had a decade before.

Zumwalt came in personally under difficult circumstances, because he was the first non-aviator CNO since 1961. He was very young; he didn't have a service constituency in the same way that some of his predecessors had.* He was made CNO over the objections of the CNO at the time, and he depended a great deal on civilian authority, because it was a courageous Secretary of the Navy, Chafee, who decided that for a number of reasons Zumwalt was the right man to bring in.** And in addition to the other difficulties, the previous CNO, Admiral Moorer, was made Chairman of the JCS, so he had a shortened term as CNO, which had an effect, too, on the continuity of command, and on the change in CNO policies which eventually took place.***

On the personnel side, Zumwalt--a younger man--and seeing many different kinds of Americans in Vietnam, judged their war experience to have a potential impact on the Navy and on all the armed services. What he saw was a different kind of social outlook among the young Americans in Vietnam, which was manifested in the U. S. in many ways in the Sixties but really was only starting to become evident in the armed services. But the armed services inevitably always reflect the citizens' views, so he thought it was important that he take that forehandedly into account. He didn't think evident approaching change could be handled in the same way that it had been done in the past. The Navy,

---

*Admiral Zumwalt was 49 years old, the youngest man chosen to be Chief of Naval Operations.
**John H. Chafee.
***Admiral Thomas H. Moorer, USN, Chief of Naval Operations from 1967 to 1970 and Chairman of the Joint Chiefs of Staff from 1970 to 1974.

being quite aristocratic and quite conservative, having a lot of the mores of the southern United States, would probably now have to think in a much broader way, and the transition probably would have to be undertaken dramatically to get people to think in less conservative ways. So he did a number of things which became very controversial before it was over, because he anticipated and hoped to avoid those more basic social problems.

I think that there can be some debate about whether he acted too fast, whether he did it right, or whether the problem that he saw existed as deeply as he thought. But I think that most reasonable people agree the changing social problems existed and that something had to be done to make changes in the Navy. He took some measures, and a large number of those altered policies still exist. And the ones that have drawn the most criticism have been those that had to do with the chain of command, which really is a small part of it. The thing in all of that to keep in mind is that Zumwalt had one objective, and that was to make it easier for professional naval men—enlisted men in particular, but the younger officers also—to do their jobs. So he wanted to create the mental atmosphere, the social atmosphere, and the professional atmosphere that would enhance motivation to get the professional job done in the most effective way. And he thought—considering all the other force and readiness problems that existed at the time--that manpower management was a crucial part of his overall policy to strengthen the Navy.

Q: Admiral Zumwalt told me that in picking people who would be close to him, especially after he was jumped over the heads of so many seniors, he went particularly to those whom he could count on for personal loyalty. Did he have a particular reason to count you among that category?

Admiral Bagley: He had a reason to, from the standpoint that I agreed fully with the origins of the Project 60, which had to do with looking and deciding on a prospective strategy that made sense, conferring with the Secretary of Defense and others on the validity of that strategy, and then taking a look at force levels and trying to design a Navy that would satisfy the real and not apparent interests of the United States. So he could count on my loyalty, because we had the same intellectual approach and the same thoughts about these issues.

Q: How had he been able to find out that about you before then?

Admiral Bagley: For one thing, I worked in 1966-67 as executive assistant to SecNav Paul Nitze, a close associate of Zumwalt's.*

Q: How much had been accomplished toward those goals by Captain Turner by the time you came?

Admiral Bagley: Turner had done a lot of good work, and he'd gotten people stirred up in OpNav to give attention to the study so it didn't look like, and wasn't, a back-room operation. So I think he, working with Zumwalt, did the basic work and the rounding out of the concept. In my time with Project 60, we fiddled around with the early drafts and made some strategic adjustments to it, made some parallel adjustments to the kinds of force changes that we ought to make but didn't intrude on the already prepared policies for personnel and how those should develop.

Then, over my period, I had a lot to do with trying to sell these evolved ideas inside and outside the Navy and to get them into the program. I did that for two or three months. Then I moved into OP-90, the program office, where I was in a position to have a say on seeing that those things were done, because that's where the programs and the

---

*Paul H. Nitze served as Secretary of the Navy from 1963 to 1967 and as Deputy Secretary of Defense from 1967 to 1969.

money converge.* And later on, as Director of Program Planning, I just carried on in that function. But during the whole period, it's worth saying that we had a common and clear perception, from the Project 60 product, of what was to be done. There wasn't one single policy paper that I can remember in three and a half years there in which it wasn't perfectly clear from the Project 60 work the direction of decision that should be taken.

In that process certain things were done differently than other CNOs do them. There was a lot of thinking, stimulating, and initiating from the top, and a number of CNOs before and after Zumwalt were much more comfortable in having any idea generated from the bottom--within the staff. There are advantages and disadvantages in the Zumwalt concept, as seen in his years. One, he developed the useful ideas that weren't coming from the bottom and set an exemplary tone. Two, in initiating ideas and then passing them down, he didn't always get full loyalty of support.

You have to match those consequences against the CNO who asks for the ideas from the bottom, which go through four or five different staff levels, and if they ever get to the CNO are so compromised that they're really not ideas

---

*OP-90, the General Planning and Programming Division, is a portion of the CNO's extended staff. The division reports to the Director, Navy Program Planning (OP-090), a billet later held by Worth Bagley after he was promoted to vice admiral.

related to real problems. The CNO then buys those positions, because he's gotten them from his staff rather than because they are ideas that make sense within a larger and finely defined concept. And since OpNav is splintered by function and experience, too, it's difficult for each part of OpNav to keep a specific concept in mind, although the CNO, Zumwalt, went to great pains to explain the overall concepts and ideas and the connections he saw between strategy and forces so that everybody on the staff would understand them. There was every opportunity for disagreements from the staff to emerge forthrightly, but usually they did not.

Q: Are there some specific cases you might use as illustrations to show how this process of interaction worked--things that the admiral would propose, and then you would staff or whatever work you would do on them?

Admiral Bagley: It wasn't always me. We're talking about past the Project 60, I believe. The CNO's ideas were passed down to the proper part of OpNav for staffing, for development of the ideas, and for recommendations on what sorts of actions would give the CNO's initiative its final form. And there was mixed success in that for the reasons that I've already stated. But when the staff product came back up to the CNO and there were obvious compromises, then

I was involved in helping see that the response was put in context and that the supporting actions that were required were formulated and instituted. And then the CNO would usually approve that paper in that form.

Q: How did the transition work between Project 60 and then going on into implementing things?

Admiral Bagley: Project 60, after we did the initial work of dealing with OpNav and getting Secretary of Defense approval, the tasks for implementation and monitoring their accomplishment were placed under a separate organization which, as I remember, was called 09C.* OP-09C took on responsibility for a whole series of following actions and having them done. But that process, in the situation I've described about the CNO getting from the staff either incomplete or altered or misunderstood kinds of action and policy papers, was never a perfect operation. So I was involved during this whole three-and-a-half-year period in altering substantively those papers and staff perspectives involved, to conform with the CNO's design, even though the administrative responsibility for pushing people to do certain things had moved to another office.

Q: In that summer of 1970--not long after he had taken

---
*OP-09C was the Special Assistant to the CNO/VCNO for Decision Coordination.

over--came the Jordanian crisis in the eastern Mediterranean. What effect, if any, did that have on your work?

Admiral Bagley: I think those kinds of problems in the eastern Mediterranean had been anticipated. And I think the general ideas and the issues that were involved in that are fully explained, and I think accurately, in Zumwalt's book.

Zumwalt, during that period, became more conscious than he'd been before of two things about the highest authority of the United States. One, that President Nixon understood perfectly well that we needed to do something about beefing up our strength, partly because of what the Soviets were doing to stretch our strategic requirements, partly because we'd hit a point of no advance in capabilities during this Vietnam period. But, secondly, in understanding that Nixon also recognized that the Vietnam experience was eroding his defense constituency slowly but surely, a condition that prevailed through and beyond his big reelection in 1972. He didn't feel that he had the political power with which to undertake defense strengthening that he told Zumwalt he thought ought to be done. And Zumwalt used the Jordanian crisis and others which followed it to try to convince Nixon that rearming was the essential U. S. need. And each of those crises in the eastern Mediterranean--and I can think of no exception to this--regardless of what we thought were our strategic responsibilities around the world, always drew off a very large part of the Navy available for deployment.

So it became apparent through the experience of these crises that much of what Zumwalt had said in Project 60 in terms of strategic requirements--the sorts of forces and the sorts of procedures and concepts that would have to be followed to meet those strategic interests--were proven in these crises to be right, not yet satisfied. So I think all of these lessons supported his ideas and what he thought, and he used these real events as occasions to press on higher authority to do something about strengthening the Navy. The following period, however, became very difficult. Our history shows that between '70 and '74 Nixon lost his ability to act as needed on defense, a lapse that only now under President Reagan is being corrected.

Q: Part of this process of modernization involved getting rid of current ships in order to raise some money for future acquisition. How could this be accomplished when, as you say, the Navy was already stretched thin to begin with?

Admiral Bagley: That sort of decision, I don't think, is ever reached with ease, but it came from two or three of those elements that I've already mentioned. One, a Navy that was tired and attrited and worn out from the Vietnam years still in progress, a President and an administration which believed that we needed to become stronger for various reasons--both our interests and what the Soviets were doing--but was unable politically to act, and a Congress which was only partly cooperative because of various things, not the least of which was the discussion that had been going on since 1968 and was going on in the early Nixon years about arms control. And that always generates more hope than dedication about security--at least in the early, optimistic stages of arms control talk--than is warranted by the result.

The kinds of funds needed for modernization weren't going to come forward and would not materialize otherwise unless something was done to help make them available. So Zumwalt decided that one of the ways to do it was to decommission some of the old ships which had been particularly worn out during heavy operations in Vietnam and transfer into the procurement appropriations those operations monies that would normally be used to overhaul those ships and keep them operating. And he was able to raise the procurement account considerably--two or three times, as I remember--by that tactic and the admiring support it evoked among decision-makers in the executive branch and in the Congress. One result is the Navy became the highest funded service, attracting monies previously given the Army and Air Force.

Those kinds of improvisations were not untypical during his time. Another one that's not unrelated is the whole question of how you meet strategic requirements with a Navy that's too small and worn out. And that was the genesis for this idea of homeporting overseas, which avoided long transits and relief ships. We could cut down on the numbers of total ships that we needed in order to keep an X amount of ships forward in an area to serve as deterrents in peacetime and hopefully have force that was suitable to deal with the threat if the deterrent didn't work.

Q: Is overseas homeporting one of the programs you worked on in OP-90?

Admiral Bagley: Yes, we worked on that.

Q: What were some of the ramifications that you had to address?

Admiral Bagley: The first thing was to deal with the country concerned and see if there was a receptivity, and that varied. This was tried in two or three different places. Secondly was to see the suitability of the country for homeporting the ships in terms of ship security while they were in port and in getting easily in and out of port. There were some instances where this wasn't going to be easy. Bremerhaven was a good example of where there was a long voyage in and out, and that just didn't look like it'd be a good thing.

But to meet criteria of this kind, as well as narrowing the options to practical factors of relations between the United States and the prospective host foreign countries, it was pretty simple to decide on a few choices. Japan became one. We proceeded with homeporting there, and ships are still in Japanese ports, including a carrier. And, secondly, Greece appeared to be the best option in the European area, although possibilities were examined outside of the Mediterranean as well as in. But for various reasons, including growing interest in the Middle East, Greece became the dominant choice.

As you know, we started homeporting destroyers there, but it really wasn't successful, given the unstable internal politics emerging again in Greece, the change of government there, and the move from an administration in Greece that was very sympathetic to our presence to one that couldn't survive unless we got out. As a consequence, we left. I'd say that was an embarrassing result, but it wasn't invalidated on strategic grounds. And I can say without any qualification that the fact that we don't have that facility now, even with the Navy in its current size--it's a little bit bigger now than it was in the early Seventies--we're not able to meet our strategic requirements in that region without undue over-stretching of our resources elsewhere.

Q: You've used the term "strengthening the Navy." Typically, one of the ways of measuring the strength in the past has been numbers of ships, and this trend was going against that. How, then, do you sell the idea that you're strengthening the Navy by getting rid of ships?

Admiral Bagley: You trade off ships to reduce the Navy today in order to have the monies to have a larger Navy in the next three to eight years, while, concurrently, you develop better weapons for the future. It's that simple.

Q: Was Congress generally receptive to that idea?

Admiral Bagley: The Secretary of Defense was receptive, and the Congress was receptive, yes. Partly they were receptive because in deciding on priorities in the Navy, in order to meet the strategic requirements, the CNO emphasized control of sea-lanes. This was seen as relevant to protecting U. S. interests in the Middle East and Persian Gulf, as I've mentioned, as well as responding to an analysis of our deficient capability to move reinforcements and resupply to NATO. So it was possible to talk about new ships that were more inexpensive than the kinds of ships that you put in carrier task forces. They would be less, on the whole, able to fight in an intense war environment than the carrier and the battle group, but you would be building specifically for combat outside those areas. So all of that made enough sense that the authorities went ahead with giving the Navy procurement funds in compensation, and more, for the operations monies saved by decommissioning old ships.

And it wasn't, of course, that every idea was approved. Escorts--the FFG-7 program--went forward.* The idea of having a sea control ship (SCS), which would probably have V/STOL aircraft, would also be medium-sized-- probably around 15,000 to 20,000 tons--and inexpensive, didn't go.** And there are internal reasons for the failed SCS idea that had to do with the Navy bureaucracy, often leery of a new idea, which on its own merits might be a sound idea but, when compared to something that already

---
*Originally the escort was designated as the PF-109 class of patrol frigate. A change in the Navy's hull numbering system made it the FFG-7 (<u>Oliver Hazard Perry</u>) class of guided missile frigates.
**V/STOL--vertical or short takeoff and landing aircraft. These were principally embodied by the AV-8 Harrier, which underwent sea control ship suitability tests during the Zumwalt years on board the USS <u>Guam</u> (LPH-9).

exists, may be seen to compromise that traditional ship or weapon system. In this case, the issue was the relationship of the sea control ship mission and that of the carrier. So there was enough opposition from OpNav and other sources generated on the Hill so that the SCS never made it.

Q: Was this opposition primarily from the aviators?

Admiral Bagley: You know, they didn't all come up and tell me, "I'm opposing it," so I would just have to guess. But it was people who, I'm sure, had various reasons, ranging from the air mission to the size and form of the ship designed to avoid high-cost nuclear propulsion.

Q: Those seem to be the two main thrusts of the high-low program: the patrol frigate and the sea control ship, one of which came into being and one didn't.* Would you say that was the kind of thing that made the difference between the two--internal OpNav opposition?

Admiral Bagley: I think it certainly had a role, yes. Over this Zumwalt period was the opening of the era when

---

*The concept of the high-low mix was that in high-threat areas the Navy would use high-capability ships and weapon systems; a larger number of less capable units would be built for lower threat environments.

weapon technology was being transformed into the forerunners of small, very accurate, very long-range weapons. And while there wasn't heavy discussion on these possibilities for land-target cruise missiles, it was clear that you would be able to put strike capability of a different order on ships that were smaller, less sophisticated, and much less expensive as time went on. So I presume some people looked at ideas like the sea control ship, which might carry a large number of cruise missiles, as something that might grow beyond what they might want it to become.

As early as 1967, when I was executive assistant to Secretary of the Navy Nitze, he was proposing that conventional missiles be fitted in the nuclear-powered cruiser Long Beach, an idea opposed by then-CNO Moorer. By the early Seventies, there was a sense that that kind of capability was here; it was the kind of thing we could talk about; if we could reach our way through the bureaucracy and traditional prejudices, we could start planning for it. However, that didn't occur, other than short-range antiship missiles. But, obviously, the land-target cruise missile idea was a substructure for the pros and cons that people had toward various programs that Zumwalt was proposing.

Zumwalt tried sincerely, for separate reasons, to head off this opposition by being a staunch supporter--because in the near term he believed in it deeply--of naval aviation and big carriers. He was responsible for having the F-14 fighter approved and procured and was a key element in having the program for large nuclear carriers continue on.

He saw, I think probably as fast as anyone--and I don't think it's gone its full course yet--the potential value in a whole series of missions for the attack submarine. And he immediately moved that procurement program from one or two a year to five a year. He had no opposition on that, because he was dealing with a submarine constituency in and out of the Navy which was strong itself. And there was general appeal in the submarine, because it was easier to see that the submarine couldn't be detected, while surface ships looked vulnerable.

Q: In his book, Admiral Zumwalt certainly talks about the difficulties he had in dealing with Admiral Rickover.* How much were you involved in that kind of a squabble?

Admiral Bagley: In my position, I could and did try to minimize contacts with Admiral Rickover. I dealt with him necessarily at times, but it was always difficult and usually unproductive to have a discussion with him. You often had to listen to a unilateral discourse rather than

---

*Vice Admiral Hyman G. Rickover, USN (Ret.), was then head of the Navy's nuclear power program, both submarines and surface ships such as aircraft carriers and cruisers.

reason on an issue. His mind was always made up. It was not easy to make arrangements with Rickover directly on particular programs, particularly if he had some reservations. But his reservations during that time--which Zumwalt goes into--were more related to concern over programs for combatant ships which by size, form, or cost projection might not fall into the Rickover criteria for mandating nuclear power. And the sea control ship was one of those. So was the DD-963.* Each of these new ship ideas bordered the parameters arguing for or against nuclear power, so there was always a fight. The FFG-7 was too small for nuclear power, so pro-nuclear power people sought to head it off entirely, but unsuccessfully.

It's interesting, because now--12 or 13 years later--Rickover is saying some of the same things that Zumwalt said at the time--that we can't put all our eggs in the high-value carrier battle group basket, and that we've got to have other and more ways of doing things.**

Q: You talk about Admiral Zumwalt supporting these things. Was the idea that if he would support these that he might hope to get support for his programs from the constituencies that were in charge of them?

---

*DD-963 is the hull number of the lead ship of the Spruance class of destroyers, which are powered by gas turbines rather than nuclear reactors.
**In his farewell statement to Congress upon leaving active duty in early 1982, Admiral Rickover talked about the vulnerability of aircraft carriers to modern threats.

Admiral Bagley: I'd say it was a convergence of two things. One, he believed that the carrier programs should proceed, because we didn't have anything else, and we had some big strategic problems that we weren't going to solve any other way in the next 10 to 15 years, so the carrier ought to go forth. There was the difficulty with the F-111, so it was important to get another fighter in order to make this carrier effective in the coming years, so he had to support the F-14.*

But in doing that, on its merits, I'm sure he felt that that was contributing to the sort of politicking that had to go on in the Navy bureaucracy, unfortunately, to get agreement and support for other important naval systems.

Q: Did you and Admiral Zumwalt feel sort of betrayed that those programs went ahead and not all of your program did?

Admiral Bagley: I don't know and can't speak for Zumwalt. These things never happen, you know, on one day. They all happen over a long period of time, and your pessimism, optimism, disappointment, and exhilaration all come over a long period of time. I regret that a unique instance of a

---

*The F-111 was the result of Secretary of Defense Robert McNamara's effort to achieve a common fighter plane for both the Navy and the Air Force. It did not work out as a carrier plane, so the F-14 was developed by the Navy for fleet air defense, using the AWG-9 weapon system.

CNO giving intellectual strength to strategy and naval power was not better accepted nor more honestly debated.

Q: In retrospect, then, how would you feel about that?

Admiral Bagley: I don't have any bad feeling about the carriers and the aircraft; we needed them at the time to do the job that was required. I think that the fact that we didn't go ahead with the sea control ship is unfortunate. I think in a number of variants it would have an important use today. And it would have had a lot to do with bringing along the V/STOL aircraft for defenses and attack use in lesser areas and less intense combat. I think the escort program was done well and was accepted. There were some difficulties in getting it going, as I suggested earlier, but it was done. But the important thing about the opponents to Zumwalt is that they contributed to inferior U. S. conventional strength today.

The FFG program, incidentally, as an aside, was probably the best managed ship program the Navy had seen in 50 years, and it was all due to Vice Admiral Frank Price, who did an exceptional job.* He was loyal, because he believed and agreed with Zumwalt that we had to get an

---

*Rear Admiral Frank H. Price, Jr., USN, headed OP-03D as program coordinator of new construction of destroyer-type ships. Later, as a vice admiral, he was OP-03, Deputy Chief of Naval Operations (Surface Warfare).

effective but less expensive ship to increase naval ship numbers, and he and the CNO fought every element in our procurement process that would change specifications and raise costs. When Zumwalt was trading off old ships in order to get procurement money for new ships, he was in no position--and Price understood that as well as anyone else--to let these new ships cost so much that you would only end up getting two or three ships while you're turning in 20 or 40 to pay for them. So that was one of the happier kinds of support and association that Zumwalt had during this whole time--with Frank Price.

This is an appropriate moment to say that in the OpNav staff Zumwalt received comparable loyalty, support, and, also, constructive criticism from other senior naval officers. A VCNO during the period--Admiral Weisner--was a tower of wise strength and counsel, really a giant of that Navy.* Vice Admirals Shear (ASW) and Houser (air) gave thought, advice, and a genial spirit to an almost revolutionary naval transformation that Zumwalt hoped to impose.** Vice Admiral Bagley (personnel) never let up in probing, testing, and questioning to prove the validity and

---

*Admiral Maurice F. Weisner, USN, Vice Chief of Naval Operations.
**Vice Admiral Harold E. Shear, USN, Director, Antisubmarine Warfare and Tactical Electromagnetic Programs, OpNav; Vice Admiral William D. Houser, USN, Deputy Chief of Naval Operations (Air Warfare).

realism of the CNO's manpower initiatives.* There also were others, but the OpNav bureaucracy is large, strangely immutable, and no single and repeated order would assure that a rudder change would be made.

Q: Would it be fair to say that the Falklands was in a sense an operational test of the sea control type?

Admiral Bagley: No, I don't think so. The whole question of the Falklands lessons is a separate discussion. We're talking about the sea control ship to escort supplies and to keep control of sea lines and communications that we wanted to use in an environment where the intensity of combat was medium or low. And the whole business of SCS strike, either with aircraft or landing troops, was not an initial part of that idea then, though cruise missiles emerging now would have changed the SCS concept. But in the early 1970s that wasn't what the sea control ship was to do.

You could argue that the ships that the British have--through-deck cruisers or ASW carriers, which have changed names several times--were a manifestation of the sea control ship idea and, incidentally, a manifestation that they're quite pleased with. Where it failed was not so

---

*Vice Admiral David H. Bagley, USN, the brother of the interviewee, served as Deputy Chief of Naval Operations (Manpower and Reserve Affairs).

much the performance of the V/STOL--which they've done a good bit of work with the ski jump and other things to improve--but had to do with logistics, tactical surveillance, the need to protect the one or two V/STOL ships available, and the absence of long-range air or missile strike weapons. And deficiencies in the Falklands involved inadequate self-defense weapons on ships (which Zumwalt made great strides on for the U. S. Navy) which the British allowed by delays in defense expenditures. But Britain didn't plan on that kind of a war, did not have the naval or air forces best suited to it, so it's hard to compare these two things. I would be leery of getting new lessons from the Falklands experience--either for the carrier or against the carrier, or for or against the sea control ship.

Q: One area of considerable concern around the time Admiral Zumwalt took over was the surface-to-surface antiship missile. The Soviets had pushed out ahead in that with the "Styx." Was this a concern of your program?

Admiral Bagley: Yes, on two counts: the thinking ahead to how cruise missiles could evolve for land-target strikes and for the near-term antiship capability. A major element in the Zumwalt program was the Harpoon missile. And that's one of the points I was trying to make, that underneath all of these things that were going on was the possibility of getting something well beyond what the Harpoon did. Sure, the Harpoon was the immediate program and was something we had to do. But the technology was there to go way beyond it, as I say, going back as far back as 1967.

But the Harpoon in the early 1970s was the dominant element. Project 60 helped bring it along. It's an effective weapon now, providing an over-the-horizon way to strike at other ships. The Harpoon introduced collateral problems of target surveillance, communications, command and control, some of which have been solved and some not. Importantly, it was the forerunner of the Tomahawk--not only against ships at perhaps eight times the range of a Harpoon, but also against land targets from ranges twice that of sea-based attack aircraft, reopening the whole Zumwalt question of how the Navy can strike land targets, defend regions, and provide strategic defenses in several regions at once with a modest-size Navy.

Q: I had understood you to say that Secretary Nitze was concerned about a land-attack missile? Was there also a ship-to-ship missile?

Admiral Bagley: No, this was a land-attack missile that he was talking about.

Q: So what time did the antiship missile come up?

Admiral Bagley: The Harpoon started before Zumwalt got there--in the Moorer years or maybe before. So there wasn't anything that Nitze had to think about in 1968, because development had already started. Zumwalt carried it along, added priority and resources to it, initiatives he took with a series of other development programs he inherited as he matched strategic thought with requisite capabilities. So his regime was a combination of reassessment, carrying on, and giving the right priority and precedence to things that had already begun, selecting new systems from those in development, and starting new developments.

Zumwalt's uniqueness was that he had the ability and courage to think about what the Navy should do for the nation more than the normal CNO.

Q: In a sense he was his own action officer on some things, wasn't he?

Admiral Bagley: He can be said to have been his own action officer, but the thing to remember is that action he directed was something that fit within an intra-Navy concept which he was the leader in devising and had persuaded SecDef, key people in the Congress, and the

Secretary of the Navy to approve. He used as his own and for others' guidance this link between strategy and the kind of Navy you'd need, and interposed in the middle was help from other services--a provision that gave economy and speed to his goals.

And there wasn't anything that couldn't be said to fit or not fit in that concept, so it's perfectly clear what was to be done. So when he became action officer, that was either as a result of someone not understanding the relationship between this particular item and the concept or not wanting to proceed with that concept. But it isn't always because somebody was fighting him that he would become action officer to get something done. It's just like in any other level of life--there are people that either don't have the energy, don't have the comprehension, don't have the intelligence, and they just can't get it done right. And some of that exists, unbelievably, in the Navy, too.*

Q: How would you describe your working relationship with him--the kinds of things that you and he would deal with personally?

Admiral Bagley: You're talking about two people who

---
*Readers of this transcript should know that Admiral Bagley said this sentence with a twinkle in his eye, a chuckle, and tongue quite near his cheek.

understood the intellectual umbrella on which anything would be done, so it had to be a good relationship. I understood what he was trying to do, so I understood all the details that could be conceived that would help fulfill that general concept, and if something that we hadn't anticipated, hadn't thought of, came up from any source, it was simple to tell whether or not that should go or shouldn't go in terms of the concept that was understood between us. So the relationship between us in dealing with those kinds of things couldn't help but be good. But I think others helped similarly, perhaps even more effectively, by not being seen as so committed to Project 60.

Q: It seems to me that a lot of things that might have required explanations with someone else you could do in a sort of shorthand when speaking with Admiral Zumwalt, because you had many of the same assumptions. Would that be a fair statement?

Admiral Bagley: Yes. Very simply. Because we were talkng from the same language. I mean, that was the advantage I had on the Project 60 in dealing with him in putting this thing together. So in saying these things about others' lack of comprehension and all the other things, I had an advantage in that, because I was involved in helping put it together. But there was a great effort put forward by the CNO to explain it to others, some who understood and gave support. So that's why I sort of sift out of this opposing group, if there were any inefficiencies, two categories. One, those who can't comprehend (of which there are some), and two, those who choose to oppose for various reasons of their own.

Q: Did it become your mission to try to explain to those who couldn't comprehend and to convert those who opposed?

Admiral Bagley: Well, I did that to the extent that it can be done, and there were a series of allies that the CNO could count on in OpNav. Those people who either because they comprehended and agreed or because they were loyal or because they had a common sense of what the country required in its sea power--those sorts of people became very supportive. You didn't have to do much about prompting it. And there were some people like that in every naval community.

Q: I'm trying to get at specifics of your relationship. Do you have examples of the kinds of things you would interact with him on personally?

Admiral Bagley: As the Director of Program Planning, I

interacted with him on everything that was done in the budget--every program and every budget item. And I would see that this supported his concept. I would brief him on important details and trade-offs. And it was never a matter of having to go in and have a formal presentation on issues, along with half the OpNav staff, in order to explain and settle these issues. So it was very simple. I had immediate access at any time. We had a very easy relationship, and it was simple to disagree or agree, and if he wanted to shut me off or alter a tentative decision or add a new direction, he could say it very easily. I understood what the genesis of the difference was or what the genesis of the decision was.

And sometimes he made some decisions or altered others for external reasons. It's worth, incidentally, talking about CNOs and measuring them on their ability to deal externally in the Navy, because a lot of what the Navy gets done depends on how good CNOs are at that. So it was a very close relationship, very easy relationship, and one in which he gave me requisite leeway to act without in any way abrogating his ultimate responsibilities nor creating a situation where he did not retain control. In sum, he continued to think hard about what was to be done.

And before it was all over, he had me engaged in going over every paper, proposal, or emerging action or other aspects touching on his naval concept. I wasn't left in the 090 program cubbyhole, because eventually--and I guess this grew--he had a lot of faith in my judgment on what he would want done, and he was an extremely busy man, and he had this OpNav which was mixed in its level of support. So before it was all over, I was looking over everything that went up to the CNO's office that had any importance, regardless or whether it was in the specific area of which I had responsibility.

Q: Did that include people programs and that sort of initiative?

Admiral Bagley: No, I'm thinking more on the OpNav side in terms of strategic and aviation policy, logistics policy, research policy, and those things.

Q: You said some things were decided on external considerations. Do you have some cases in that regard, some examples?

Admiral Bagley: Well, I guess it's important to say that he spent a lot of his time being sure that he had a decent relationship both with the Secretary of the Navy and the Secretary of Defense, and when the Secretary of the Navy became extremely hostile to him--in the case of Warner--with mainly the Secretary of Defense.* And his relationship with the Secretary of Defense went on uniformly, I think, during the whole period he was there. He also saw Kissinger in the White House on a regular basis; he saw the Undersecretary of State on a regular basis; he had regular visits with people on the Hill who had important influence on national security matters.** He met regularly with civilian advisors brought together as the CNO Executive Board. And there were times, I think, when he did some conscious trading off about what we might do in order to get something more important done. It's the play of priorities when you have to deal with someone who has perhaps higher authority and responsibility for the resources on which either of these options depend.

Q: Can you cite some examples of those trade-offs? We've talked about sort of a high-low trade-off in getting rid of old ships. But what about these considerations, dealing with higher authority or what have you?

Admiral Bagley: Those trade-offs were not often explicit or obvious. But they existed. And it's because he was so active externally. That had a lot to do with his success. And his success, you know, in addition to being measured by

---
*John W. Warner replaced Chafee as Secretary of the Navy in 1972 and served in that capacity until 1974.
**Henry A. Kissinger was special assistant to President Richard M. Nixon for national security affairs from 1969 until he became Secretary of State in 1973.

the fact that he was externally respected, also internally in OSD in terms of getting resources for the Navy.* You know, his first full budget, the fiscal year '72 budget, was the first time for some 20 years that the Navy got the biggest share of the defense budget, a record Zumwalt maintained during his tenure. And that was because of his thinking, expressed in the Project 60, his continuing liaison with and the relationship he built with these people, and then his intellectual persuasiveness.

He didn't, as many Navy people do, rely on assertions; he had a good, compact reason for each proposal he made. And he is very rarely given credit for that--convincing higher authority and also the public that the Navy was the principal service on which we had to depend for future security, and that was the service that should get the bulk of the defense resources. Now, people can talk about other reasons for Zumwalt's succes. One, the restraints on Nixon--his inability politically to do some of the things that he might have done for the other services, originating from the disappointments in Vietnam and the resulting idea of his Guam Doctrine that we weren't going to fight on Asian land again. There was a whole series of things that were in coincidence with what I would call the Zumwalt persuasiveness. It helped him, but much was gained on his own.

---

*OSD--Office of the Secretary of Defense.

Q: Under Admiral Hayward, the long-range planning group was created, and this was sort of a renaissance of something that had been under Admiral Burke.* In the time that you were with Admiral Zumwalt, how much consideration was given to that sort of long-range thinking?

Admiral Bagley: I think a lot, but it wasn't formal in the sense of the way it had been under Rear Admiral Miller.** Zumwalt did it more through OP-96.*** He had established and led OP-96 in 1967; he had manned it so they could deal with current problems and, as an extension, think with continuity into the future. He thought that way of looking at things was sound, its product would be more persuasive, and it avoided being termed "pie in the sky," no matter how imaginative the previous method might have been. So he was able as CNO to capitalize on his recent experience in OP-96, depend on it more, put the right people in there--one of whom was the brilliant and courageous Stan Turner--and

---

*Admiral Thomas B. Hayward, USN, Chief of Naval Operations from 1978 through 1982, reestablished the presence of a formal, dedicated branch within OpNav to carry out the function of long-range planning. Admiral Arleigh A. Burke, USN, CNO from 1955 through 1961, had set up such a group during his tenure. See Commander Gordon G. Riggle, USN, "Looking to the Long Run," U. S. Naval Institute Proceedings, September 1980, pages 60-65.
**Rear Admiral George H. Miller, USN, performed the function in Admiral Burke's time.
***OP-96 was the Systems Analysis Division of OpNav.

he turned to that.

He used OP-06 and the strategic plans people, working with them, so there was a lot of coordination within OpNav on looking outward.* I think it was effective. I guess you'd measure it first by how much can you predict about what you want to do 15 years out? Though there was no crystal ball, there was always that element of the program planning process, too, that looked 15 years out. So it had that kind of input from these analytical parts of OpNav. I don't think that anybody has foreseen the future. But, at any rate, Zumwalt did promote thought and exploration, because it was a different kind of intellectual naval planning atmosphere that he was creating. He thought a lot about the future himself, and he had a group in OP-96 that he also thought could think. So he did it that way.

When he left, this sort of process began to deteriorate, because there wasn't a spark anymore; the spark had left. And, as a consequence, after a while, certain people--and, incidentally, these people were external to the Navy--said, "You've got to have some kind of organization that does some thinking out in front." But the result of that has been curious. Once established--it now, I think fair to say, is delinquent in terms of looking ahead, because it's tied down with immediate problems,

---
*OP-06 was the Deputy Chief of Naval Operations (Plans and Policy).

current budgets, programs within five years or less. And that in that evolving post-Zumwalt process, the organism that Zumwalt depended on to do his thinking, OP-96, has been cut down to a very small size. So now you've gotten rid of the spark; you've gotten rid of the mechanism which was OP-96 working with OP-06; you've generated another thing which doesn't have any spark--the long-range objectives group, or whatever it's called now--and you've tied it down with daily problems.

Q: When you were Director of Navy Program Planning, how much of your view was on the immediate--the one-year and five-year--and how much consideration to the long range?

Admiral Bagley: We gave consideration to two parts. The first part was the five-year program. No question, that draws a lot of attention. But OP-96, which was under 090, did look at the second part--into the future. And with the Project 60 guidance, the current period was defined, allowing more time to look beyond it with the benefit of the Project 60 strategic assessment.

Q: SALT, I believe, came up during that period.* How much did that drive your considerations?

---

*SALT--Strategic Arms Limitation Talks with the Soviet Union.

Admiral Bagley: SALT drove little of my considerations, but OP-06 spent most of the time on SALT. That's one thing, frankly, I didn't then get into in any great depth. Zumwalt was his own action officer on SALT I. And he had a close relationship with Nitze, who was on the negotiating team, so he was up on what was going on.* He became very disabused with the entire process, but it had little effect on what we were saying about the Navy, which was to strengthen it.

As I suggested to you earlier, SALT--and arms control in general--does have an effect on ways the Congress and other people look at Navy goals. One thing came up during that time which reemphasizes this idea of sensing and analyzing what would be useful in the future. Kissinger wanted to give up cruise missiles entirely--the nuclear cruise missiles--in the post-SALT negotiations at Vladivostok. If pursued and agreed, that would in turn have preempted the possiblity of having conventional cruise missiles, on the argument you cannot verify one from the other, as well as the nuclear ones. On that issue and one or two more, Zumwalt had a crisis with Schlesinger and the White House.** Two weeks before his term was to expire as

---
*Zumwalt had been executive assistant to Paul H. Nitze when the latter was Secretary of the Navy in the mid-1960s; in the early 1970s, when Nitze was involved in the arms limitations negotiations, the two men continued to have high mutual regard, as they do to this day.
**James R. Schlesinger was Secretary of Defense from 1973 to 1975.

CNO, he forwarded a letter saying the U. S. negotiating position was absolutely wrong, despite the warning from SecDef that it could lead to his being fired from office.

Q: You mentioned Admiral Miller before. One of the studies he worked on was the ULMS, which eventually evolved into the Trident.* Was this a concern of your office during that time?

Admiral Bagley: Yes, we did look at that. And in that sense the SALT process and the discussion on the various concepts for deterring nuclear strike did get into our planning deliberations. Let me give you one example. A question arose about how accurate you wanted the missile to be. And that became a very subtle argument that went on, because the country's nuclear policy was tied to a concept of mutual assured destruction. We'd made unilateral decisions in the past that we wouldn't make our missiles accurate enough to destroy their missiles. And we were talking about a new survivable kind of ballistic missile system that could be made accurate and would have an invulnerable first-strike capability. So it wasn't a trivial kind of decision to make. And there were pros and

---

*ULMS--underwater long-range missile system; the Trident missile system was initially deployed in the Ohio (SSBN-726)-class strategic deterrent submarines in the late 1970s.

cons and all sorts of shades being introduced into the discussion, all being manipulated for or against a change in nuclear policy. The missile ended up not being pushed for accuracy, the decision being taken outside the naval hierarchy.

And then also there was the related argument at the time about how big the submarine ought to be, which was an important consideration for survivability as well as cost and force size. The decisions that were involved in that were decisions that the Navy could try to influence but wouldn't have the last word on as long as force security was safeguarded. And Zumwalt did a lot of talking on his own. In that kind of national program, the SecDef likes to reach into the services and deal directly with some of the people. And in this case he dealt often with the project office that was going to make the missile--Levering Smith.* So there were a lot of things going on that weren't working right through Zumwalt.

Q: What was the outcome on the accuracy decision?

Admiral Bagley: There wasn't going to be a push for accuracy. And you couldn't just turn on accuracy then, but you could make a promising effort to get it. That effort was made low key for about five years after Zumwalt left

---
*Rear Admiral Levering Smith, USN, Director, Strategic Systems Project Office, Naval Material Command.

and then accelerated right at the end of the Carter term.* And now it's attainable with the Trident II missile.

Q: In the Sixties there had been discussion of a sea-based anti-ballistic missile system. Was that a dead issue by the time you came in?

Admiral Bagley: Yes. That was one of Rear Admiral Miller's favorite things. I wouldn't dismiss it, but it isn't something that anybody's going to support or push, even in the current debate about what kind of nuclear weapons we ought to have or, lately, the question of defense against nuclear ballistic missiles in the next decade or two.

Q: The amphibious forces in providing a lift capability-- how did this figure in your calculus in program planning?

Admiral Bagley: It was a high priority. Zumwalt came at a time when the modernization of the amphibious force had started. It had to continue, or at least he had to make the decision to continue and had to make a decision about what kind of lift was involved. As I remember, he raised

---
*Jimmy Carter was President of the United States from January 1977 to January 1981.

the lift to one and a third divisions, and it had been lower before that. And he put a lot of money on it.

But that wasn't his top priority at the time, because his strategic assessment had to do with more areas that we had to protect, longer distances to get there, and a Navy which was oriented around a relatively few number of carriers and carrier battle groups and inferior sea-lane protection forces. He felt we had to do something about what he called the sea control side. It's just not an academic thing to say that Zumwalt was the first non-aviator to be CNO since 1961, because there's a lot to that. We'd had a period of nine years in which aviators had emphasized carrier battle groups and the strike capability, in the early part of which there was very little opposition at sea from the Soviet Navy. That threat at sea increased as the period went on and had something to do with the way Zumwalt talked about it.

But the aviators had a fervent mission. They'd gone through the late Forties and early Fifties throwing away careers and doing everything possible to convince the country and the Congress that they had to stay with carrier sea power. So once they got past that, in which a number of careers were lost--and if you look at that period, there were non-aviator CNOs then, with the exception of Forrest Sherman--mainly because of what had fallen by the wayside in this no-holds-barred argument, so when the aviators got back into the CNO position, they had a mission.* And that mission was carried forward with dedication all through the Sixties and Seventies. So Zumwalt not only had the traditionalists, he had something that was imbedded in concrete that he had to deal with. And that's why he dealt with it, I think--aside from the merits of it--in a compromising way to some degree in order to reachieve a balance in what he thought the Navy ought to have. He still gave high priority to the sea control side.

Q: I guess that explains why the LHA was already in force before he came on, and then there have not been any significant new amphibious lift programs until the LSD-41, which really was later. So that couldn't have been too important a concern relatively.

Admiral Bagley: These modernization efforts go in cycles and should be judged on their whole rather than their regularity. Zumwalt had a clear perception that the lift he preferred--the 1.3 divisions--was a requirement for the modernization of the amphibious force, even though modernization had started. A great deal of emphasis had been put on it during the Moorer years and the two years before.

---

*Between 1945 and 1961, the only naval aviator to be Chief of Naval Operations was Admiral Forrest P. Sherman, USN, from 1949 to 1951.

Q: Yes, indeed.

Admiral Bagley: So what Zumwalt did was carry on what was going on, and there wasn't any need for a major tilt unless he'd stopped them, which he didn't do. He kept the elements of a balanced navy, which the CNOs all like to pontificate on, but what he argued was that it's not in balance, so we'll keep balancing parts that are not in balance, and we'll take the part that is obvious in any kind of a strategic assessment has to be improved and strengthen and work on that. And that, I think, shows more integrity than talking solely about a balanced navy, which doesn't--unless similarly defined--mean a thing.

Q: What about the mine force--mine countermeasures? That seemed to go very heavily in the direction of airborne and to neglect ship types, which since have had something of a resurgence.

Admiral Bagley: Well, he walked in, and mine warfare was almost zero. I think even the command had been disestablished. He re-established the command. He also said, "We need a mine warfare capability now. It isn't something that we need ten years from now, allowing us to make an orderly ship construction program to get it." He said instead: "We've got to do it right now." So he put together the program of helicopters and the minesweeping equipment that would go with it. He also did some positive things about increasing the readiness and the capabilities and the fitting out of the reserve minesweeping ships, of which there were something like 27, and then looked at the possibility of what could be done in the future. I don't remember any really new departure being taken for the future except the very reasonable policy to continue to beef up the air mining abilities--a policy proved and re-proved in the crises which have followed.

There's a good strategic argument for the air minesweeping capability, because it can move to where you need it quickly. And we saw that in the '73 war.* That was Zumwalt's squadron that went there, and it was flown there in C-5s and was able to the job very quickly.** So I wouldn't belittle the air initiative and say that's all he did. Because there's a good argument for it if you believe that mines can be laid rapidly and covertly, and you can't necessarily have the strategic or tactical patience to sit around and wait for something slow to arrive and slowly sweep them.

---

*This is a reference to the Yom Kippur War between the Arabs and Israelis in the autumn of 1973. U. S. mine countermeasures helicopters were subsequently used for hunting mines in the Suez Canal.
**C-5s are huge Air Force cargo planes capable of loading the mine countermeasures helicopters and transporting them rapidly to places where they are needed.

Q: But the question is why then don't you also do something with ships?

Admiral Bagley: I said he did work with the reserve minesweeping ships, and there were 27 of those, and if you could make them deployable and effective, that was an important and economical step.

At the time, remember, people were talking very seriously about the whole question of choke points being cut off and how easily that could be done, particularly at the southern end of the Red Sea, which governed whether or not we could get in and out of the Indian Ocean or whether we could get into the Red Sea itself. And it just seemed to make a lot of strategic sense at the time to have something that could be deployed quickly by air and operate from land or sea bases and be perhaps just as effective as any foreseeable alternative.

We have trouble with the ships themselves in sweeping every kind of mine, so if you intellectually walk through each kind of a mine and say, "Okay, how am I going to deal with that?" it becomes difficult to deal with all of them with a helicopter sweep, and it becomes difficult to deal with all of them with a ship sweep. And you may have to bring in other assets to get some of them--particulary until new sweep equipment was developed for helos--and you have to be very patient. And if you have to make a lot of passes by air, if that's the way that you actuate or disable the mines to sweep them, that's better than doing it with a ship. Sixty to 120 knots is better than five knots.

Q: Was it a case, then, of not being able to afford both?

Admiral Bagley: Well, everything is a trade-off. I mean, you're trying to modernize the Navy in which the ship procurement had gone down to around a billion dollars. And while he was there, he got it up close to three billion. And you put things in priorities, and you look, as I say, at your strategic responsibilities. You can make an argument either way, depending on your strategic assessment of the risks. But what he didn't do was ignore it. He got a way to sweep that was different than they'd done before, but it was deployable. We had the C-5s at the time, and, as I say, we saw it used in '73. Some ships went there in '73 also. And accelerated programs were started to develop and procure sweep gear for various modern mines.

Q: Where did the logistic support forces fit in the overall strengthening of the Navy?

Admiral Bagley: There was an effort to increase logistic

force levels significantly, because they were far too small for the separated threats. These areas in which we wanted to defend U. S. interests and would have to accordingly deploy naval ships, were increasing. So he was the instigator of chartering and putting at sea MSC replenishment equipment into existing supply ships rather than relying solely on the time and the expense to build new ones.* So he would take them from the merchant force or MSC, do some work on them, put them all under the MSC, and then deploy them in order to do the replenishment work for various areas, and he advanced towards an improved logistics capability much quicker that way.

Q: There was a build-and-charter program then, in which the private companies would build the ships with an agreement that the Navy would charter them for a considerable period of years, that Congress has looked somewhat askance at.

Admiral Bagley: I don't remember that during the Zumwalt time.

Q: I thought it was with the Sealift-class tankers. These were about 25,000-tonners.

---

*MSC--Military Sealift Command, which is part of the Navy but operates its own vessels and chartered merchant ships with civilian crews.

Admiral Bagley: I don't recall that there was a program to build them during his time. There was a program to pull them out of the merchant marine, fix them up, and put them in the MSC and use them. We had one in the Med during the 1973 war; it was not built; it already existed.

Q: Another important part of that initiative was taking ships that the Navy had been running for fleet support and putting MSC merchant crews on them to cut costs.*

Admiral Bagley: That's right. That was another thing that was done to cut costs. A lot of the effort to cut cost-- those sorts of things got some visibility and worked. There were a lot of other things that were proposed to cut costs that he lost because of lack of support within the bureaucracy. And those things became desirable, but in isolation, each of them became less important than some of the other things he was trying to do. But I can tell you that there was a whole series of things which had to do with cutting back administration, cutting out the number of commands, things that had to do with personnel that wouldn't affect the morale or effectiveness of personnel,

---

*For an assessment of this initiative, see Lieutenant Sidney W. Emery, Jr., USN, "Civilian-Manned Support Ships: A View from the Fleet," Proceedings, April 1977, pages 34-40. To this day, a number of the Navy's replenishment ships have largely civilian crews.

like travel and some other things that had a mixed success.

Q: What were some of those--can you recall--that didn't get implemented?

Admiral Bagley: The one that I think is most dominant in my mind is the one of cutting back the sizes of commands. Commands had swollen to huge sizes, and there were many more people that we had to pay for in staffs than were being productive or were compatible with the mission of the command. Large staffs required big headquarters buildings and overhead, required command and control and that kind of thing. And the effort to cut those back was made quite forcefully, but I think the real impact or the real possibilities of that were lost in the throes of the CNO staff. People just dragged in implementing the CNO goal. It was done--there were some cutbacks made in lots of commands and staffs--but I just never was very confident that it was really working.

Q: Was the phasing out of the naval districts part of that initiative?

Admiral Bagley: Streamlining was. There were so many people, including OSD, in on that naval district thing, I can't remember whether that was something that was suggested from above or whether it was something that Zumwalt thought of. But it was not inconsistent with what I'm trying to describe.

Q: Did you have any problem in trying to sell a program to congressmen who maybe didn't understand or appreciate what you were trying to do but whose vote you vitally needed to implement it?

Admiral Bagley: I don't remember any particular incidents on that. As I say, he was for the carriers and F-14; he got that through. And that had some opposition, too, at the time, because people were trying to save some money.

He got his new escort program through, and he got additional P-3Cs through as part of the sea control business. He got new weapons. He got his new mining helicopter squadrons financed, his logistics initiatives, and more research. And the only thing that he really lost that had that kind of visibility was the sea control ships.

Q: This was during a period of detente. Did that have any effect on your planning and thinking?

Admiral Bagley: It depends on what you mean by detente. It was a period that I tried to describe very briefly to begin with that had its ups and downs. At the beginning of the time, the Middle East was very upset. There was some discussion starting with the Russians about SALT. Within two years prior to 1970, we had the crisis with the Russians going into Czechoslovakia and the efforts that Lyndon Johnson was making towards arms control petering out, and then being resuscitated by Nixon, and still in the process of resuscitation.* Over this period, the Soviets built up force in Europe. We saw that the Soviets started in 1969 putting ships in the Indian Ocean, and by the early Seventies they had a reasonable force, which they didn't have five years before that.

And so detente at sea or strategically was sort of in the eyes of the beholder. But I don't think that detente had any real impact on the way that Zumwalt put together his idea of what our strategic responsibilities were and what kind of force we needed to do it, because he assumed that we were competing with the Russians--whatever it was called. And in detente the Navy competes with presence, to show the U. S. will to protect its interests, and he gave as much emphasis as he could to that and brought it out in a much clearer fashion than other people did. But always he had to plan to build the Navy for the time when you have

---

*In early 1968 a wave of liberalism spread through Czechoslovakia and led to the takeover by Alexander Dubcek as the new leader of the country's Communist Party. He declared his intention to institute democratic reforms. As a result, armies from the Soviet Union, Poland, East Germany, and Hungary invaded Czechoslovakia in August 1968.

to fight.

Q: Even though they may be friendly now, they're still the enemy.

Admiral Bagley: Well, we talk about capabilities, you know, more than words or intentions. And the same thing goes with the issue today about whether any kind of presence is enough, because the Soviets, if they see you there, will see greater risk in generating any confrontation. But you should distinguish between whether you need to have a presence that serves to indicate your interest in peacetime, on one hand, or on the other could fight if you had to fight. And Zumwalt would look at it the second way. But we didn't yet have the resources to be confident about that. And that's why all these other things came in--the sea control force, the replenishment ships that you raise, the question of overseas homeporting--everything that would make the forces you had go further and deal with these additional regions strategically by presence and a means for combat.

Q: Could detente have been a factor to the extent that you're saying that you're deliberately going to weaken yourself in the short term in order to make yourself better in the long term—the idea being that you have to assume that nothing is going to happen in the short term?

Admiral Bagley: No. I think you take the risk; many of the decommissioned ships went into the reserve, not to a trash yard. If without the trade-off there is no prospect of beginning to strengthen a Navy, which—in addition to being small—is worn out, then it would appear to be irresponsible not to deal with that in the near term and take a prudent risk. You don't know when anything's going to happen. But the Soviets have the capability of making it happen whenever they want. But, at the same time, pay some attention to the other things that have to do with the nuclear deterrent to conflict, which Zumwalt did in a very concentrated way by following and understanding what was going on in the arms control talks about nuclear strategic forces. And the last thing that he would allow to have happen during the time that he was there trying to build the Navy up—and taking some risks in the process—was any action or any agreement that would put into question our ability to deter any kind of nuclear war which, if deterrence was weakened, would put more pressure on conventional power to discourage crises.

Q: And hence his concern about the cruise missiles.

Admiral Bagley: Yes, for both the nuclear strength then and conventional power later. If he thought that we were giving them a leg up in negotiating talk, he would fight it. As it turned out, of course, the SALT I did give them a leg up. Congress had to come back with a resolution saying that we consider SALT I to be a first step only and that all of these deficiencies were to be corrected in a forthcoming agreement, which we would undertake rapidly and aggressively and forcefully and all the rest. And Zumwalt's role in the next follow-on talks at Vladivostok, as I say, was a letter just prior to the time that he left office in 1974 saying, "You've got to do better than this."

Q: Did the opening of China during that period have any effect on your program?

Admiral Bagley: I think the view of China was that it helped validate Nixon's Guam concept of no ground war in Asia, and it relaxed some of the pressures on Western Europe. The general perception at the time was that we had fallen behind in Western Europe. So the general idea was, "Well, the Chinese now are going to draw off some of the Soviet troops, so that's going to help us." But it didn't have a lot to do with the premises the Navy was talking about. They still had to reinforce Europe, still had to deal with this growing of potentially hostile forces in the

Middle East and the Indian Ocean, and still had to deal with the Western Pacific from the standpoint that everybody felt that it would just be a matter of time before Vietnam would start doing some aggressive things as we left, a move for which we were preparing. And I guess there was always a certain amount of skepticism about how permanent the agreement with the Chinese would be or how coordinated our strategies could become.

And we're still talking--we did then, and we're still talking with them now--about the general idea of strategic cooperation. We've never been able either to define or pin that down. Whatever strategic advantage we got out of it appears to be accidental, I thinks it's fair enough to say. It is probably temporary or, at least, variable as our common interests come and go. But it didn't have any important effect on what the Navy was trying to do to build capabilities.

Q: What do you remember about the 1973 Middle East War and the effect that had?

Admiral Bagley: Effect on what?

Q: On what you were doing--the interaction between you and the CNO.

Admiral Bagley: I wasn't in the CNO staff then. But the point I tried to make earlier was that each of these crises--and that was one of them--all it did was help show--and this one was particularly important, because it had come after the time that Nixon had said we're going to have to depend more on sea power (or essentially that's what he was saying)--it drew off 95 ships out of maybe less than 200 that could deploy anywhere. It served to underline what Zumwalt had been saying about the force limits on American sea power, both for combat and logistics and about our strategic fragility.

Q: You're saying you were gone. Weren't you CinCUSNavEur then?*

Admiral Bagley: Yes, but I thought you put it in the context of OpNav and my relationship with Zumwalt there. In London I worked first for CinCEur.**

Q: We're trying to touch on your whole relationship with the CNO.

Admiral Bagley: First, I've told you what I thought that

---
*CinCUSNavEur--Commander in Chief U. S. Naval Forces Europe, including command of the U. S. Sixth Fleet in the Mediterranean.
**CinCEur--Commander in Chief Europe, the joint service commander of U. S. military forces in Europe.

crisis did for the CNO. And that also helped him argue the other important points described later in his book--argue that we weren't paying enough attention to our nuclear relationship and that we were letting it deteriorate at the same time that we had deficiencies in our conventional forces, that the combination of the two was very dangerous.

The relationship between him and me during that crisis was very good. We were on the telephone every day, and we'd talk over some of the things that were happening, and what were some of the supporting things that we could do. But that was in the early stages of it, and that crisis really evolved under the tight control of Admiral Moorer as the Chairman of the Joint Chiefs working with the White House and directly with ComSixthFlt.* Even the rest of the JCS had, I'd say, limited influence.

Q: I think this is what I'm trying to get at. How much role can or does a CNO have in an operational kind of situation?

Admiral Bagley: Directly--very little. In the Arleigh Burke days, the CNO had a lot, but in these days with the way this has evolved, the CNO acts through and with the JCS. And in this instance, Moorer decided--or was prompted by the White House--that he would take this next to his own

---

*ComSixthFlt--Commander Sixth Fleet.

bosom, and he could talk easier and deal easier with the President and with Kissinger. And I don't know that there's anything wrong with that in some crises, as long as it is controlled. I got the sense, without being present, that the other chiefs weren't being brought along on every little detail or in every subtlety of what American policy was attempting to do.

Q: During that time that you were having these daily phone calls with him, was that more on friend-to-friend basis than a CNO to theater commander?

Admiral Bagley: No, I was in contact with Murphy in the Sixth Fleet, and Zumwalt was on the JCS, so it was a natural thing, whether we knew each other very well or not, to be talking, so that's what went on.* But, again, you're after something here I'm not really sure I'm clear about. But it was the frankest kind of discussion, and we'd say what was going on--"Who's saying what to whom and what's happening? And what are the uncertainties and what don't we know? What are the advantages and disadvantages of the Sixth Fleet where it is now? What are the Soviets doing, and are we restricting ourselves too much or not restricting ourselves too much? Do the Soviets seem to have similar restrictions? How much problem are we having

---

*Vice Admiral Daniel J. Murphy, USN, Commander Sixth Fleet.

with access to other bases for our aircraft and for ship repair? How long should we keep the Navy out here, or should we move other relief ships in so current ships get some maintenance? How much should we prepare to defend ourselves against a preemptive attack as the Russians came fairly close during a portion of this thing? Do we need a change in the rules of engagement in order to be safe in what's evolving here? If we want to move in closer to the Israeli coast, do we do it regardless of the Soviet force there?" (And then later on the Soviet force kind of interposed themselves between the Mediterranean coast and our ships which were around Crete.) Those kinds of questions were discussed.

Q: What I'm after is a comparison, perhaps, between how much of a role Admiral Zumwalt had vis-à-vis that situation compared with what Admiral Burke had 15 years earlier.*

Admiral Bagley: A lot less.

Q: What kinds of things would Admiral Burke have done that Admiral Zumwalt couldn't?

Admiral Bagley: Burke would move the forces. He wouldn't

---

*Fifteen years earlier, in 1958, Admiral Arleigh A. Burke was Chief of Naval Operations when there was another crisis in the eastern Mediterranean; it involved the landing of U. S. Marines at Beirut, Lebanon.

worry about anybody else. But, see, we've had a number of documents which would prevent Admiral Burke from doing what he did then, where the operational control of the forces has moved from a service chief to the Joint Chiefs and to the Secretary of Defense. So there's been an official change in that procedure.

Q: This was the 1958 law, was is not, that changed that?

Admiral Bagley: Burke left there in '61, but his dramatic moving of ships--that's the greatest thing about the Burke regime, the ability to do it. Unbelievable. And he often did it without any political link, assuming that if you showed power quickly, the other side would pause or withdraw in pushing a crisis.

There was another crisis, however, in which the CNO had a good deal of influence, and that was in the Indian Ocean in the war of late 1971 between India and Pakistan. And under his recommendation, the Joint Chiefs sent a carrier task group into the Indian Ocean, off the eastern side of India. And he had a great deal to do with how that task group was put together, and he decided that at the time it was important to send a couple of attack submarines there, because he was concerned about what the Soviets might send down from Vladivostok. They didn't have anything that he couldn't see or was particularly worried about in the Indian Ocean at the time. So he had a lot to do at that time in how it was structured, how it operated, how it protected itself.

The presence there was a political decision, and all he did was make sure that there was no possibility of the Soviets either creating an incident or doing something else, depending on how this crisis evolved. And he had more control over that crisis and the use of the Navy than he did in the '73 one which we just talked about, which was much less.

Q: What makes the difference in how much control the CNO does have in a case like that?

Admiral Bagley: I think it depends on where the crisis is; it depends on the national interest in the crisis and the urgency and the degree of effect expected. I think it depends on the degree of crisis possibilities for confrontation with the Soviets; it depends a little bit on how visible the presence is and what kind of influence it might or might not have and when or how fast. And in this case the ships were well outside the sight of land. There had been a press release, as I remember, that they were there. At the beginning the Soviets weren't there. They did send ships down from Vladivostok later. So I just don't think that it was the kind of direct and close confrontation between the Soviets and the U. S. that the '73 business in the Mediterranean turned out to be, and obviously it did not include the nuclear alert of that time.

Q: Does it make a difference also how much control those higher in the chain of command choose to take?

Admiral Bagley: Yes, it's part of what I just said, and what they choose to take seems to me to have to do with those considerations that I went through, among others. There is much disagreement on this issue in the military who like the comfort of chains of command and who fear mistakes if usual consultations are curtailed.

Q: We've talked on the program planning aspect. That certainly didn't happen in a vacuum, because there were many other things going on--the people initiatives, race, women's greater role, Watergate came along. How much can a CNO devote to a specific aspect such as the one you were involved in with so much else going on?

Admiral Bagley: I think the way that all the services are organized is that the chief of service spends an inordinate time on programs and budget. So no matter what is going on in the rest of the world, the whole future life of the service depends on what programs are put together and why they're put together and how much money is allocated to them. And then you go up and you consult with the civilian hierarchy in the Pentagon. The process is absolutely crucial to the Navy. So, no matter what else is going on, the CNO is involved. And I'm sure--while there was no world war while we were there--I'm sure if you were in a war you'd be doing the same thing, except it'd be more urgent and easier, so you wouldn't have to argue so much.

Q: Could you describe the job of the Director of Navy Program Planning--the things that you did and the relationship with the CNO?

Admiral Bagley: Essentially, you start with the concept of what the Navy has to do--what is the function of the Navy and what kind of strategic purposes does it serve? And then secondly you take a look at the force structure that you have, and you decide where that fits into satisfying this concept and you analyze the changes that should be made or what modernization/updating of what you already have should be undertaken. And you usually do it on a time sequence. Do you want some measure of improvement and greater capability in six months, or do you want it in 15 years? And that has something to do with how you go about it. And then there's a whole series of details that then are meshed that have to do first with the procurement--which looks to the future--and then secondly with the readiness kinds of items which improve the maintenance of the forces you have now and their readiness to get under way, fight, sustain combat, and all of that.

Related to that is what you can do in a short term in putting better weapon systems, better radars, and all the rest on a ship so they become more capable with the same kind of hull or airframe while you're waiting for some of your ship and aircraft procurement programs. Depending on fund resources and strategic needs, you either build your Navy bigger or replace things that are starting to get old--hulls and airplanes--and keep the Navy at about the same current size. You always take into account the question of how effective the opposition is, and you try to calculate the kinds of situations where you might have to fight, and when you fight to try to calculate how our weapons and our sensors and all the rest do against the opposing capabilities. And from that you attempt to decide what sort of attrition you'll take and what kind of attrition you'll give, what effect, if any, the way you employ your forces and the tactics you use might modify these conclusions.

And you come up with a series of issues. When you think about attack submarines, how do you proportion your capability between maritime air, escort ships, SOSUS, mines, and the other things that you might be able to do?* And in strike, you look at the question of where you might want to land amphibious troops, what naval force you'd have to land them in, where you've got the troops in the United States now--do you have to move them to get them to ships? What kind of division of amphibious ships do you require between oceans, and what impact does that have on the total size of the amphibious force just because of the positioning in peacetime? And then you look at the strategic question of what are the areas that you want to protect? Where are your interests? Do you have to have continual presence, how capable should that presence be to be credible, and how quickly can you reinforce?

You put all these things and more together and try to decide what to buy and with what priority, and what are your alternatives, depending on various levels of funding that you might be able to get? How would fund availability change what you think is perhaps an optimum arrangement for amphibious strike, and, then, for other naval power? So that's one thing--it has to do with the budget, it has to do with programs, and it has to do with analysis that kind of pulls it all together. And I think that's the heart and soul of the 090 thing, but from the CNO standpoint, it's also the heart and soul of what he's trying to do.

---

*SOSUS--sound surveillance system, an underwater network of listening devices designed to detect Soviet submarines.

There also are a lot of things around this process that have to do with coordination with other services and have to do with bases, have to do with nuclear weapons, and those kinds of things which the CNO deals directly with the OP-06. But the two--OP-090 and -06--ought to be meshed pretty well, because one has an influence on the other. If you get 15 bases overseas, you may need less ships, etc. And that kind of coordination always went on and always does go on. But, in a nutshell, I'd say that's about what 090 did then.

Q: One thing about the various places that you get inputs from--like possible attrition--is this something that you would draw on the War College for?*

Admiral Bagley: The War College was involved to some degree in those kinds of things, but OP-06, in working themselves and through contractors, would work up war gaming scenarios that they would run through the computers. I think there's a limit on the value of the results--the limit that you can depend on them. But at least they give you some kind of guideline in relative effectiveness and on the marginal issues on which combat might depend.

But all of that is manipulable. An argument for or

---

*The Naval War College in Newport, Rhode Island, holds war games and has analytical groups studying various Navy problems.

against something can be made without too much trouble by those in control over the war game. And even in the analysis of the results of it, of an analytical assessment of an engagement or of a war, you may by prejudice, background, or aim, do different things with it. So there's a lot of room for professional judgment to balance what civilians in OSD, contractors, or Navy analysts come up with. That's when it becomes important to have some people that have the best possible judgment.

I'd say Zumwalt did it both ways. I think that in some instances he applied what I think is uniquely good judgment. In other cases where he had the instinct that something would be beneficial for the future Navy but wasn't fully supported outside the Navy by the available facts when he went forward to try to persuade others, I think he would build the analytical argument to emphasize elements of particular interest to others. But I think McNamara and his people did the same thing--tailoring arguments and emphases--so it was a little bit of a game. I wouldn't call it dishonest, but I think that it was a game contested by generally sincere advocates for American security and well-being.

Q: Do you remember any of these instincts that Zumwalt had that became part of the program?

Admiral Bagley: One argument that always went on where there was plenty of room for instinct was the question of how much of your money you ought to put into nuclear-powered ships versus conventionally powered ships. And when you deal with numbers and programs to look at what they can do in combat and what they can do in terms of daily cost to operate and all the rest, there's a lot of room to have judgment. And I think in that particular case that he slanted the available facts--which I would say maybe were 60% of what you might need in order to have a persuasive argument that anybody would buy--in such a way that it worked against the nuclear-powered ships. And in the same sense, Rickover used the same available 40% of uncertainties to support it and manipulate his own argument for nuclear-powered ships, and the other guy wanted a bigger Navy, because he felt he had the strategic requirements that demanded it. So that's one example, involving different perspectives and responsibilities.

Q: To what extent did OP-090 rely on its own resources and expertise in judgment, and to what extent did it go outside?

Admiral Bagley: Well, OP-96, you know, was part of 090, and it was formed to increase the Navy capability to do analysis on its own. So the CNO relied on OP-96, and OP-96 used some selective contracting. CNA was under the supervision of OP-96, too, so it did much work for and with OP-96, reducing the need for outside contracting.* And OP-96 used the "wise-man" advice of the CEB and coordinated with similar or related studies that were done in the OP-06 area who had their own study money, and they would also use contractors, so that there was an interface there that had to jibe.**

One of the toughest things for a CNO is to go down to the JCS and present the program of the kind of Navy and force levels that he dreams he needs, based on a whole series of studies which, let's say, have a 40 to 50% vacuum within which you can throw instinct and extra judgment and perhaps a pretty cynical eye into. And what he presents up the other chain, through the Secretary of the Navy and the Secretary of Defense, for this budget and the budget over the next five years, is much more fiscally constrained, and there's rarely an intellectual link between the two. But, nevertheless, there's a kind of informal coordination that goes on, and each side tries to help the other. But it's not what I would call a very forthright nor a very solid connection between various dreams and a fiscal budget.

---

*CNA--Center for Naval Analyses, an outside organization that works for the Navy on a contract basis.
**CEB--CNO Executive Board.

Q: What can you say about the value of the Center for Naval Analyses?

Admiral Bagley: I think it's very valuable. It's valuable, and has been since the mid-Zumwalt years when the management was altered such that it came under a university and outside the substantive influence of the Navy.* Zumwalt went to a great deal of trouble to set that up so that it could be objective and not be under prejudiced influence inside or outside the Navy. Since that time until now it's been very good indeed. The quality of the work depends on the quality of the people there, but on the whole, they've had a high quality of people. And if we're beginning to see emerging an attack to put it more under the influence of the Navy, that's a critical mistake--not only because it _appears_ to be the wrong thing to do but because it _is_ the wrong thing to do.

Q: Contractors and consultants in general have come in for criticism. What would be your assessment of their value and contribution?

Admiral Bagley: I think that the contractors are good if they are given a problem that they think there's some

---

*Subsequent to this interview with Admiral Bagley, management of the Center for Analyses has been shifted from the University of Rochester to the Hudson Institute.

operative, authoritative level which will act on the results. But, unfortunately, a very high percentage of the kinds of operational studies that we contract out for are contracted out for on the material side of the Navy rather than the policy side of the Navy. As a consequence, some bad and some good things are done and never see the light of day. And the contractors are not really held to account. They could be held to account if what they submitted was measured on whether their conclusions either contributed to a decision to do something or contributed to a decision not to do something. But if it was set aside as being irrelevant or not important, then they ought to get a bad mark or not get another contract.

But I've found--particularly since I've been out of the Navy and seen it from their standpoint--that they don't care whether they're studying something that ever has an effect on a decision as long as they get the contract. And we should be a lot tougher at the contract-letting end, and preferably have it related to policy if that's the kind of study we're asking them to do. And if it's just to decide whether to make a rectangle or a triangle or a leg on some kind of a piece of equipment, then that ought to be done on the material side but not how to use and employ the equipment--and they do a lot of that over there. Just wasted money.

Bagley/Zumwalt Staff - 307

Q: Would it be better if the Navy did more of these things itself so that it would have greater control?

Admiral Bagley: Yes, and it does, as I explained, with some limits on results. How big of an analysis organization do you want to build up, and how does it develop once you build it up? Another way to say it is, as I said earlier, that this whole process can be manipulated. So, to avoid that, you want to be sure how you go about it. The more centralized it is, the more analysis can be manipulated. And I don't think you want that. So if you can find contractors--and there's some good contractors--and they know that they've got an important audience rather than an unimportant audience, some of them can do a fine job.

Q: How big an input did the National Security Council have into Navy program planning during your time there?

Admiral Bagley: Well, obviously, the NSC during the arms control deliberations had an input on what we did on the strategic nuclear side of the Navy, which was not unimportant, because that takes a share of the Navy budget which becomes vital if you compare the trade-offs with building conventional forces instead. Zumwalt tried several times to see if he could get the strategic costs of the Navy put into a separate pocket somewhere. He always had to fight the implication of that, that our ballistic missile submarines would be given to the Air Force, and of course he couldn't live with that in the Navy, even if he felt himself that it might make some sense.

But nuclear arms are expensive things when compared to other needs that are not adequately funded. So as the NSC is able to say, "We're going to make the following arms control proposal, and it's going to be heavy on submarines," or "heavy on ICBM" at the penalty of increasing or decreasing one or the other--that has an effect on what you can do. If you're spending, say, $10 billion a year on ballistic missile submarines, and the NSC says that you're going to have to modernize that and have a new missile and build new submarines, you know that that's going to increase costs.

You're probably going to get the same general proportion of a budget, so you're not going to get a representative rise in order to take care of this, and your conventional forces are going to go down. So that's an impact that's important and you follow and you monitor and try to have it balance out so that you don't lose needed and also relevant nonnuclear capabilities. It's important to have the nuclear forces, but it's important to have the conventional power, and your preferred situation is not to have the two compete within your own service, particularly because the nuclear is more of a national-level kind of thing, and the Navy does not have like impact on nuclear policy as it does on sea power policy.

NSC had a role in the overseas homeporting to the extent that they had their own judgments about who could be talked to about this sort of thing, whether we could talk to the Germans, or whether we could talk to the British, whether we could talk to the Greeks and the quids and pros involved. State got into this, too, and had an influence on the NSC side--about the kinds of rules that would assure that we didn't become ugly Americans, that we were good Americans if we did get in, and how could we assure that, and what sorts of provisions would we take, how would these people live, and was that good or bad? So NSC got in pretty deep in the whole overseas homeporting matter.

Alliances obviously may have something to do with it also. If we walk into the NSC, OSD, and other authorities and say that we see the strategic interests that we've got to protect are the following; we don't have the forces to do that, so we've kind of thinned things out, and we're not terribly satisfied with it, but the thinning-out could be offset to some degree if you could get airbases and put U. S. Air Force airplanes into, say, Oman, then that might help offset the fact that we can only put one carrier battle group into the Arabian Sea when we feel that we ought to have three. The NSC is a logical place to perhaps raise that issue, and Zumwalt did raise those kinds of issues with Kissinger quite often.

Q: How much did you work--particularly in establishing a sea control force to support the NATO allies--how much consideration do you give to what they can contribute to the overall force?

Admiral Bagley: Let me just say it's kind of a trade-off. One, you'd like to say, "Okay, this is what they're going to do, and this is what's left, and this is what we have to do." But, unfortunately, the United States has got a lot more strategic responsibilities than the European countries, focusing on Europe alone. We have to worry about getting to the Persian Gulf over long sea lines and protecting and using the South Atlantic as well. And then in the Pacific, using sea lines of communication from the West Coast to Korea. If you start adding up all of those requirements, if they happen simultaneously, or two or three at a time rather than one at a time, you end up with a large logistics and force problem. So you can't meet them all. You do the best you can in a compromise, but it always ends up being a lot more force--if we can manage to fund it--than we would require to fill the difference in the North Atlantic between what the allies are doing and what the total requirement would be. But that's always a fight to get forces for this sort of broad strategy.

There's always been an element of debate within the Navy about whether to plan a Navy based on the European and the NATO context or to be perfectly clear that it involves other things, like the Pacific and Northeast Asia and the Arabian Sea, although the analytical support for the latter two is never as strong and is easier to overturn or rationalize away than the NATO one is. There should not be that sort of dilemma. It reflects national confusion about strategy. Zumwalt and Project 60 sought to give needed clarification, but change comes hard. Nixon's political problems and Vietnam worked a toll on all this.

Q: What can you say about the initiative of building up our capability in the Indian Ocean during the Zumwalt years?

Admiral Bagley: Well, because of his initial interest--and, as I say, the first person to point out this growing reliance on high oil imports at a time when things were looking unstable--he started deployments out there, but they were few and far between, because there weren't many ships available from other commitments for regular deployment. We had been in the Indian Ocean before, obviously, before he came around. But he didn't have the resources to do a lot, so he did what he was able to do, usually with deployments from the Pacific Seventh Fleet, and still not weaken things for too long a period in the Pacific, where, you know, we then had a firm commitment in Southeast Asia.

And then if you get back again to the whole argument process in the Pentagon--which is nothing I'm particularly proud of--but you make your progress through strategic concepts that people understand and accept. And they understood, accepted, and were accustomed to the Western Pacific (Southeast Asia). But if you start taking forces away from there to put into a new place, then you're undercutting with budget-makers what you said you required for Southeast Asia in the Western Pacific. These are the kinds of considerations that should never get into rational discussion, but in the Pentagon they get into rational discussion all the time, no matter how irrational they are.

So he started Mideast deployments, he did it irregularly, he was helped by the India-Pakistan War, as I've mentioned to you. He went out himself and visited the West African countries, just looking into the question of bases and things of that sort. As I remember, he went to Kenya, which was then friendly, and, of course, has been used a lot more now, to see if he could find some economical way to increase base and crisis support possibilities there.

Q: In dealing with Diego Garcia also.

Admiral Bagley: Moorer did that. Zumwalt finished it up for him.

Q: How much frustration is there in the program planning business in that very little of what you do is likely to come to fruition in your time there?

Admiral Bagley: That is worrisome as much as it is frustrating. Suppose you make a lot of mistakes. Suppose you look at things the wrong way or, say, you give the wrong priorities. Maybe you cut back readiness instead of procurement, or maybe you go too heavy on readiness and slack your procurements such that you're not ready when something really happens six, seven, eight years later. So I don't think it's so much frustrating--maybe to some people, but it's not to me.

But I think that you do worry about whether or not you have the proper balance between the future and the present. And that's something that Zumwalt really thought about deeply in Project 60 and later, and that's why some of those compromises that you mentioned earlier were made-- near-term risk for long-term benefit, and then hope you can realize the expected gain. The risk is that even if you have a long-term perspective and you're wiling to take near-term risks, you can always find somebody who will take the near-term risk with you, because it appears to be the possibility of saving some dollars, although in this case we took every dollar from the short-term savings and put them into the long-term thing. But you never can be sure that after you leave that everybody will still have that long-term interest, and the actions initiated in the short term have to be a continuing program in the out years.

And there's no question that those kinds of difficulties arose, and particularly after four years, which is a relatively short period of time for a CNO like Zumwalt, who has big plans, big ideas, big concepts. To have a new CNO come in, often with less will and less perspective, it would be pure luck if it continued on. Pure luck. So you can lose something by a new CNO, and you can lose something by congressional impatience or changing the availability of funds, applying different perspectives, or seeming to apply different perspectives. Most of the things that CNO said in 1970 are important today in 1983 and not yet satisfied. I think that's the most important thing about him. He had a good look into the future, and it was more accurate than not.

Q: Looking back now with ten years of hindsight and perspective, how do you think you did?

Admiral Bagley: It isn't how I thought I did; I did what I was intended to do at the time. The question here is whether or not the things that were set in motion with Zumwalt--first, do you agree with them? Were they sound? I say, "Yes, they're sound." And you have to put them down on a piece of paper and evaluate each one. But I think each one was sound.

Then, secondly, was what he set into motion given support after he left? And then the answer to that is "yes" or "no." I say more "no" than "yes."

And then the third logical question is, "Why not? What other perspective, what other concept, what other idea that substituted for those he made in the early Seventies makes what was sound no longer sound or makes it ignored or let it tail off after he left?" And that's a whole different story.

I think that on the whole his ideas about trying to build a Navy that could control the seas as we dealt with more trouble spots, more points of critical interest to the United States, have gone forward fitfully but inevitably. Whether people believed in it or not, events have cascaded to make it more clear now even to those who weren't perceptive enough at the time to see it. So that's happened.

There is also the question of the resources which have evolved in the Navy.

The programs that he wanted to undertake for sea control went forward--the main ones, except for the sea control ships. I'm talking about the escort program and the P-3C, the minecraft, the CAPTOR mine, more submarines--all of those things have gone forward.* So that's it, even if in sum Zumwalt would have done more. Essentially, faith was held in that.

The business of the right strike capability related to the proliferation of strategic interests in the regions in which we had possibly to use the Navy--I think that has not gone forward right. There's been too many resources put into carriers on a continual basis, and there should have been a shift, a more perceptible shift, towards cruise missiles and distributing of strike capabilities so you could cover more areas with strike resources and still have a credible way to make a difference.

And that, of course, as I've mentioned, is this ingrown feeling which was born in an almost irrevocable way in the late Forties and Fifties, where naval aviation felt they saved naval aviation. And there's no aviator CNO who would sit at the demise of naval aviation; it's impossible to do. So that's the first priority for the non-Zumwalt Navy, and it's covered by words like "balance" and all the rest. But in the last analysis, it's going to have to be

---

*The P-3C is a long-range, land-based maritime patrol aircraft with specialized antisubmarine sensors and weapons. CAPTOR stands for encapsulated torpedo, a type of mine intended to shoot a torpedo at an enemy ship.

shot down just like the battleship was shot down--it's got to be done both inside and from outside the Navy. And it can't be an either-or sort of thing. The cruise missiles have got to be presented, as they are being presented in some of the sounder forums, to complement the aircraft carrier, just as the aircraft carrier was a complement to the battleship in the Twenties and Thirties. That's the only way that this thing will move forward. I think it's happening, but it's just slow as glue. It's a terrible blight on Navy thinking.

Q: The idea of revitalizing the diesel submarine comes up every now and again. What consideration was given to that during your years?

Admiral Bagley: They had about four studies on it. I think the tendency in the hierarchy of the Navy is to accept the professional submarine view on that. You know, there are pros and cons, and I think the diesel submarines might have had two valid uses--at least based on the studies' analysis done then. One is for a very long-range carrier of ballistic missiles, mainly to save money, because, in general, it could still be made safe. And then, secondly, for a coastal attack submarine--you know, shorter range, regional sea control. But if you're dealing with a power with as many interests as we have and argue, as I've argued, that these interests are proliferating in terms of overseas regions, you want to keep maximum mobility, it seems to me. You're going to have to do some trading off in costs, but nuclear submarines sell.

The surface ship is a different matter--you know, the nuclear power versus nonnuclear power. Nonnuclear power doesn't sell as easily.

Q: What was your relationship with the Marine Corps during your time as far as supporting Navy programs they were interested in?

Admiral Bagley: I think, on the whole, we were fair with the Marine Corps. There were always arguments about whether more should be done, but the genesis of Zumwalt's outlook was that we needed to be able to put naval force into these regions, and that if we couldn't do that, then there was no way you were going to be able to do some of the other things like put one carrier in or put one division or one BLT or one regiment of Marines in and land them.* So the advancing priority was given to the naval side. You had to get the troops there, you had to protect them to get them there, you had to protect them when they were there, and you had to supply them. And his judgment

---
*BLT--battalion landing team.

was that we weren't in a good position to do that.

Q: Why was not more done to give them a major-caliber gunfire support program?

Admiral Bagley: There was a great deal of effort going on at the time for the long-range 8-inch gun. And that was canceled after Zumwalt left. But the 8-inch gun was in the Project 60 concept. And development went on slow but sure, and finally there was a ship earmarked to put it on. Though an active program was supported by Zumwalt, I don't think he felt down to his socks that it was that important, but nevertheless offered advantages we didn't have now. The 8-inch gun was lightweight and usable on more ships than the old 8-inch gun. But that was really killed after Zumwalt left. I wouldn't put it in the category of great disappointments. Some would, but I'm not sure I would.

Q: Are there any aviation programs that particularly stand out in your mind that we haven't discussed?

Admiral Bagley: Stand out in terms of what?

Q: In terms of things that you were considering that worked or didn't work or that had high priority. You mentioned the F-14.

Admiral Bagley: The F-14 was a high priority. It worked. Zumwalt earlier had gone through that period with the F-111, you know, where he'd had a role in OP-96 in deciding that the F-111 could make it. But I think that all the analysis around the F-111 wasn't terribly persuasive on either side. The gut reaction of the aviator who had to fly the airplane was probably right. I don't know, since we never put it on a carrier. But Zumwalt came into office having that experience behind him, and it was perfectly clear there wasn't going to be an F-111, so he had to do something, and he supported the proposal for the F-14, which had really germinated before he was in as CNO. But he gave it full support, pushed it over a very crucial period when if he hadn't, it may never have gone into production, because it was in the development phase about the time he came in. He always supported the other kinds of things—the A-6 and the A-7 and the S-3s.*

He was a heavy proponent for the idea of putting the ASW aircraft into the attack carriers and having the CV

---

*The A-6 and A-7 are carrier-based attack aircraft, and the S-3 is a carrier-based antisubmarine warfare aircraft.

concept.* And that went on during his time. There was some opposition to that, but it wasn't heavy, because it made intellectual and strategic sense that was very difficult to refute, because nobody was going to have every force or system available at any one time in a crisis. It was going to be a tailored wing that had to do with the kinds of problems that you were trying to deal with. So if you were looking at a strategic strike and ASW problem which heretofore wasn't feasible in dealing with, this was another kind of economy that made you more feasible--made meeting those crisis requirements more feasible than you would have been without it.

Q: One thing that I've been trying to get and we haven't really touched on too much is sort of the personal relationship between the two of you in doing your respective jobs.

Admiral Bagley: What kind of things do you want? I've talked about quite a few. What would you like for me to say?

Q: Well, I'm sort of interested in specific cases, the

---

*ASW--antisubmarine warfare. With the demise of the dedicated antisubmarine carriers, fixed-wing and helicopter antisubmarine squadrons were moved aboard what had previously been exclusively attack carriers. CVAs were thus redesignated CVs.

kinds of discussions you would have, how often you would see each other. Did you see each other socially?

Admiral Bagley: During a normal working day, there's a process where each morning the CNO receives the VCNO in his office, and then they bring in others, including intelligence officers that brief him on what is going on.* Zumwalt expanded that to include me every morning, so I'd go up there with the VCNO. That's one thing. That's been carried on, incidentally, since that time by subsequent CNOs. Zumwalt and I talked on the phone every day or saw each other every day, and I worked also closely with his aide, because the CNO is busy. He's running around. He's not always there. But, anyway, the contact--usually a personal contact each day in addition to the morning reunion with the VCNO and then other times during the day or working through the aide if the CNO was out of the building or gone somewhere.

I used to get notes from him all the time. When I'd write a note up on something, I'd get it back from him with some comment, and sometimes on the bottom, "GOYA." It means, "Get Off Your Ass," and get this done. So, anyhow, it was a relaxed kind of communication. I've been known to put in an envelope the same message to him. And then socially we saw each other occasionally.

---

*VCNO--Vice Chief of Naval Operations.

The relationship only became close from the late Sixties on, but there was a lot of mutual trust. I have a high admiration for the guy. He's honest and forthright. He's brilliant. There hasn't been his kind of brains in the Navy in a very long time. There's a few but not very many. He's got the courage of a lion, or he wouldn't have even tried what he tried to do.

He showed--probably more than anybody else, in my opinion--that the Navy's not as great as it thinks it is. It's got too many small people, too many inadequate people, and too many dumb people who react only from the gut. So I admire him for bringing that out, to cause the Navy to realize it could think more deeply and objectively, which should have been self-evident in any other organization, but the Navy likes to sit back and talk about how wonderful it is, rather than what it could be. And it's not that wonderful now. And he was one of the few CNOs that could walk around anywhere--whether it was the White House with Kissinger, the State Department with the Secretary of State, or sitting down talking with Schlesinger or other Secretaries of Defense on a man-to-man basis--where there was an easy exchange and that there was a mutual respect. That doesn't happen very often.

In addition to a strong fleet background, he had had much experience with civilian authority before he became CNO. He had a better sense of how to deal with civilians and how civilians thought--their prejudices about the military and how to deal with those prejudices and still get the message across. And no one else that I've seen in at least 15 years could touch him on that.

In the old days, before 1940, we had a number of CNOs who could do that. But it was a different kind of organization then. They had a Secretary of the Navy (in the Cabinet), and they were the CNO, and that's all there was. And then there was the President. So that kind of relationship was much easier. But after the reorganization into a Defense Department, the whole accompaniment to those relationships was a prejudice against the military, sparked, in part, by a separated personal and professional relationship. Part of it was because the less familiar military was looked on as not being adequate, for one reason or another. And very often when you make generalities like that, why, you end up tarring everybody with that and triggering similar hostility from the military towards the civilian leader.

But Zumwalt more than others--I think that Forrest Sherman, if I had to reach back since the '47 act--Forrest Sherman and maybe Arleigh Burke were the others who broke through that. And it takes a unique kind of man to do it.

The others I haven't mentioned, unless I've forgotten one, never did it. So Zumwalt was a very unique guy. There have been some lousy CNOs, and there have been a very few good ones since World War II; he's one of the two or three that are good, in my humble opinion. I've seen them since I was a boy in the middle Thirties, in one form or another.*

So it was easy to have a relationship with a man that you respected and with whom there was mutual respect. We saw each other regularly and saw each other socially, mainly in official events. We talked at night a lot on the telephone after we were away from the office. That's something that goes on all the time. It's a sort of communication that is economical in time spent and promotes understanding.

Q: Did he use you as a sounding board?

Admiral Bagley: Yes--me as well as others.

Q: For areas outside your normal billet?

Admiral Bagley: Oh, yes. As I say, before it was all over, I was going over every paper that went to him. And when there were ideas or he was talking with someone from the outside who he'd invited in--and he did a lot of that--civilians, intellectuals, university people, think tank

---

*The interviewee grew up in a Navy family. His father, David W. Bagley, was a Naval Academy classmate (1904) of the famous Admiral William F. Halsey, Jr. His father eventually retired in the rank of four-star admiral.

people, businessmen who were going to discuss something that would have some relevance to Navy problems that he thought might be enlightening and would give us germs of ideas, he'd invite me down, invariably. I'd be the only other person there. But I don't like to overdo this. You know, I am telling you that Zumwalt's a fine CNO, and all the rest about me is not terribly important, I don't think. Others had key roles and strong influence.

Q: It's important in the sense that it sounds as if you were probably closer to him than almost any other three-star admiral of the period.

Admiral Bagley: There's no question that I was close, yes. There were few who had the same professional relationship. But that may be good or bad, you know. Maybe I was the wrong influence, too. Maybe there are some people that would argue that relationship was not useful. So I don't like to overemphasize it. Zumwalt can stand on his own.

Q: You cited briefly the instance of his sense of humor in "GOYA." What are some other examples?

Admiral Bagley: I don't know that I can think of many examples, but he's always had a good sense of humor. He was smiling more than he wasn't. But he could see the irony and the humor of a lot of these things that we've talked about as problems. You know, the lack of support and people making gestures of resistance or trying to be subtle and being unsubtle. They were dealing with an extremely sophisticated, smart man. So there was always a lot of laughter at some of that, as well as disappointment that he was not making his points intellectually.

But there was laughter up, too. There was an individual in OP-06 at the beginning--a wonderful and talented person, Vice Admiral Blouin.* Zumwalt came in like a whirlwind and asked him about everything in the whole world. He used to run up and down the corridors and say, "We don't have a CNO; we've got CinCWorld." Zumwalt had very broad interests.

****

A portion of the transcript at this point in the interview has been omitted from the released version at the request of the interviewee. It will be released at a future time, when authorized by Admiral Bagley.

****

*Vice Admiral Francis J. Blouin, USN, Deputy Chief of Naval Operations (Plans and Policy).

Q: Zumwalt said in his book that he deliberately picked you as a brilliant surface officer rather than a brilliant aviator or a brilliant submariner for his program. Do you think he got what he hoped for in making that kind of choice?

Admiral Bagley: I don't know. That's for him and others to decide. But the point is that in this command business of aviators and submariners and surface ship people--there are whole different spectrums of motivations that go into that. And the important one to remember is that we're all victims of our background. So even those that try to break away from their background aren't going to understand everything else. So that's one thing. The second is that I've always felt that the aviators have this mandate of 1950 that just was in stone, and there was no flexibility there. I mean, that was something that even they should have felt bad about and still should. But I don't think they're able to break away from it. It's got to be done from some external source.

And the submariners--it's a whole new world, you know, the possibilities. It was recently that nuclear power came. The ships can be adapted for ballistic missiles, for cruise missiles, and for every other thing. There's no evidence that the submarines are going to be vulnerable. I think they had the impetus of something that was good. They knew it better than anybody else, and they ought to be the advocate of it. In many ways, they were the most hidebound, but when there were exceptions in the submarine force from being hidebound, they were absolute gems. I'm not going to give names, but just people whom the Navy couldn't do without. But they were the exception in that group, at least when measured by the general well-being of sea power.

The aviators had some gems and fewer exceptions. They were able, except when they had full responsibility for producing these carriers that they'd gone to the death for in 1950. They had some very brilliant and exceptional people who could do anything, in my humble opinion.

So it isn't all cut and dried when you look at the CNO's staff perspective, and it isn't continually a bureaucratic war, and it isn't that everybody is working against everybody in the Pentagon. But there is a whole series of different kinds of influences that come out of it, and it's hard to describe what lies behind the result. But you can affect the result in some cases, and in other cases you can't.

I think Zumwalt had much more success than he's given credit for. I think people look on Zumwalt more for his personnel policies and more for the thing about chain of command--which I don't think ever was fully described or critics fully thought out--but was meant to facilitate getting a job done without necessarily compromising the chain of command. But it came out in a different way, and that's been in everybody's craw. You have to have your whole being depend on the chain of command to have some of the reactions that some people have to Zumwalt because of that. To me it seems unbalanced.

Q: There have been various critics of the programs of Admiral Zumwalt. How would you respond to them?

Admiral Bagley: I think that there was one conversation which throws some of that into perspective. Arleigh Burke one night--to me and to me alone, when no one else was within earshot--said that he thought that the entire Zumwalt program was as sound as it could be, but there was one critical point of it that he didn't particularly admire, and that was that Zumwalt used "I" too much. And I think that that sort of perception has had some effect on the way people evaluate what Zumwalt did. And it seems to me, on balance, a rather minor point, or at least an unimportant one, particularly in terms of a historical assessment, because most of the people that are in authority--whether they're in the military or outside the military--have egos that certainly are above average. So I think that that was a conscious compliment to what Zumwalt did, and it came from one of the greatest CNOs of the 1900s.

Q: So it had to be gratifying.

Admiral Bagley: It was.

Index

to

Reminiscences by

Staff Officers to

Admiral Elmo R. Zumwalt, Jr., U.S. Navy

Volume I

Abrams, General Creighton W., Jr., USA (USMA, 1936)
    As Commander U.S. Forces Vietnam in the late 1960s, relationship with naval forces commander, Rear Admiral Kenneth Veth, 17-19, 35, 206; attitude towards Navy's role in war, 33-34, 56; relationship with Vice Admiral Elmo Zumwalt, 35, 45-46, 53-54, 86-87, 134, 140, 173, 177, 204-206, 208; at meeting with joint service advisors in the fall of 1968, Abrams very forcibly made point that he was under presidential orders to implement Vietnamization as soon as possible, 47-55; signed some Navy fitness reports, at Zumwalt's request, 63; protection when he would go into the field or travel about Saigon, 79, 114; came to Zumwalt's aid when Navy channels disapproved his requests, 88; changed quarters in 1968 to be closer to his headquarters, 111; discussed troop reductions with new Secretary of Defense, Melvin Laird, in early 1969, 132; pushed for permission to raid enemy sanctuaries in Cambodia and Laos, 132-133; requested reassessment of policy options from service heads in Vietnam, 137-138

Air Force, U.S.
    Air Force colonel drew General Creighton Abrams's ire during briefing that showed slow turnover of Air Force assets to the Vietnamese in the fall of 1968, 48-50, 53, 204-206; CNO Elmo Zumwalt fought suggestion that Navy's ballistic missile submarines be given to the Air Force in the early 1970s, 308

Amphibious Force
    CNO Elmo Zumwalt increased force in the early 1970s, but it was not a top priority, 275-278

Antisubmarine Warfare (ASW)
    CNO Elmo Zumwalt a strong supporter of putting ASW aircraft into attack carriers in the early 1970s, 320-321

Arbo, Captain Paul E., USN (USNA, 1944)
    As senior advisor to the Vietnamese Navy in the late 1960s, tried to discourage Zumwalt's plan for rapid turnover of Navy assets to the Vietnamese, 43-44, 183

Arms Control
    CNO Elmo Zumwalt strenuously opposed U.S. negotiator Kissinger's intention to give up nuclear cruise missiles at Vladivostok meeting, 272-273; <u>see also</u> Strategic Arms Limitation Talks

Army, U.S.
    Army personnel in Saigon were better trained than Navy men to protect their compound in the late 1960s, 114; better rapport with and support to Navy under VADM Elmo Zumwalt, 177

Bagley, Vice Admiral David H., USN (USNA, 1944)
    Value to CNO Elmo Zumwalt in the early 1970s as Deputy Chief of Naval Operations (Manpower and Reserve Affairs), 257-258

Bagley, Admiral Worth H., USN (Ret.) (USNA, 1947)
    Relationship with Admiral Elmo Zumwalt, 232-233, 239-240, 263-266, 322-323, 325-326, 328; Bagley's duties as Vice Chief of Naval Operations in the early 1970s, 243, 265-266, 325; duties as director of program planning, 271

Ballistic Missiles
    CNO Elmo Zumwalt fought the suggestion that the Air Force take over the Navy's ballistic missile submarine program in the early 1970s, 308

Bernique, Lieutenant (junior grade) Michael, USNR
    Junior officer chased a Viet Cong on foot at gunpoint in to Cambodia in the late 1960s, 103, 109-110

Blouin, Vice Admiral Francis J., USN (USNA, 1933)
    As Deputy Chief of Naval Operations (Plans and Policy) in the early 1970s, anecdote about his assessment of CNO Elmo Zumwalt, 327

"Body Count"
    Judged to be of low significance to Navy by Commander Naval Forces Vietnam Elmo Zumwalt in 1968, 127-128, 222-223

Brown, General George S., USAF (USMA, 1941)
    Commander Seventh Air Force pushed for the mining of Haiphong Harbor in early 1969, 133; criticized by General Abrams for Air Force briefing on Vietnamization, 205

Bureau of Naval Personnel (BuPers)
    See Naval Personnel, Bureau of

Burke, Admiral Arleigh A., USN (USNA, 1923)
    Comparison of his power as Chief of Naval Operations from 1955-1961 compared to Admiral Elmo Zumwalt's in the early 1970s, 292, 294-295, 324; assessment of Zumwalt, 330-331

Air Force cargo planes used to ferry Navy minesweeping equipment to the Suez Canal in 1973, 279, 281

Cambodia
Infiltration into IV Corps through Cambodia in 1968, 17, 30; junior officer chased a Viet Cong on foot into Cambodia, not realizing the political implications, 103, 109-110; General Creighton Abrams pushed for permission to raid enemy sanctuaries in Cambodia in early 1969, 132-133; President Richard Nixon criticized for raids into Cambodia in 1970, 136-137

Ca Mau Peninsula, South Vietnam
U.S. set up a fire base in the peninsula to rid it of Viet Cong as part of Operation Silver Mace in the late 1960s, 197

Center for Naval Analyses (CNA)
Used in the early 1970s for program planning, 304; value to Navy assessed by Bagley, 305

Chafee, John H.
Bagley credits Secretary of the Navy Chafee with a courageous decision to appoint Elmo Zumwalt as Chief of Naval Operations in 1970, 237

Chief of Naval Operations (CNO)
Admiral Elmo Zumwalt compared to other CNOs, 241-242, 261, 292, 294-295, 314; CNO's power during national crises, 294-298

Chief of Naval Operations's Executive Board (CEB)
Discussion of duties in early 1970s, 162, 304; CNO Zumwalt held regular meetings with this group, 267

China, Peoples' Republic of
Thawing U.S.-China relations in the early 1970s didn't lessen drain on U.S. Navy requirements, 289-290

Chon, Admiral Tran Van
South Vietnamese naval head seen as aggressive and willing to fight during the late 1960s, 71; social life with Americans, 169; relationship with VADM Elmo Zumwalt, 190, 192

CinCPac
see Commander in Chief Pacific

CinCPacFlt
    see Commander in Chief Pacific Fleet

Clark Air Force Base, Philippines
    Kerr and VADM Elmo Zumwalt undergo survival training prior to leaving for Vietnam in late 1968, 20-21; Zumwalt visited his family here while serving in Vietnam, 186, 199-200

Commander in Chief Pacific (CinCPac)
    Gave wide-ranging briefing to Zumwalt before he arrived in Vietnam in 1968, 16; established rules of engagement for Navy in Vietnam, 84

Commander in Chief Pacific Fleet (CinCPacFlt)
    Briefing to Zumwalt before he assumed duties as naval commander in Vietnam in 1968 paid little attention to in country matters, 15-16

Command Histories
    Quality of histories from in-country units in South Vietnam during the Vietnam War era, 90-95

Contracts
    Discussion of quality of material and analytical services procured from civilian organizations in the 1970s and 1980s, 305-307

Corcoran, Major General Charles A., USA
    As General Creighton Abrams's chief of staff in Vietnam in 1968, offered to delay a Navy presentation on Vietnamization after his boss blew up at the Air Force talk, 52, 205

Cruise missiles
    Discussion of land-target cruise missile argument in the late 1960s-early 1970s, 252; CNO Elmo Zumwalt opposed Dr. Henry Kissinger's intention to give up nuclear cruise missiles during 1974 negotiations with the Soviets, because it could have led to the end of conventional cruise missiles as well, 272-273, 288-289; discussion of accuracy of missiles in the early 1970s, 273-275; Bagley feels too much interest has been put on aircraft carriers, to the detriment of cruise missiles, 316-317; see also Harpoon; Trident II

Decision Coordination, Special Assistant to the CNO/VCNO for
    Implemented ideas initiated by Project 60 in the early 1970s, 243

Defense Department
    Reorganization of separate military establishments into the Defense Department in the 1940s may have served to broaden gap between military and civilian hierarchy, 324

Destroyer Squadron 26
    Admiral Elmo Zumwalt revealed his concept of giving young officers a shot at early ship command to Kerr at a party in mid-1970, 144-145; mixed success at original concept of inspiring young officers to stay in service, 146-147, 152

Detente
    Influence of world situation in early 1970s upon CNO Elmo Zumwalt's policies, 285-290

Diego Garcia
    CNO Elmo Zumwalt furthered CNO Thomas Moorer's initiative to establish this U.S. outpost in the Indian Ocean in the early 1970s, 313

Emery, Lieutenant Commander Thomas R.M., USN (USNA, 1955)
    Recommended to join VADM Elmo Zumwalt's Vietnam staff by Glenn, 184

Falkland Islands
    Lessons learned by the U.S. Navy from the 1982 British-Argentine action, 258-259

F-14 Tomcat
    CNO Elmo Zumwalt was a proponent of this fighter partly to garner support for his own proposals, 253, 255, 320

F-111 (TFX)
    RADM Elmo Zumwalt's analysis of this dual Navy-Air Force plane concept in the late 1960s influenced his strong backing of the F-14 as CNO in the early 1970s, 320

Fitness reports
    VADM Elmo Zumwalt used fitness reports to reward those officers who served well in Vietnam, 63

Fletcher School of Law and Diplomacy
    Discussion of Kerr's postgraduate degree from this institution in the mid-1960s, 1-3, 9; Kerr's master's thesis on the escalation of U.S. involvement in Vietnam, 3-5

Fonda, Jane
    Strident anti-war activist seemed to have no impact on Americans stationed in Saigon in the late 1960s, 115-116

Ford, Gerald R.
    Vice President Ford excluded from many issues by national security advisor, Henry Kissinger, in the mid-1970s, 156; credited for classy handling of Admiral Elmo Zumwalt's retirement ceremony in 1974, 157-159

IV Corps, South Vietnam
    Infiltration through Cambodia in 1968, 17, 30-31, 75; U.S. Marines would have been better suited to serve in this sector, rather than in I Corps, 77-78

Giant Slingshot, Operation
    Interdiction of Viet Cong moving supplies in the Parrot's Beak became one of VADM Elmo Zumwalt's first operations when he assumed command in 1968, 172-178, 197, 213-214, 220

Glenn, Captain W. Lewis, Jr., USN (USNA, 1962)
    Early Navy service, 165-166; assigned as aide to Commander U.S. Naval Forces Vietnam, Rear Admiral Kenneth Veth, in mid-1968, 167; duties as aide to Vice Admiral Zumwalt, 179, 207, 209-211; travelled extensively through Vietnam, 196; suffered food poisoning in Vietnam, 199; misgivings about leaving job in Vietnam, 229; relationship with Zumwalt after Vietnam service, 230-231

Guam Doctrine
    Discussion of President Richard Nixon's idea that the U.S. would not fight again on Asian land, 268, 289

Guns--8-inch
    CNO Elmo Zumwalt was a proponent of the 8-inch gun program to provide better gunfire support, but the program was canceled after he left office in 1974, 319

Haiphong Harbor
    U.S. military leaders pushed for the mining of Haiphong Harbor in early 1969, 133

Harpoon Missile
    Development in the late 1960s, 259-261

Hawkins, USS (DD-873)
    Unit of Destroyer Squadron 26, an experiment in giving greater responsibility to more-junior officers, in 1971, 145-146; reenlistment under skipper, Kerr, 147; difficulties caused by Z-grams, 148-150; racial problems in the early 1970s, 150-152

Hayward, Admiral Thomas B., USN (USNA, 1948A)
    Characterized as having an excellent memory for details,
    214-215

Hoffman, Captain Roy F., USN
    Assessed as Commander Task Force 115 off Vietnam in
    1968, 26-27, 182, 221; heroic dismissal of order to
    protect himself during swift boat operations, 76;
    reaction on RADM Kenneth Veth's staff to one of his
    inshore actions, 172, 174; relationship with VADM
    Elmo Zumwalt, 180

Homeporting
    See Overseas homeporting

Houser, Vice Admiral William D., USN (USNA, 1942)
    Loyalty to CNO Zumwalt in the early 1970s as Deputy
    Chief of Naval Operations (Air Warfare), 257

Humphrey, Robert
    Civilian contracted advisor briefed Zumwalt on how to
    overcome cultural difficulties in Vietnamization
    process in the late 1960s, 68

I Corps, South Vietnam
    Unsuccessful attempts to move U.S. Marines from I Corps
    to IV Corps in the late 1960s, 77-78

Indian Ocean
    Growing Soviet presence in the Indian Ocean in 1968 of
    concern to the U.S. Navy, 235; concern with choke points
    in the early 1970s that could have blocked access to the
    Red Sea, 280; CNO Elmo Zumwalt's influence on U.S. Navy
    actions during India-Pakistan conflict in 1971, 295,
    312; CNO Zumwalt's initiatives to buildup U.S. presence
    here in the early 1970s, despite some resistance in the
    Pentagon, 311-313

Intelligence
    Intelligence officers on VADM Elmo Zumwalt's Vietnam
    staff in the late 1960s studied how the Viet Cong were
    infiltrating the Mekong Delta, 126

Johnson, Lyndon B.
    Cut back on bombing North Vietnam towards the end of his
    term to help Vice President Hubert Humphrey's chances of
    getting elected, 136

Joint Chiefs of Staff (JCS)
    When CNO Elmo Zumwalt wrote a critical letter about
    President Richard Nixon's handling of the SALT issue in

1974, the JCS mildly agreed, but thought the wording was too strident, 155-158, 160-161; at Zumwalt's retirement ceremony in June 1974, 159; except for the chairman, Admiral Thomas Moorer, somewhat left out of U.S. alert during 1973 Yom Kippur War, 292

Jordan
Effect of mid-1970 trouble in Jordan on new Chief of Naval Operations, Admiral Elmo Zumwalt, 243-245

Kennedy, John F.
Conjecture on President Kennedy's plans for handling the Vietnam War, had he not been killed in 1963, 4-5

Kenya
CNO Zumwalt visited Kenya in the early 1970s to evaluate potential for support during an Indian Ocean crisis, 312

Kerr, Captain Howard J., Jr., USN (Ret.)
Education and early service duties, 1-5; circumstances of his selection as Commander Naval Forces Vietnam's aide in 1968, 6-9, 11; duties on Zumwalt's staff, 13-14, 20-21, 39-40, 100-102, 211; suffered food poisoning in Vietnam, 112, 199; commanding officer of the Hawkins (DD-873), a unit of the "Mod Squad," in 1971, 145-153; aide to various political officials in the early-to-mid-1970s, 154; relationship with CNO Zumwalt when Kerr was working in the White House, 155-159; worked on CNO's Executive Panel staff briefly in 1970, 161-162

Kerrey, Lieutenant (junior grade) Joseph R., USNR
Kerr's recollections of future Nebraska governor as SEAL officer in Vietnam in 1969, 114

Kissinger, Dr. Henry A.
As instructor at the Fletcher School of Law and Diplomacy in the mid-1960s, 3; as national security advisor to President Richard Nixon, exerted strong control over his boss, to the exclusion of his military advisors, 155-156; had regular meetings with CNO Elmo Zumwalt, 267, 310, 323; favored giving up nuclear cruise missiles during Vladivostok negotiations in 1974, 272-273

Laird, Melvin R.
Nixon's Secretary of Defense discussed troop reduction with General Abrams during early 1969 visit to Saigon, 132-136

Laos
General Creighton Abrams pushed for permission to raid

enemy sanctuaries in Laos in early 1969, 132-133

Logistics
See Military Sealift Command

Long Beach, USS (CGN-9)
CNO Thomas Moorer opposed fitting this nuclear cruiser with conventional missiles in the late 1960s, 252

Long-Range Planning
CNO Elmo Zumwalt's organization and handling of long-range planning, compared to his successors, 269-271

McCain, Admiral John S., Jr., USN (USNA, 1931)
Benevolent attitude towards steward who spilled beef juice on the admiral's shirt during Vietnam dinner party hosted by VADM Elmo Zumwalt in the late 1960s, 208-209

McNamara, Robert S.
Effect of Defense Secretary's austerity measures on the Navy in the late 1960s, 234-235

Marine Corps, U.S.
Would have been better utilized in Vietnam in IV Corps rather than I Corps in the late 1960s, 77-78; Kerr saw mixed blessing when Marine guards were assigned to protect Admiral Elmo Zumwalt, 114-115; Bagley feels that the Marine Corps got fair consideration during CNO Zumwalt's term, but concedes that higher priority was given to naval issues, 318-319; see also Guns--8-inch

Market Time, Operation
North Vietnamese adjusted strategy to compensate for success of these operations, 32; use of swift boats in the late 1960s, 75-76, 170

Medals and Decorations
Kerr accompanied Vice Admiral Elmo Zumwalt to the scene of action with a briefcase containing medals in 1968-69, 79-81

Meese, Lieutenant Sam, USN
Description of Glenn's predecessor as aide to Commander U.S. Naval Forces Vietnam, Rear Admiral Kenneth Veth, in mid-1968, 168

Middle East
CNO Elmo Zumwalt recognized in the early 1970s the inconsistencies between U.S. policy in the Middle East and our increasing need for oil, 235

Military Sealift Command (MSC)
    CNO Elmo Zumwalt's use of the MSC to meet his logistics requirements, 282-283

Miller, Rear Admiral George H., USN (USNA, 1933)
    Interest in sea-based anti-ballistic missiles in the 1960s, 275

Mine Warfare
    U.S. military leaders pressed to be allowed to mine Haiphong Harbor in early 1969, 133; CNO Elmo Zumwalt reestablished mine warfare command in the early 1970s, 278--279-281; Zumwalt's interest in the reserve minesweeping ships, 279-280

Missiles
    See Styx; Harpoon; Cruise missiles; Ballistic missiles

"Mod Squad"
    See Destroyer Squadron 26

Moorer, Admiral Thomas H., USN (USNA, 1933)
    Opposed selection of VADM Elmo Zumwalt as his successor as Chief of Naval Operations in 1970, 237; as CNO in the late 1960s, opposed fitting the nuclear-powered Long Beach (CGN-9) with conventional missiles, 252; handling of U.S. response to 1973 Yom Kippur War, 292-293; CNO Moorer initiated effort to establish U.S. outpost at Diego Garcia in the late 1960s, 313

National Security Council (NSC)
    Effect on Navy program planning in the early 1970s, 307-309; involved in overseas homeporting question, 309-310

Naval Advisory Group, Vietnam
    Initially fought VADM Elmo Zumwalt's desire to speed up turnover of Navy assets to the Vietnamese in the late 1960s, 43-44

Naval Aviation
    Hold of aviators on CNO billet since 1961 presented difficulties for non-aviator Elmo Zumwalt in the early 1970s, 276-277, 316-317; support of aviation community for CNO Zumwalt, 329

Naval Forces Vietnam, U.S.
    Prospective Commander Naval Forces Vietnam, Rear Admiral Elmo Zumwalt, briefed by West Coast commands on his way to Saigon in 1968, 12; significance of upgrading Zumwalt's billet to three stars, 18-20; Navy's staff structure seen as ineffective prior to Zumwalt's

arrival, 21-22, 29-32; Zumwalt's early effects on staff, 38; Zumwalt's effect of attitude of other services toward Navy in Vietnam, 56-57; quality of naval personnel sent to Vietnam, 58-62, 166-167, 181-182; casualties increased with expanded Navy involvement, 33-34, 83; moral dilemmas, 83-84, 103-105; relaxed appearance and discipline of naval personnel, 85; morale under Zumwalt, 44-45, 86; Kerr's efforts to upgrade official command history from Vietnam, 90-95; accommodations for Zumwalt and staff, 110-111; difficulties getting stateside naval operations to adapt to needs of Navy in Vietnam, 124-125; intelligence group the strongest function on Zumwalt's staff, 126; Zumwalt's measure of success of Navy in Vietnam, 127-128; abrupt firing of Zumwalt's first operations officer, 130; daily schedule under RADM Kenneth Veth, 169-170; routine under VADM Zumwalt, 95-98, 176-180; "working" social life, 180; "insiders" and "outsiders" on staff, 185; lack of air support for brown-water troops upset Zumwalt, 203; Zumwalt's successes and failures in Vietnam, 219

Naval Personnel, Bureau of
Kerr's difficulties changing his orders to command a gunboat after he had decided to join Rear Admiral Elmo Zumwalt's Vietnam staff in 1968, 11-12; deceptive claim that only cream of Navy's officer corps were being sent to Vietnam, 58; Zumwalt fought to get the brightest officers sent to Vietnam and to reward those who had served well, 59-61, 63-65, 183

Navy, U.S.
Status of the service when Admiral Elmo Zumwalt became Chief of Naval Operations in 1970, 234-239; decommissioning of older ships in the early 1970s to loosen up additional funds, 245-246, 249, 257; CNO Zumwalt was successful in getting a bigger slice of the defense budget for the Navy, 268; streamlining and cost-cutting measures suggested by CNO Zumwalt, 283-285, 307-308; see also Naval Advisory Group, Vietnam; Naval Forces Vietnam, U.S.; Naval Personnel, Bureau of

News Media
Accessibility of Americans in Vietnam to news and to reporters, 115-121; VADM Elmo Zumwalt's relationship with the media, 118-121, 225-226; as hindrance to war effort, 227; see also Time magazine

Nicholson, Commander Richard E., USN (USNA, 1948B)
Assessed as operations officer on Elmo Zumwalt's Vietnam staff in the late 1960s, 129-130, 141, 181-182; as

commander of Destroyer Squadron 26 in 1971, whose units were commanded and manned by more-junior officers, credited with instilling harmony instead of competition, 145-146

Nitze, Paul H.
    As Secretary of the Navy in the mid-1960s, favored fitting the nuclear cruiser Long Beach (CGN-9) with conventional missiles, 252

Nixon, Richard M.
    VADM Elmo Zumwalt saw his election in 1968 as directly affecting what actions the Navy should take in Vietnam, 36; changes in U.S. handling of Vietnam War after his election, 131-134, 228; criticized for authorizing raids into Cambodia in the early 1970s, 136-137; CNO Zumwalt drafted a letter critical of Nixon's handling of SALT issues in 1974 that eventually led to the admiral's retiring, 155-158, 272-273, 289; Zumwalt felt Nixon was aware of eroding defense capabilities in the early 1970s, but the President didn't think he had enough political power to do anything about it, 244-246, 268, 311; see also Guam Doctrine

North Atlantic Treaty Organization (NATO)
    Presence of allies in the North Atlantic factored into Navy's worldwide requirements in the early 1970s, 310-311

Nuclear Power
    Nuclear proponents often opposed any type of ship that was not suited to nuclear propulsion, 254, 328-329

Nuclear Weapons
    Discussion of accuracy of nuclear missiles in the early 1970s, 273-275; impact of expense of nuclear weapons on the Navy's conventional weapons programs, 307-309

Oliver Hazard Perry (FFG-7) Class
    Escort ships proposed and accepted during Admiral Zumwalt's tenure as Chief of Naval Operations, 250-251, 256; class opposed by proponents of nuclear power, 254; quality management of program, 256-257

OP-06
    See Plans and Policy Division

OP-09C
    See Decision Coordination, Special Assistant to the CNO/VCNO for

OP-96
    See Systems Analysis Division

Orme, Captain Samuel T., USN
    As BuPers detailer for captains in the late 1960s, did
    unusual thing in sending himself to Vietnam, 58; as
    chief of staff to Rear Admiral Kenneth Veth,
    relationship with his boss, 171; worked well with new
    boss, VADM Elmo Zumwalt, but rotated from Vietnam as
    scheduled, 181

Overseas homeporting
    Studied within OpNav in the early 1970s, 247-249;
    influence of various government agencies on Navy's
    ability to choose overseas locations in the early 1970s,
    309-310

Plans and Policy Division (OP-06)
    Worked on long-range planning in conjunction with OP-96
    in the early 1970s, 270-271; see also Blouin, Vice
    Admiral Francis J., USN

Powers, Lieutenant Commander Robert C., USN (USNA, 1960)
    VADM Elmo Zumwalt often used this staff officer as an
    alter ego in Vietnam in the late 1960s, 98-99

Price, Captain Arthur W., Jr., USN
    Assessed as Commander Task Force 116 in Vietnam in
    1968, 27, 182, 221; relationship with VADM Elmo Zumwalt,
    180

Price, Rear Admiral Frank H., Jr., USN (USNA, 1941)
    Credited with outstanding management of FFG-7 program in
    the early 1970s, 256-257

Program Planning
    Discussion of Navy program planning under Bagley in the
    early 1970s, 298-304. 313-318

Project 60
    Bagley discusses Admiral Zumwalt's strategic philosophy
    program, 233-234, 239-241, 243, 260, 263, 267-268, 313,
    319

Racial Tensions
    Admiral Elmo Zumwalt credited for his sensitivity to
    racial problems, 151-153; troubles on board Kerr's ship,
    the Hawkins (DD-873) in the early 1970s, 150-152

Rauch, Captain Charles F., Jr., USN (USNA, 1948A)
    Given more responsibility by Vice Admiral Elmo Zumwalt

when he went along with the admiral's plan for rapid turnover of Navy assets to the Vietnamese, 43-44, 72, 182-183; initially negative on idea of advice from social scientists to aid in Vietnamization, 70; advised on political and strategic considerations, 141

Rectanus, Captain Earl F., USN
As highly regarded intelligence officer on VADM Elmo Zumwalt's Vietnam staff in the late 1960s, conjectured on how Viet Cong were infiltrating the Mekong Delta, 126, 128; as political and strategic advisor, 141; kept on by Zumwalt, but Glenn considered him an outsider, 185

Rickover, Vice Admiral Hyman G., USN (USNA, 1922)
Bagley recalls difficulties dealing with the "czar" of the Navy's nuclear power program in the early 1970s, 253-254

Riverine Warfare
Background of effort in Vietnam, 82

Rizza, Captain Joseph R., USN
Replaced in 1968 as VADM Elmo Zumwalt's chief of staff in Vietnam because of a difference in working styles, 40-41; 181

Royal Navy
Preparation for 1982 Falkland Islands action, 258-259

Rung Sat Zone, South Vietnam
One of Zumwalt's goals in Vietnam in 1968-69 was to get some operations going in this area, known as the Forest of Assassins, 42; Zumwalt upset about lack of air support available to cover U.S. troops in this area, 203

SALT
See Strategic Arms Limitation Talks

Salzer, Captain Robert S., USN
Impressive looking and savvy as Commander Task Force 117 in Vietnam in 1968, 26-28, 221; at VADM Elmo Zumwalt's request, took the lead in launching an early SEA LORDS mission, 42, 72-75, 82-83; selected for flag rank on the heels of his Vietnam tour, 62; Salzer's call sign, "First Sea Lord," caused a small mix-up with London, 72-73; relationship with Zumwalt, 180, 182, 323

Schlesinger, James R.
In a quandary over how to handle CNO Elmo Zumwalt's retirement ceremony in June 1974 when the admiral was at such odds with President Richard Nixon, 158-159; trouble

between Schlesinger and Zumwalt over U.S. arms control position on nuclear cruise missiles, 272-273

Schreadley, Commander Richard L., USN
Chosen to upgrade quality of official command history of in-country naval forces in Vietnam in the late 1960s, 92-94

Sea Control Ship (SCS)
SCS concept, promoted by CNO Elmo Zumwalt, failed to appeal to the internal Navy bureaucracy, 250-252, 254, 256, 258, 276-277, 285, 315-316; lessons learned from the 1982 Falklands action, 258-259

SEA LORDS
One of Elmo Zumwalt's three goals for Vietnam in 1968 resulted in this effort to get the three task forces to interact in joint operations, 42, 73-77; Zumwalt particularly pleased with acronym, which he originated, 72-73; effect on morale, 86

SEALs
Identity of enlisted Navy SEALs generally kept secret during Vietnam War, 106-107; Kerr accompanied SEALs on several night missions as an observer, 107-109

Shear, Vice Admiral Harold E., USN (USNA, 1942)
As Deputy Chief of Naval Operations (Antisubmarine Warfare) in the early 1970s, loyalty to CNO Zumwalt, 257

Sherman, Admiral Forrest P., USN (USNA, 1918)
As first aviator to become Chief of Naval Operations after World War II, credited for unusual control he was able to wield, 276-277, 324

Sihanouk, Prince Norodom
Cambodian head of state filed protest when an American officer chased a Viet Cong at gunpoint into Cambodia in the late 1960s, 103, 109-110

Silver Mace, Operation
See Ca Mau Peninsula

Smith, Rear Admiral John V., USN (USNA, 1934)
As Amphibious Force Commander in Vietnam in 1968, briefed the new Commander Naval Forces Vietnam, RADM Elmo Zumwalt, 13; a latecoming supporter of Zumwalt, 88-89

Smith, Rear Admiral Levering, USN (USNA, 1932)
As director of the Strategic Systems Project office in

the early 1970s, dealt directly with Defense Department personnel on the question of submarine-launched missiles, 274

South Vietnam
    See Vietnam, South

Soviet Union
    Firm presence in Indian Ocean by 1968 a cause of concern to the U.S. Navy, 235; President Richard Nixon realized need for stronger defense against the Soviet Union in the early 1970s, but felt he didn't have enough political power to compensate, 244, 246; U.S. was cautious of the Soviets during 1973 Yom Kippur War, 293-294; U.S. Navy response to perceived Soviet threat during India-Pakistan conflict in 1971, 295-296

Stefencavage, Lieutenant George, USN
    Credited with plan for waterborne ambush as part of Giant Slingshot in South Vietnam in 1968, 175-176, 220

Strategic Arms Limitation Talks (SALT)
    CNO Elmo Zumwalt wrote letter critical of President Nixon's handling of SALT issue in 1974, 155-156, 160-161, 272-273, 289; Zumwalt ordered by Nixon not to discuss SALT on "Meet the Press" in June 1974, 157-158; while courting the Soviets with SALT, the Nixon administration was hesitant to give military its full support, 246; OP-06 was Navy division concerned with SALT, 272; the Soviets came away with an advantage after SALT I, 289

Styx (surface-to-surface antiship missile)
    Concern of Soviet missiles to the U.S. Navy in the early 1970s, 259-260

Submariners
    Support of CNO Zumwalt in the early 1970s, 328-329

Submarines--Attack
    CNO Elmo Zumwalt quick to recognize potential value of multi-mission attack submarines in the early 1970s, 253

Submarines--Ballistic Missile
    CNO Elmo Zumwalt fought suggestion that the Air Force take over this Navy program in the early 1970s, 308

Submarines--Diesel
    Discussion of value of keeping diesel submarines as nuclear subs grew in prominence in the early 1970s, 317-318

Survival Training
    Zumwalt and Kerr underwent survival training in the
    Philippines prior to leaving for Vietnam in 1968, 20-21

Swift Boats
    Use in Market Time operations, 75-76; subdued reaction
    to swift boat successes on Commander U.S. Naval Forces
    Vietnam staff prior to VADM Zumwalt's arrival in 1968,
    172; Zumwalt was discouraged from riding swift boats for
    his safety, 198; used in Giant Slingshot, 214

Systems Analysis Division (OP-96)
    Given charge of long-range planning by CNO Elmo Zumwalt
    in the early 1970s, 269-271, 303-304

Task Force 116
    Participation in the first SEA LORDS operation in South
    Vietnam in 1968, 74-75

Task Force 117
    Mobile Riverine Force's participation in first SEA LORDS
    mission in South Vietnam in 1968, 74-75; see also
    Salzer, Captain Robert S.

Tidd, Captain Emmet H., USN
    As Zumwalt's replacement chief of staff in 1968, worked
    well with his boss, 40, 66-67, 181

Time Magazine
    Time reporter apologized to Kerr for negative slant
    magazine editors had take on a story about Navy's role
    in Vietnam in the late 1960s, 117

Train, Captain Harry D. II, USN (USNA, 1949)
    VADM Elmo Zumwalt tried to get Train for his staff in
    Vietnam in the late 1960s, but Train had already been
    tapped to be Chief of Naval Operations Admiral Thomas
    Moorer's executive assistant, 65

Trident II Missile
    Accuracy improvements developed from discussions in the
    early 1970s, 275

Turner, Captain Stansfield, USN (USNA, 1947)
    Assessed as officer in charge of Project 60 in 1970,
    233, 240, 269-270

Veth, Rear Admiral Kenneth L., USN (USNA, 1935)
    Relationship with General Creighton Abrams, 17-19, 25,
    35, 206; relationship with Vice Admiral Elmo Zumwalt,

25; somewhat distant as Commander U.S. Naval Forces Vietnam, 29, 78-79; adamant about seating arrangements at his change of command ceremony despite protocol, 37-38; personality and role assessed by his aide, Glenn, 168, 170

Vertical-Short Take-off/Landing (V/STOL)
Failure of the British to protect their V/STOL ships during 1982 Falklands action, 258-259

Vietnamization
One of VADM Elmo Zumwalt's three major goals during his tour in Vietnam, 42-45; necessity for Vietnamization not recognized by the other services as early as Zumwalt foresaw it for the Navy, 44, 47-56, 204-206, 228; overcoming cultural difficulties, 67-70; effect on morale, 86; quality of Vietnamese units not interchangeable with U.S. units by mid-1969, 131; election of President Richard Nixon bought time for turning over U.S. assets, 131-132; Zumwalt took level of technical expertise into account when planning facilities that would be turned over to the Vietnamese, 190-191

Vietnam, North
VADM Elmo Zumwalt's assessment of Hanoi's strategy in the late 1960s, 137-138

Vietnam, South
Perceived as reluctant to fight their own war, 71; Americans served Vietnamese food, 112-113; news available to Americans stationed here, 115-121; see also Vietnamization, Vietnam War

Vietnam War
Kerr wrote his master's thesis in the mid-1960s about the period from 1950 to 1962 when U.S. involvement escalated, 3-5; U.S. Navy seen as underutilized prior to 1968, 17, 22, 33-34, 169-171; Kerr's opinion of VADM Elmo Zumwalt's attitude towards war, 23; lessons learned in war, 31; war was being fought by young officers who were looking for leadership, 32; rules of engagement, 84, 109, 219-220; quality of U.S. military leadership, 87; political sensitivities in Southeast Asia, 103; changes in U.S. policy after Nixon elected, 131-134; role of politics in war, 137-140; intensity of random rocket attacks on Saigon in mid-1968, 168; joint U.S.-Vietnamese operations, 193-194; Navy was in better position to intercept enemy supplies than Army, 224; hardship on Navy in terms of hardware, 234, 246; see also U.S. Naval Forces Vietnam

V/STOL
    See Vertical-Short Take-off/Landing

War Games
    Used by Navy planners to judge possible attrition that would be wrought by programs under consideration in the early 1970s, 301-302

Warner, John W.
    As Secretary of the Navy in the early 1970s, relationship with CNO Elmo Zumwalt, 266-267

Weisner, Admiral Maurice F., USN (USNA, 1941)
    As VCNO in the early 1970s, credited with loyalty to CNO Elmo Zumwalt, 257

Yom Kippur War
    Use of U.S. minesweepers to clear the Suez Canal in 1973 reflected back on CNO Elmo Zumwalt's determination to get mine warfare forces back into shape, 279-281; U.S. merchant ship sent to the Mediterranean to provide logistic support, 283; crisis tightly monitored by the Chairman of the Joint Chiefs of Staff, Admiral Thomas Moorer, 292-293; close contact between Zumwalt and Bagley, 292-294

"Z-Grams"
    Kerr dealt with problems caused by Admiral Zumwalt's special messages as commanding officer of the Hawkins (DD-873), 148-150; Glenn's interpretation of the spirit of Z-grams, 216-217

Zumwalt, Admiral Elmo R., Jr., USN (USNA, 1943)
    Turned down by Kerr when he invited the lieutenant to join his Vietnam staff in 1968, 6-9, 11; negative attitude about Zumwalt held by some in Bureau of Naval Personnel, 12; briefings before assuming duties as Commander U.S. Naval Forces Vietnam/Commander Naval Advisory Group Vietnam from 1968 to 1970, 12-17; frocking ceremony to vice admiral aboard a commercial jet, 15; ramifications of early promotion, 18-22, 24; survival training in the Philippines prior to arriving in Vietnam, 20-21; credited with sensitivity to Vietnam situation, 23-24; toured Vietnam upon arrival, 25-32, 172; leadership style, 39-44, 46; goals in Vietnam, 42; relationship with General Creighton Abrams, 35, 45-46, 53-54, 86-88, 134, 140, 204-206; led effort to reward officers who served well in Vietnam, 59-60; spent great deal of time in the field, where he often decorated men on the spot, 78-81, 123-124, 176-179, 187; never wore a

weapon, 79; assessed by Kerr, 95-99, 111-112, 154, 160, 162-164; attempt on Zumwalt's life, 113, 187; relationship with news media, 118-121, 225-226; impact of Vietnam duty on policies as CNO, 121-123; impressive in meeting with Defense Secretary Melvin Laird in early 1969, 134-136; sensitivity to politics, 137-141, 226-227, 255; received no fanfare when he returned to the States in 1970 between Vietnam and CNO duties, 143-144; discussion of "Mod Squad," 144-153; credited with enlightening Navy about race relations, 151-153, 163; drafted a letter critical of President Richard Nixon's SALT policies in 1974 that eventually led to his retirement, 155-160, 272-273, 289; political aspirations, 156-157, 160-161; daily routine, 95-98, 176-180, 198-199, 322; assessed by Glenn, 178-180, 186-189, 199-200, 202-204, 211, 213-218, 231; as own operations and action officer, 129, 189, 261-262, 272; dealings with Admiral Tran Van Chon, 190; proponent of joint service operations, 193-194; concern for safety, 193, 195-196, 198; family, 143-144, 186, 199-200; health, 201-202; relationship with his deputies in Vietnam, 212-213; used "murder boards", 215-216; success and failures in Vietnam, 219; philosophies assessed by Bagley, 237-239, 268, 323-327, 329-330; compared to other CNOs, 241-242, 261, 292, 294, 314, 324-325; as proponent of various programs, 252-255, 302, 314-316, 319-321; relationship with Navy and Defense Department secretaries, 266-268, 323; successes in getting programs implemented, 285; sense of humor, 326-327; see also "Z-Grams"

www.ingramcontent.com/pod-product-compliance
Lightning Source LLC
Chambersburg PA
CBHW080619170426
43209CB00007B/1471